AVID
READER
PRESS

ALSO BY MICHAEL RIEDEL

Razzle Dazzle

SINGULAR SENSATION

THE TRIUMPH OF BROADWAY

MICHAEL RIEDEL

AVID READER PRESS
NEW YORK LONDON TORONTO SYDNEY NEW DELHI

Avid Reader Press
An Imprint of Simon & Schuster, Inc.
1230 Avenue of the Americas
New York, NY 10020

First Avid Reader Press hardcover edition November 2020

AVID READER PRESS and colophon are trademarks of Simon & Schuster, Inc.

Interior design by Kyle Kabel

Manufactured in the United States of America

1 3 5 7 9 10 8 6 4 2

Library of Congress Cataloging-in-Publication Data is available.

ISBN 978-1-5011-6663-1
ISBN 978-1-5011-6664-8 (ebook)

PHOTO CREDITS

INSERT 1: 1, 2, 3, 14: Photo courtesy of Betty Jacobs; 4: Barry King/Alamy Stock Photo; 5, 6, 7, 10: Courtesy of Julie Larson; 8, 9: Courtesy of David Stone; 11: Courtesy of Michael Riedel; 12, 13, 15, 16: Courtesy of Anita and Steve Shevett; 17: Courtesy of Jerry Zaks; 18: Courtesy of Jeremy Gerard; 19: Courtesy Tom Kirdahy; 20: Courtesy of Jeremy Gerard

INSERT 2: 21: Courtesy of Fran and Barry Weissler; 22, 34, 35: Courtesy William Ivey Long; 23, 24: Courtesy of Michael Riedel; 25: Courtesy of Betty Jacobs; 26: Courtesy of Marty Bell; 27: Courtesy of Tim Rice; 28, 29, 30: Photo by Kenneth Van Sickle, courtesy of Disney Theatrical Productions; 31, 32, 33: Courtesy Disney Theatrical Productions; 36: Courtesy Robin Wagner; 37: Photo by Audrey Ruben

For my parents, Bob and Penny

CONTENTS

FOREWORD

I never intended the subtitle of this book—*The Triumph of Broadway*—to be ironic. *Singular Sensation* charts the success of Broadway in the 1990s, and its remarkable comeback after the 2001 attack on the World Trade Center. But around the time I turned in the manuscript, something called the *coronavirus* was stirring in China. I didn't give it much thought, and treated myself to a ski vacation in Switzerland and Italy the first week of March. Two days after I got back to New York, one of the resorts I was in, Cervinia, shut down. The virus was spreading across Northern Italy.

And then it hit New York. Many of us who work on or around Broadway were slow to grasp the implications for this business. Scott Rudin, the producer of *The Book of Mormon, To Kill a Mockingbird*, and the revival of *West Side Story*, saw his box office grosses wobble and announced any unsold seats, once priced at several hundred dollars, could be had for fifty dollars. I thought it was a brilliant move. Who wouldn't leap at the chance to see a hit Broadway show at such a bargain price?

The hot show in town was the revival of Stephen Sondheim's *Company* starring Patti LuPone. It started previews on March 2 and was scheduled to open March 22, Sondheim's ninetieth birthday. The mood of public officials was growing darker, and I remember thinking Sondheim might skip the opening. But I never thought, nor did anyone in the show, that it wouldn't open. And then Cynthia Nixon, who had run for governor of New York and was politically connected, attended a preview. Sitting in LuPone's dressing room afterward, she told LuPone and Chris Harper, the show's producer, that she had tickets for the opening but came to the show that night because "I wanted to do something fun before this city is locked down."[1]

On March 10, the Broadway League, the industry's trade organization, announced that cleaning crews would scrub down theaters after every performance. The League told actors not to mingle with audience members at the stage door after the show. And then on March 11, New York governor Andrew Cuomo prohibited gatherings of five hundred people or more. Broadway announced it was going dark—but only for a month.

COVID-19 hit Broadway hard with the news that it had killed playwright Terrence McNally, at eighty-one. He appears throughout these pages. A few days after he died, I emailed his husband, Tom Kirdahy, a line Terrence has in the book. Kirdahy wrote back, "The stories have come pouring in from everywhere, but none made me laugh out loud. Until now."

I hope when you come across Terrence's line, it will make you laugh out loud, too.

As I write this foreword at the beginning of May 2020, Broadway is still shut down, and nobody knows when it will come back. The official word is that Broadway will reopen in the fall. But many theater people think the spring of 2021 is more likely. Broadway is a $2-billion-a-year business, and the losses will be staggering. Many shows will never reopen. The big titles—*Wicked, The Book of Mormon, The Lion King, Hamilton*—will, but without those $2- and $3-million-a-week grosses. When will the tourists, who make up nearly two-thirds of the Broadway audience, return to New York, where more than twenty thousand people so far have died from COVID-19? No one has the answer.

Singular Sensation is about a happier time. My first book, *Razzle Dazzle: The Battle for Broadway,* attempted to show how a handful of people—Shubert chiefs Bernard B. Jacobs and Gerald Schoenfeld, James M. Nederlander, Michael Bennett, Andrew Lloyd Webber, and Cameron Mackintosh—rescued Broadway from the sleaze of Times Square in the 1970s and '80s. The book ended in 1995 with Bernie Jacobs's death. I didn't think I had another book about Broadway in me, but then my editor, Ben Loehnen, suggested a sequel. I realized that, as the theater columnist for the *New York Daily News* from 1993 to 1998, and then for the *New York Post* from 1998 until I was furloughed due to COVID-19, I'd covered almost thirty years of thrilling, tragic, hilarious, and tumultuous events on Broadway. I wrote about the feud between Patti LuPone and Andrew Lloyd Webber at *Sunset Boulevard.* I attended a performance of *Rent* a few days after the death of its creator, Jonathan Larson. I caught twenty minutes of a rehearsal of *The Producers,* and, after seeing Nathan Lane sing "The King of Broadway," raced back to my office at the *Post* and pounded out a column urging New Yorkers to get tickets *now.* And I watched, from my apartment in the West Village, the Twin Towers collapse.

But *Singular Sensation* is not a memoir. I interviewed more than a hundred people to tell the behind-the-scenes stories of some of Broadway's most celebrated shows and personalities. I was astounded at how much I didn't know. I strung columns together with bits and pieces of information, but after spending hours with the people who created the shows, or who took part in key moments in Broadway history, I had to laugh at how much I missed, failed to understand, or got wrong. Columnists can be know-it-alls. I certainly was. Writing *Singular Sensation* was fun. It was also humbling.

I planned to end this book with *Hamilton*. But I soon realized its length would dangerously approach Robert Caro territory, and I'm no Robert Caro. So I decided to concentrate on the 1990s, a decade of profound change on Broadway. All forms of popular entertainment have had such periods. The Golden Age of live television lasted roughly from 1947 to the late 1950s, when the pursuit of ratings led to an explosion of pretaped sitcoms. Broadway's Golden Age began in 1943 with Richard Rodgers and Oscar Hammerstein II's *Oklahoma!* and carried on through their final show, *The Sound of Music*, in 1959. Hollywood's Golden Age lasted a little longer, from 1930 until the fall of the studio system around 1948. A new era arrived in the late 1960s, as directors such as Robert Altman, Stanley Kubrick, Mike Nichols, and Roman Polanski came to wield as much power over their movies as any studio executive.

On Broadway in the early 1990s, the British invasion was still in full swing, but it came to an abrupt end with the collapse of *Sunset Boulevard*. It won the Tony Award for Best Musical in 1995. A year later, *Rent*, an American musical set in modern times and produced at a fraction of the cost of *Sunset*, won the award. *Crazy for You* and the revival of *Guys and Dolls* ushered in the return of the American musical comedy, culminating in *The Producers*. Plays, always an endangered species on Broadway, made a comeback, beginning with Tony Kushner's *Angels in America*. A new breed of producers rose up to challenge the grip theater owners had long held on Broadway. Corporations began to see how much money could be made from live theater. Disney and Garth Drabinsky's Livent moved into Times Square, changing the landscape by refurbishing long-derelict theaters. And Rosie O'Donnell deployed her enormously popular daytime television show to nudge Broadway back into the mainstream of American popular culture.

The attack on the World Trade Center threatened to upend all of that. In those grim days, the threat of more attacks loomed.

Times Square was on Mayor Rudy Giuliani's list of New York's top five targets. There were fears that terrorists might take over a Broadway theater and hold the audience hostage.* But two days after the attack, Broadway was up and running. Through a combination of strategies and events detailed in this book, it recovered much faster than anyone could have imagined.

Broadway has a knack for survival. It weathered the Great Depression largely through the maneuverings of theater owners Lee and J. J. Shubert. It withstood the onslaught of movies and television. New York City's fiscal crisis of the 1970s nearly destroyed it, but it fought back with such inspired weapons as the "I Love New York" campaign. And it faced its own pandemic, AIDS, in the 1980s. While much of America paid scant attention to what was once called "gay cancer," Broadway created Broadway Cares/Equity Fights AIDS to provide for the thousands of theater people suffering and dying from the disease.

Each of those threats presented a unique set of challenges. So, too, does COVID-19. "After 9/11, people wanted to be together," said Jed Bernstein, who ran the Broadway League from 1995 until 2006. "It became a patriotic act to see a show, to support New York. Now people don't want to be together. In fact, they can't be together."[2]

A business that attracts such talents as Jonathan Larson, Glenn Close, Rocco Landesman, Julie Taymor, Edward Albee, David Hare, William Ivey Long, Susan Stroman, Mel Brooks, Matthew Broderick, and many others you'll meet in this book is not going to die. There will be a comeback, and Broadway is good at comebacks. This one may take some time, but I'm confident the word *triumph* on the cover of this book will one day lose its bitter irony.

* Those fears were not unfounded. In October 2002, a Chechen radical military group held 850 people hostage at the Dubrovka Theatre in Moscow. One hundred and seventy people were killed.

CHAPTER ONE

I'M READY FOR MY CLOSE-UP, MR. LLOYD WEBBER

Amy Powers, a young lyricist at the start of a promising career, picked up the *New York Times* on September 20, 1991, and went straight to reporter Alex Witchel's influential Friday theater column.

The headline on the first item—A HITCH IN LLOYD WEBBER'S LYRICS—startled her. "You mean you've never heard of Sydmonton?" Witchel began. "Well, darling, don't admit it to a soul. It's the name of Andrew Lloyd Webber's estate in England where he holds an annual musical festival in late summer, very closed to the public, to introduce new work for assorted cronies . . . This year's dish is all about 'Sunset Boulevard,' Mr. Lloyd Webber's much-anticipated musical of the classic Billy Wilder movie starring Gloria Swanson."

Witchel reported in the same item that Liza Minnelli and Shirley MacLaine were the leading contenders to play Norma Desmond, the forgotten silent-movie star, in the stage musical (neither diva, though, was at the festival). Lloyd Webber's score, Witchel spies told her, was his best since *Evita*. "Some say it's simply the best he's written."

So far so good, Powers thought.

But then she read: "But the dark spot—there's always a dark spot, isn't there?—is the show's lyrics by the newcomer Amy Powers . . . [A]fter the lyrics met with a lukewarm response by the guests . . . Mr. Lloyd Webber reportedly let Ms. Powers go."

Powers gasped. She had just returned from Sydmonton. Lloyd Webber had told her he was pleased with the work they had done on the show.

"Go home," he said. "Take a couple of weeks off and then come back and we'll get started on Act Two."

And now she was reading in the *New York Times* that she'd been fired. "I don't know which was worse," Powers recalled years later. "Learning that I was not on the show anymore or learning that the *New York Times* couldn't always be trusted for reporting accurately. Nobody called me."

Witchel ended her item by writing that Powers's problem was "more inexperience than lack of talent." She quoted a source saying Lloyd Webber now needed "the lyrical equivalent of Billy Wilder."

Powers picked up the phone and called Lloyd Webber's office in London.

"Is this true?" she asked a minion.

"We don't know," the minion said. "We'll have to get back to you." Powers hung up the phone, went to her bathroom, and threw up.

Later that day the office called back to confirm that, in fact, she had been fired. Hers would not be the first head to roll down Sunset Boulevard.

Show business people love the movie *Sunset Boulevard.* Wilder's scalding story of a once-great film star tossed on the scrap heap resonates with those who work in the fickle world of entertainment. The 1950 movie features iconic performances by Gloria Swanson as Norma Desmond, holed up in her decaying Renaissance-style mansion on Sunset Boulevard; William Holden as the cynical young screenwriter Joe Gillis, who becomes Norma's lover; and Erich von Stroheim as Norma's mysterious German butler Max von Mayerling. Lines such as "I am big. It's the pictures that got small," "Without me there wouldn't be any Paramount Studio," and "All right, Mr. DeMille, I'm ready for my close-up!" are among the most famous ever written for the screen.

In 1971, Stephen Sondheim and Burt Shevelove, who had written *A Funny Thing Happened on the Way to the Forum* together, attempted a musical version of *Sunset Boulevard*. They opened their show with the scene from the movie in which Norma and Max bury her pet monkey on the grounds of the mansion.

"I wrote some music, and it was spooky," Sondheim said. "And then I found myself at a cocktail party with Billy Wilder and, very shyly, I went up to him and said that a friend and I were embarking on a musical based on *Sunset Boulevard*."

"You can't do that," Wilder said.

Sondheim thought he meant the rights were not available.

"No, no," Wilder said. "It can't be a musical. It must be an opera."

A couple of years later, Hal Prince, the director and producer of such Sondheim shows as *Follies* and *A Little Night Music*, came up with the idea of switching the setting of *Sunset Boulevard* from Hollywood to Broadway. He wanted Angela Lansbury to play a forgotten musical comedy star. Prince asked Sondheim and Hugh Wheeler, who wrote the book to *Night Music*, to write the show.

"Billy Wilder said it has to be an opera," Sondheim told Prince.

"You know, he's right," Prince said.

Prince secured the rights to the movie from Paramount, and asked Lloyd Webber if he'd be interested in writing *Sunset Boulevard*.

"Hal's idea was to update it and make Norma Desmond a sort of Doris Day character, a 1950s musical star who lived as a recluse in a house with no windows," Lloyd Webber said. "I'd never seen the movie—it wasn't a movie one knew in Britain particularly—so Hal arranged a screening. I was left with two things. I didn't like changing the time and I also thought, well, Hal works with Steve so why is he asking me to do it?"

Lloyd Webber declined.

But he admired the movie and several years later began thinking of it as an operatic musical. His biggest hit was, after all, *The Phantom of the Opera.*

Christopher Hampton, the British playwright who wrote *Les Liaisons Dangereuses*, also thought *Sunset Boulevard* could be an opera. He had interviewed Billy Wilder years before while researching his play *Tales from Hollywood*, about European émigrés in the movie business in the 1930s. (Wilder arrived in Hollywood from Germany in 1933 after Hitler came to power.) Hampton suggested the idea to the English National Opera. ENO inquired about the rights, but discovered someone had them already.

At lunch with Lloyd Webber one day, Hampton brought up *Sunset Boulevard.* He was disappointed that the rights weren't available. Lloyd Webber pointed to himself and smiled. "I have them," he said. The canny composer had snapped them up after Prince let them go.

Lloyd Webber didn't bring Hampton onto the project right away. He wanted to write some songs first, but he needed a lyricist. His friend Gerald Schoenfeld, the powerful chairman of the Shubert Organization, which had produced *Cats* on Broadway, suggested Amy Powers. She was a lawyer, but she aspired to write musicals. Her aunt knew Schoenfeld and thought he could give Amy some advice. She showed him some of her lyrics. A soft touch around attractive young women, Schoenfeld was impressed.

Not long after the meeting she got a call from "a guy with a British accent who said he was Andrew Lloyd Webber. I said, 'Come on, you're pulling my leg.' But he wasn't kidding."

"What are you doing this weekend?" Lloyd Webber asked. "Do you want to come over to the south of France? I need somebody to work on a new show, and Jerry Schoenfeld recommended you."

A few days later Powers boarded the Concorde to Paris, courtesy of Lloyd Webber, and then headed to the composer's villa in Cap Ferrat.

Powers and Lloyd Webber worked around his grand piano for two hours in the afternoon. He plucked one tune from his stash of songs that never had much exposure. It was from a musical called *Cricket* he'd written with Tim Rice to celebrate Queen Elizabeth's sixtieth birthday in 1986. Powers and Lloyd Webber thought the melody would fit the scene in the movie where Norma returns to Paramount Studios for the first time since her career ended.

Lloyd Webber wrote another soaring tune for Norma to recount her talent as a silent-screen star. She didn't need dialogue to cast a spell over the audience. She could do it with a gesture or a look. Powers came up with a title: "One Small Glance." Though Powers enjoyed working with and learning from Lloyd Webber, she had a sense that he wasn't always satisfied with their collaboration. "I think he wanted someone who would come up with the lyrics for his songs. Sort of just fill in the blanks."

Six months into their collaboration—and only weeks before the premiere of *Sunset Boulevard* at Sydmonton—Lloyd Webber told Powers his friend Don Black was joining the show. A veteran lyricist, Black had a catalog of title songs from movies—*Born Free, To Sir, with Love, Thunderball, Diamonds Are Forever, The Man with the Golden Gun*. He'd written with Lloyd Webber the musicals *Song and Dance* and *Aspects of Love*. Black was funny, affable, fast, and efficient. His songwriting motto was "If you start at ten o'clock in the morning and haven't finished by six o'clock, you're an idiot."

"The truth was Don was a godsend," said Powers. "He taught me all about hooks and titles." They spent a lot of time on the song about Norma's return to Paramount. They talked about her emotions, her thrill at being back on a soundstage. They walked around Hyde Park mapping out the song. But the title—the hook—eluded them.

Black called Powers early the next morning.

"I've got the title," he said. "'As If We Never Said Goodbye.'"

That phrase "encapsulated everything we had been talking about regarding what the song should do," Powers said. "It was just great."

Lloyd Webber kicked off the Sydmonton Festival in the summer of 1991 with a lavish lunch for invited guests at his estate. After lunch everyone filed into a church Lloyd Webber had converted into a theater to see the first act of *Sunset Boulevard*. Ria Jones, who had been in *Evita* in the West End, played Norma. She was too young for the part, even with a Norma Desmond turban, but Lloyd Webber admired her voice.

Black had only been on the show a few weeks, so many of the lyrics were still Powers's. Elaine Paige, the leading lady of British musical theater, did not like "One Small Glance." She leaned over to Black and whispered, "You've got to do something about those lyrics."*

After the performance ended, Lloyd Webber asked friends what they thought. The verdict was clear: Don should do the job.

And so Amy Powers was gone, her departure announced to the world in the *New York Times*. She consulted a powerful theatrical attorney about a possible lawsuit. "This is what will

* Eventually he did. Black changed "One Small Glance" to "With One Look." The word *look*, he thought, was more muscular than *glance*.

happen," he told her. "If you try to fight it, Andrew will destroy you. He has endless resources. You will never work in this business again."

In the end, she reached a settlement. Her credit in the *Playbill* would be, in small type, "additional lyrics by Amy Powers." As for her financial stake "you would need a microscope to see it," she said.*

Lloyd Webber brought Christopher Hampton onto the show, and work began in Cap Ferrat in the fall of 1991. "That's when *Sunset* really started evolving," Lloyd Webber said. "It was a great subject for us to tackle. Don and Chris knew Hollywood, and I was fascinated by *Sunset* as a study in madness. The way I wanted to take it was quite extreme. We went much further than the film."

"We'd meet in the mornings, and Andrew would usually have a tune written," said Black. "Then Chris and I would go off to write lyrics or a scene in the afternoon, while Andrew walked around his gardens or checked his wine cellar. Then we'd meet and say, 'We've cracked it,' and give him the lyric or the title. Andrew loves titles. I remember how euphoric he was when I gave him 'The Perfect Year.' And off he'd go to write a song."

How fast Lloyd Webber worked impressed Hampton. "I remember coming in for dinner and saying we need a song about the greatness of silent movies," Hampton said, "what it was like for Norma to be young and in at the beginning of the movie business. The next morning Andrew sat at the piano and played 'New Ways to Dream.' He'd written it after dinner."

* Powers never heard from Lloyd Webber or Black again. She was not invited to the London or Broadway productions of *Sunset Boulevard*. She did attend the opening of the 2017 revival starring Glenn Close. She saw Lloyd Webber, "but he did not see me," she said.

It took about six weeks to finish the first draft. Lloyd Webber wanted to unveil both acts at the Sydmonton Festival in the summer of 1992.

The score impressed David Caddick, Lloyd Webber's longtime musical director. "It combined two worlds," he said. "Norma's world had that very baroque quality to it. Everything was deep and rich and dark. It was counterpointed with the real world of Joe and his young friends, which was light, very California, an easy jazz sound. Andrew separated the two worlds with two distinct musical styles."

Caddick knew who should play Norma at Sydmonton—Patti LuPone, who had won a Tony Award in 1980 as Eva Perón in *Evita*. LuPone grabbed the offer. She was in Los Angeles in her fourth season on the ABC television show *Life Goes On* and "was suffocating from boredom," she wrote in *Patti LuPone: A Memoir*. "I missed singing. I missed being on stage."

The part of Joe Gillis went to LuPone's good friend Kevin Anderson, a fine actor and strong singer LuPone had met while she was doing *Les Misérables* in London and he was appearing in the play *Orphans*. They rehearsed a few days in London and then headed to Sydmonton. The people milling about the estate unnerved her. "Kevin and I thought we went over there to do a small workshop of the show," she said. "We had no idea it was going to be filmed and we would have an audience of every producer from London and Broadway!"[1]

Among the VIPs: Broadway's two most powerful landlords—the Shuberts and the Nederlanders; Disney chief Michael Eisner; producer Cameron Mackintosh; director Trevor Nunn; entertainment mogul Robert Stigwood; and, for good measure, Meryl Streep.

LuPone's performance that afternoon was, by all accounts, sensational. Meryl Streep was in tears at the end. Everyone thought *Sunset Boulevard* had the makings of a hit. "We thought this was going to be way bigger than *Phantom*," said Bill Taylor, the chief financial officer of Lloyd Webber's company the Really Useful Group.

At a lavish dinner party following the show, Lloyd Webber said to LuPone, "Name your price."

"Kevin Anderson," she replied. Lloyd Webber offered him the role of Joe Gillis on the spot. LuPone went back to Los Angeles triumphant. And then negotiations began.

"They were offering a $1.98—take it or leave it!" LuPone recalled. "I said, 'Wait a minute. Andrew offered me the part at Sydmonton. Show some respect!' It was an ugly negotiation. I should have known then that this was not a healthy environment."

The deal got done. LuPone would originate the role of Norma Desmond in London and then on Broadway a year later. One point gave her pause. There was talk of a production in Los Angeles before Broadway. It made sense since *Sunset Boulevard* is about the movies. But Really Useful did not offer LuPone Los Angeles. She thought, *I'm going to premiere it in London, but somebody else is going to premiere it in America before me?* "You're setting up a competition between two actresses and one of us is going to lose," she told the brass at Really Useful. Absolutely not, they assured her.

"Well, I fell for that," LuPone said.

Lloyd Webber assembled the rest of the creative team. Trevor Nunn, who directed *Cats* and *Les Misérables*, signed on, as did set designer John Napier (*Cats*), and costume designer Anthony Powell. The production would be enormous. The era of the British spectacle was in full swing. *Cats* had its giant tire that ascended to the Heaviside Layer. *Phantom* had its crashing chandelier. *Les Misérables* had moving barricades and a turntable, while *Miss Saigon* had a helicopter. *Sunset Boulevard* would have Norma's mansion, complete with a winding staircase and a pipe organ the Phantom would envy. Napier designed the rococo mansion, which weighed thirty-three thousand pounds, so that it could fly. A hydraulic motor and cables as thick as the ones used to tie down the *Queen Mary* would lift the mansion to the top of the theater where it would hover over other lavish sets—the gates of Paramount, a sound studio, Schwab's Pharmacy. An IBM computer and software programed for *Sunset Boulevard* would pilot the mansion.[2]

Cash was not a problem for Lloyd Webber. His empire was awash in it. Royalties poured in from worldwide productions of *Cats* and *Phantom*. "We had regular board meetings and somebody would ask how much cash we had in the bank. And there'd be twenty million pounds or something," Taylor said. "And then there would be champagne."

The Really Useful Group was so successful that Lloyd Webber floated shares on the stock market for a few years, though he bought them all back, eventually. He raised the money by selling a 30 percent stake in his company to PolyGram, the Dutch entertainment giant. It was a decision he would come to regret.

Sunset Boulevard was budgeted at $7 million, the most expensive show in the history of London's West End. While it was coming together in England, Really Useful began assembling a second production for Los Angeles. That one would cost $12 million. The plan was to open *Sunset Boulevard* with LuPone at the Adelphi Theatre in July 1993. Five months later, the show would premiere at the Shubert Theatre in Los Angeles. But who would play Norma Desmond?

Christopher Hampton suggested a genuine movie star—Glenn Close, who had recently played the evil Marquise de Merteuil in the movie version of *Les Liaisons Dangereuses*.

Close had two Broadway musicals to her credit. She played Princess Mary in Richard Rodgers's *Rex* in 1976, singing a sweet but forgettable ditty called "Christmas at Hampton Court." In

1980, she played P. T. Barnum's wife, Charity, in Cy Coleman's *Barnum*. She had a fine voice, though nobody thought she had the pipes of Ethel Merman.

Lloyd Webber knew Close could act the role, but he wasn't sure if she could sing it. He flew her to London to audition for the creative team. Before she arrived at his Eaton Square mansion, Lloyd Webber took Hampton aside and said, "Look, I've booked a table at my local Italian for the seven of us. If it all goes well, we'll go there. If it doesn't, I booked a table at the Dorchester for two. You take her there."

Close was ushered into the library. Lloyd Webber was at the piano. She sang "With One Look" and "As If We Never Said Goodbye." Lloyd Webber stood up and said, "You are fantastic. You have eclipsed your performance of 'Christmas at Hampton Court.'"

Close burst out laughing. "Andrew Lloyd Webber, you are a bastard!"

Dinner was at the Italian restaurant.

Before announcing that Glenn Close would play Norma Desmond in the American premiere of *Sunset Boulevard,* executives at Really Useful thought somebody should tell LuPone. The job fell to Edgar Dobie, who ran the U.S. arm of Lloyd Webber's empire. He called her at home. She was waiting for the limo to take her to the airport to fly to London to begin rehearsals.

Dobie knew it would be a tricky conversation, but he was a diplomat. "You're creating the role in London and we have a deal for Broadway," he said. "But I want you to know we have engaged Glenn Close for Los Angeles."

Silence. And then LuPone said, "Glenn Close? She brays like a donkey and her nickname is George Washington because if you look at her in profile her nose meets her chin."

LuPone, in an interview in 2020, disputed Dobie's recollection. "He never called me," she said. "My agent did. And I never said that about Glenn. I never said that. He made that up." Dobie shrugged and said, "Given the way she was treated, I'll let Patti have the last word. But how would *I* come up with a line like that?"

One memory they both share: When the driver arrived, LuPone handed him her plane tickets. "Take these to Really Useful," she said. "I'm not going."

"My ego was so bruised," she recalled. "I was so hurt." Three days of frantic negotiations ensued before LuPone agreed to go to London.

"Why did I get on that plane? I had five trunks already in London, and I thought if I don't go over there, I'll never get them back," she said.

CHAPTER TWO

BOULEVARD OF BROKEN DREAMS

Andrew Lloyd Webber was at the height of his power in 1991. Both *Cats* and *The Phantom of the Opera* dwarfed the success of any show in musical theater history. On Broadway alone, the two productions posted combined weekly grosses of more than $1 million, unheard of at the time. Lloyd Webber and Cameron Mackintosh, the producer of *Cats* and *Phantom* as well as *Les Misérables* and *Miss Saigon*, ushered in the British invasion of the 1980s. Their megamusicals ran for years all over the world and eclipsed, at the box office and in the press, most American musicals.* But a backlash was brewing.

It began with *Miss Saigon*. The show transplanted Puccini's *Madama Butterfly* to the war in Vietnam, telling the story of the doomed romance between an American soldier and a Vietnamese prostitute. An enormous success in London, *Saigon* had a showstopping performance by Jonathan Pryce as the Engineer,

* At the 1988 Tony Awards, Stephen Sondheim's *Into the Woods* won Best Book and Best Score. But *Phantom* won the most important award, Best Musical. Broadway could not turn its back on a show that had sold $18 million worth of tickets before opening night.

a pimp, hustler, and swindler who dreams of coming to America. The character is Eurasian and Pryce wore slanty-eye prostheses and yellow makeup. Nobody thought much of it in London, but when Mackintosh announced the show for New York, with Pryce, Asian Americans and others in the theater world were appalled. The yellowface was an affront. Furthermore, why should a Caucasian British actor play the role on Broadway? Why not an Asian American actor?

David Henry Hwang, who wrote *M. Butterfly*, the Tony Award–winning play about a French diplomat who falls in love with a Peking opera singer he thinks is a woman but turns out to be a man, and BD Wong, who played the opera singer, filed a complaint with Actors' Equity. To the shock of Broadway, the union denied permission for Pryce to play New York. Equity cannot "appear to condone the casting of a Caucasian in the role of a Eurasian. This is a moral decision," the union said. Mackintosh, furious that he and his show were being portrayed as racially insensitive, canceled *Miss Saigon* on Broadway. Only a producer as rich and powerful as Mackintosh could scuttle a show that had a $25 million advance.

But it was a brilliant move. The cancellation of *Miss Saigon* made headlines all over America. "If Cameron had planned it and paid for it, it couldn't have worked out better," said Richard Maltby Jr., one of the show's writers. "We were on the local news in Shreveport. Everybody in America knew there was a show with a helicopter in it and a controversy around it."

Broadway's power brokers lined up behind Mackintosh, denouncing Equity for killing a show that would bring millions of dollars to New York City and employ many actors, including more than thirty Asian Americans. "The nicest thing I can say about [Equity's] decision is that it's stupid," Rocco Landesman, who ran the Jujamcyn theater chain, told the *New York Times*.[1]

The union's position was untenable. Many of its members, concerned about the loss of jobs, revolted. Two weeks later the union reversed itself and gave Pryce permission to play Broadway, though not in yellowface. To the hundreds of actors who had protested the show, the defeat was humiliating—another example of just how powerful the British had become on Broadway.

Mackintosh caused another stir by raising the top ticket to $100, the highest in Broadway history, at a time when America was in the midst of a recession. Reviewing *Miss Saigon* for the *New York Times*, Frank Rich called it "a show with something for everyone to resent."[2]

At the 1991 Tony Awards, *Saigon* squared off against *The Will Rogers Follies*, a charming but slight celebration of Americana directed by Tommy Tune. It opened shortly after America had defeated Saddam Hussein in Operation Desert Storm, and it waved the flag of patriotism. *Will Rogers* had nowhere near the financial prowess of *Saigon*, but it won six Tonys, including Best Musical. *Saigon* won three. At last an American musical, however fluffy, scored a victory against a British megamusical.*

While the insular theater community may have had its fill of British shows, ticket buyers still had an appetite for them, or so it appeared. Andrew Lloyd Webber's *Aspects of Love* arrived in New York from London in 1990 with advance ticket sales of $12 million. Based on a slender book by David Garnett, a minor member of the Bloomsbury circle, the show told the story of a group of bohemians jumping in and out of one another's beds in the south of France. It was an intimate story and Lloyd Webber wrote some romantic songs, including "Love Changes Everything," which hit number two on the UK singles chart. But every British show had to be huge in those days and so *Aspects*, budgeted at $8 million, had a set featuring the Pyrenees mountain range.

* *Will Rogers* ran a respectable 981 performances. *Miss Saigon* ran ten years on Broadway—impressive, to be sure, but shorter than *Cats*, *Les Miz*, and *Phantom* (which is still running).

The mountains were jagged and sharp and rolled on and offstage on a conveyor belt. "It was a dangerous set," said Alex Fraser, who worked in Lloyd Webber's New York office. "The prop man said to me, 'You know, for a show about love, if you fall down on the set you'll die.' "*

The New York office saw a run-through. "It was turgid and overblown," Fraser said. "We were heartbroken. There was a sense that something had to be done to fix it." Not much was, though Lloyd Webber and director Trevor Nunn did come up with a new number in the second act for some peasants to sing about the land. A batch of new costumes arrived, as well as thirty baskets of fruit for the peasants to carry. The song was "pretty," Fraser said, "but all it did was make the show longer and more turgid."

Opening night was glamorous, with a lavish party at the Rainbow Room in Rockefeller Center. But there was concern about the reviews, especially the *New York Times*. Frank Rich had been leading the charge against Lloyd Webber. He called *Phantom* "long on pop professionalism and melody, impoverished of artistic personality and passion." He ended his *Phantom* review hoping the Lloyd Webber era was "poised to go bust."

Heading into the party, Don Black, who wrote the lyrics to *Aspects*, said to Nunn, "I'll be thrilled if he only hates it." Rich destroyed it. "Andrew Lloyd Webber, the composer who is second to none when writing musicals about cats . . . and falling chandeliers, has made an earnest but bizarre career decision. . . . He has written a musical about people. Whether 'Aspects of Love' is a musical for people is another matter." He dismissed Lloyd Webber's score as "easy-listening pop," zinged the lyrics as "translated . . . from the original Hallmark" and called the scenery "oppressive."

* The set was indeed dangerous. In London, leading lady Ann Crumb's foot got caught in the conveyor belt and was mangled. "I heard this huge screaming over the orchestra, and it was me," she told reporters at the time.

"I remember looking at Andrew's face when the review came in," Black said. "It was ashen." *Aspects of Love* ran ten months. It lost its entire $8 million investment, making it, at the time, the most expensive flop in Broadway history.

Excitement surrounding *Sunset Boulevard* eased the disappointment of *Aspects of Love*. At the Really Useful office in New York, staffers were calling the new show "The Female Phantom."

Although Billy Wilder, the director, had no control over the movie (Paramount had the rights) or the stage adaptation, Peter Brown, Lloyd Webber's closest friend and public relations chief, sought Wilder's blessing. He knew of Wilder's gift for wisecracks: "He had Van Gogh's ear for music," "Hindsight is always 20/20," "Shoot a few scenes out of focus. I want to win the foreign film award." Brown worried that Wilder might make a crack about the musical with which the press could bludgeon Lloyd Webber.

Brown and Lloyd Webber flew to Los Angeles to show Wilder the video of LuPone's performance at Sydmonton. They bought expensive video and sound equipment and a large screen. When Wilder arrived at their suite in the Hotel Bel-Air, Lloyd Webber, always worried about sound quality, began fiddling with the equipment. "Why is Mr. Webber moving around so much?" Wilder asked in his thick German accent. "He's nervous," Brown said. "This is a film—and you're a great director." Lloyd Webber hit the on button. Nothing happened. Finally he got it to play, but only in black and white. "Andrew was beside himself," Brown recalled. But Wilder didn't mind. "Tell Mr. Webber I like it in black and white," he cracked.

Wilder was "polite" about the video—"not gushing, but polite," Brown said.

* * *

Back in London, rehearsals began in an atmosphere of hostility. LuPone, still furious about Close, arrived with a list of demands. Number one: Close could not attend her opening night in London or be anywhere near her while she was creating the role.[3]

"Everybody was walking on eggshells," Lloyd Webber recalled, "and I was frankly utterly shaken. None of the work we might normally have done in rehearsals got done because we were afraid we might upset Patti. That was the time when one wished one had a strong producer like Cameron [Mackintosh]. He might have replaced her. Looking back on it, when she said she wouldn't come over, that's probably what should have happened."

Lloyd Webber, through his Really Useful Group, produced *Sunset Boulevard*. But his primary job was writing it. And he wasn't calling all the shots. His producing partner, Paramount, studiously guarded one of its most famous titles. In addition to working on the show, Lloyd Webber was also trying to manage his expanding empire, and keep his 30 percent partner, PolyGram, happy with the cash flow. (PolyGram had an option to acquire 50 percent of Really Useful by 2003.)

"It was a very difficult time for me," Lloyd Webber recalled. "I felt I was in danger of losing control of my company."

Under Nunn's direction, rehearsals went well, but when the cast moved into the Adelphi Theatre "the shit hit the fan," LuPone said. She was not happy with the mansion. "It was heavy," she said. "The whole set was too heavy for an art form that is celluloid."

The mansion turned out to be a bigger diva than Norma Desmond. During technical rehearsals, it would fly in without warning or take off without warning—with terrified cast members on it. The problem, it turned out, was that the radio frequencies used to operate the set were the same frequencies used by taxicab dispatchers. As LuPone put it, "Anybody passing by the Adelphi could give me a thrill ride just by picking up the phone."[4]

Sunset Boulevard opened July 12, 1993, at the Adelphi. A few days before, Bill Taylor, the CFO of Really Useful, had attended the opening of the revival of *Grease*, which turned out to be a surprise hit in the West End. "It was great fun. It was big and brassy. It captured the zeitgeist. I thought it was everything *Sunset Boulevard* was not."

Wilder and his wife, Audrey, attended the *Sunset* opening. Peter Brown sat with them. After the first act they went for a drink. Wilder said nothing. But during the second act, when LuPone sang "As If We Never Said Goodbye," Audrey cried. After the show Wilder told Brown, "Mr. Lloyd Webber did a good a job." He told Black and Hampton, "You guys are very clever. You didn't change a thing."

The opening-night reception was warm, but not ecstatic. The show hadn't quite landed with the audience, Taylor thought. Walking across the street to the party at the Savoy Hotel, Cameron Mackintosh said to him, "The thing about this show—it's a fantastic score—but there's not one character in this show that I actually like."

The reviews were mixed. Most of the critics praised LuPone's performance. But the most important one, Frank Rich, did not. "Despite her uncanny delivery of Gloria Swanson's speaking voice and her powerhouse delivery of the score's grand if predictable ballads, she is miscast and unmoving," he wrote. He criticized her for acting and looking like "her own spry 40-something," adding that she failed to convey Norma's status as a legendary movie star. In the climactic scene, when Norma goes mad, LuPone did not "snap into the heartbreaking Blanche DuBois manner called for."

A few days after Rich's review, Jeremy Gerard, the theater editor at *Variety*, reported that Lloyd Webber was going to ditch LuPone for Broadway. Lloyd Webber's press agents denied the story. But *Variety* stood by it. An already poisonous atmosphere became even more lethal.

* * *

The atmosphere in Los Angeles, where *Sunset* went into rehearsal in August, was joyous. The creative team cut scenes that dragged, sharpened lines, deepened characters. The look of the show changed as well. The London production was bright, its colors—tangerine, chartreuse, turquoise—drawn from David Hockney's paintings of Los Angeles in the 1960s. But that vibrant palate was at odds with the eeriness of the story. Inspired by the long shadows the setting sun casts in Southern California, the designers darkened the production. Wilder's *Sunset Boulevard* was film noir. Lloyd Webber's L.A. production would be, too.

The L.A. production would also have something London did not: a 1929 Isotta Fraschini, the luxury car that brings Norma to the Paramount gates. In London, the car was projected on a screen. Billy Wilder told Lloyd Webber, "You gotta have the car." The composer ordered up an exact fiberglass replica, at a cost of $90,000.*[5]

Rehearsals took place in the basement of a church on Fairfax Avenue in Hollywood. Glenn Close's approach to the role was "fearless," said Judy Kuhn, who played Betty Shaeffer. "There was a total lack of vanity. She didn't care what she looked like. To play the part of an aging screen actress—in Los Angeles, where every movie star and everybody else in the business was parading through to see her—was incredibly brave."

Close modeled Norma's grotesque look on Walter Matthau's wife, Carol. Close didn't know her, but she'd heard that when Carol was young she had porcelain skin. As she got older, she

* The production team located the real car used in the movie and put it in the lobby of the Shubert Theatre. Trevor Nunn was not pleased, Edgar Dobie recalled. He didn't want the replica being compared to the real thing. "Get rid of it," he said.

applied white makeup to her face, which made her look odd, even a little frightening. "But I'm sure when she looked in the mirror she saw that porcelain skin," Close said. "Norma's makeup morphed into something grotesque. But she was seeing something different in the mirror. She was seeing what she looked like in the 1920s."

Tense and distracted in London, Lloyd Webber was happy and relaxed in Los Angeles. He moved into a rented mansion on North Alpine Drive in Beverly Hills with his new wife, Madeleine, and their small children. One day he had employees bring a camel to the house. The camel had appeared in a publicity stunt for a revival of *Joseph and the Amazing Technicolor Dreamcoat* that was then running at the Pantages Theatre. Everybody had a camel ride around the pool.

Excitement mounted for the premiere. Massive billboards advertising the show lined Sunset Boulevard. "I'm ready for my billboard, Mr. DeMille," read one. Items about the show appeared in the papers almost every day. Two thousand people showed up at Tower Records to have Lloyd Webber sign the London cast recording. "There could not be a billboard on Sunset Strip big enough, there could not be enough wine flowing, there could not be a big enough party—everything was heightened," said Rick Miramontez, who handled publicity.

All of Hollywood was curious to see if Close could pull off the role. A dress rehearsal was held one Monday night at the Shubert for a small audience. Close insisted everybody sit up in the mezzanine. Miramontez noticed a woman standing outside the theater with her face pressed up against the glass door. "Can I come in?" the woman said. It was Meryl Streep. Miramontez took her to the mezzanine.

Sunset Boulevard was due to open December 13, 1993, in Los Angeles. Barbara Davis, the wife of 20th Century Fox owner Marvin Davis, had taken over a preview performance as a fundraiser for her charity. Surveying the audience that night, Peter Brown saw all the biggest names in Hollywood. *Oh my God,* he thought. *They have upstaged us. Everybody's here tonight, so they won't come to our opening.* He needed something special for the *Sunset* opening that would top Davises' charity preview. A friend had the answer. Why not get someone from the Golden Age of Hollywood who hadn't been seen in a long time? The friend suggested Lana Turner, the beautiful MGM star of the 1940s. She was living as a recluse in Century City. Turner had been at the center of one of Hollywood's most infamous scandals—the stabbing of her lover Joey Stompanato after a violent argument at her Beverly Hills mansion in 1958. It resonated eerily with Norma's shooting of Joe Gillis at the end of *Sunset Boulevard.* (Turner and her teenage daughter, Cheryl Crane, were exonerated of all charges.) Brown, who was close to another star from old Hollywood, Nancy Reagan, gave the order to Miramontez: "I'll deliver the Reagans. You get Lana Turner."

Miramontez tracked down Cheryl and invited her and her mother to the opening. "My mother has not been well," Crane said. A few minutes later she called back. "My mother is so excited!" As the opening-night audience settled into their seats, Turner came down the aisle. People started whispering, "It's Lana." Nancy Reagan turned to Brown and said, "There's Norma Desmond."

The opening-night party was held on the Paramount soundstage where *Sunset Boulevard* was shot. Turner didn't make the party, but the Reagans did. As they arrived, a reporter shouted, "Mr. President, what did you think?"

"Best show I've ever seen," Reagan said.*

* Reagan had not yet gone public with his Alzheimer's diagnosis. But to Christopher Hampton, who met him on opening night, he seemed confused. "You must remember the movie," Hampton said. "There was a movie?" Reagan replied. "Yes, with Bill Holden." Reagan turned to his wife and said, "Nancy, Bill Holden is in the movie of this. I can't wait to see how it comes out!"

Brown got them away from the press quickly. He had just gotten the perfect sound bite.

The reviews were mixed. For Close, they were glowing. Frank Rich had left the drama beat at the *New York Times* to become an op-ed columnist. Vincent Canby, the paper's longtime movie critic, had replaced him. "When the curtain came down," Canby wrote, "Glenn Close had suddenly become a big, exciting new star of the American musical theater of the 1990s."

"That review," said Miramontez, "was the nail in Patti's coffin."*

Don Black had just gotten into bed when the phone rang.

"Don, Don!" said a voice that was "absolutely manic," Black recalled.

It was LuPone.

"What is it?"

"Glenn Close is going to play Broadway and I'm not!"

"Just calm down, calm down," Black said.

"Calm down? I won't stop shaking for six months!"

Though rumors of LuPone's demise had been swirling for months, Lloyd Webber's publicists denied them all. But that morning in New York her agent, Robert Duva, picked up Liz Smith's gossip column and read that Close would open on Broadway. Smith cited no sources. But everybody on Broadway knew she would not run such an incendiary item if she hadn't confirmed it.

Duva now had to tell his diva. She was getting made up for the Wednesday matinee when he called.

"I started screaming," LuPone said. "I couldn't believe it. They

* There was another nail as well. An executive at Paramount charged with overseeing the show attended a performance in London. He told Lloyd Webber, "I can't understand a thing that woman is saying." (LuPone's diction, which can be slurry, has been the butt of impersonators, drag queens, and the revue *Forbidden Broadway* for years.)

didn't tell me. They didn't talk to me. They just announced it. And then I had batting practice in my dressing room. I threw a floor lamp out the window." Then she left the theater.

The next day in New York, the Really Useful Group confirmed the story. "In view of the expense of the production, and that our investors have been vocal about this, the consensus was that the wisest course for us on Broadway, which is the preeminent place for a musical to be, was that we had to go with Glenn," Peter Brown told the *New York Times*.[6] Close did not comment, but Brown said she did not want to be seen as "some kind of Eve Harrington," a reference to the conniving understudy in *All About Eve*.

Close had nothing to do with the decision to fire LuPone, and she vowed never to speak about it. But she was upset that Brown had described her position. She called him up and said, "You have no authority to speak for me."[7] Brown apologized.

The dethroned diva, meanwhile, was holed up at the Yew Tree Inn, an elegant seventeenth-century hotel and pub in Newbury, an hour or so outside of London. She was crying "buckets of tears." But she made a crucial decision. She knew that in show business if you quit, you get nothing. But if you're fired, there's usually a settlement. She returned to London for the Friday-night performance.

Duva, her agent, recommended she hire the best theater lawyer in the business, John Breglio. His clients included the Michael Bennett estate, Stephen Sondheim, and the playwright August Wilson. Breglio flew to London to mediate. LuPone often called him from the theater a half hour before the show. She was furious and humiliated.

"This is not the best way for you to go onstage tonight, is it?" he asked.

"It's the perfect way for me to go onstage!" she said.

Breglio hammered out a settlement in a few days at Really Useful headquarters on Tower Street. He negotiated with Patrick

McKenna, the head of the company. Lloyd Webber was in another room and "Patrick would have to go back and forth," Breglio recalled.

LuPone's settlement, as reported at the time, was $1 million, though a source close to the actress says it was more than that.* She played her final performance in *Sunset Boulevard* on March 12, 1994, to a thunderous standing ovation.

The feud between Patti LuPone and Andrew Lloyd Webber gripped the theater world for years to come.

Asked about the feud in 2017, Lloyd Webber said, "I know I'm cast as the villain in her mind. But I wish she had come to London and been part of the process and not behaved like a diva. The atmosphere she created was poison."

LuPone said, "It's more fun to have this feud than make up with him—so much more fun. And my husband wouldn't have it. People always say what would you do if you saw Andrew Lloyd Webber. And I always say it's not what *I* would do. It's what my *husband* would do. He would flatten him."†

The L.A. production of *Sunset Boulevard* was a smash, shattering box office records at the Shubert every week. Close was due to play her final performance June 26, 1994, before heading to New York. The question in Los Angeles became, Who could replace her? Gossip columns percolated with divas—Meryl Streep, Madonna, Diana Ross, Michelle Lee, Diahann Carroll, Loretta Young, Debbie Reynolds, even Olivia de Havilland.

* LuPone used part of the settlement to build a pool at her house in Connecticut. She dubbed it the "Andrew Lloyd Webber Memorial Pool."

† LuPone and Lloyd Webber did meet on January 24, 2018, to rehearse her performance of "Don't Cry for Me Argentina" at the Grammy Awards. LuPone swept in and said, "Hello, Andrew." Turning to the rest of the room, she said, "This is détente, ladies and gentlemen."

"We made endless lists," said press agent Rick Miramontez. "Most of it was all made up, but we always got the names in print!"

Close's success taught Lloyd Webber an important lesson: a movie star, not a Broadway star, should play Norma Desmond, especially in California. As it happened, a real movie star, one of the biggest of the 1970s, was interested: Faye Dunaway. Everyone agreed she was perfect for the part. But could she sing it? Lloyd Webber flew to Los Angeles to test her out with his trusted music director David Caddick. "She didn't have Glenn's range, but she could sing," said Caddick. After Dunaway left, Lloyd Webber said, "You know, clearly what's most important for the role of Norma is the acting ability. If we don't have the actress, we don't have the piece."

Dunaway, who had a reputation for being difficult, was a delight in rehearsals, driving herself to the theater in her snappy Mercedes sports car and "looking like a million bucks," said Miramontez. She was strong in the dramatic scenes, performing the role her own way rather than mimicking Close.

"You could see why the camera loved her because when she made that face come alive in the character it was completely compelling," said Caddick. "What she couldn't do was bring the same kind of flair to the music." Caddick expressed his concerns to Lloyd Webber. Caddick and Dunaway flew to London to make sure the composer was still comfortable with her. Lloyd Webber, Caddick recalled, again emphasized the importance of the acting.

But back in Los Angeles, where Dunaway was rehearsing under the direction of a stage manager, her performance became halting and unsteady. She could land a song once, but not consistently. "It robbed her of her confidence," said Caddick.

Trevor Nunn arrived to fine-tune her performance before her opening on July 12. Her acting impressed him. Her singing did not. The financial people monitoring the box office were not impressed either. Close opened with an advance of more than $10 million. Dunaway's stood at $4 million.

Miramontez snuck into Dunaway's first run-through at the Shubert Theatre. What he saw was "shocking and heartbreaking. She was lost. She was just lost."

(Somebody in the theater secretly videotaped the run-through. A few weeks later the video made the rounds of all the bigwigs in musical theater. Duva, LuPone's agent, saw it. Dunaway made him think of Florence Foster Jenkins, the socialite and amateur soprano pilloried by critics for her self-funded Carnegie Hall debut in 1944.)

After the rehearsal, Nunn called Lloyd Webber. "She can't go on," he said. "There will be ridicule and there will be laughter."[8] Once again *Sunset Boulevard* was thrown into turmoil. The $12 million L.A. production had not turned a profit. If it opened with Dunaway, the critics would destroy it. Lloyd Webber could fire her and let an understudy go on until he found another star. But that would be expensive. In the end, he dismissed Dunaway and closed the L.A. production, at a loss of more than $6 million.[9]

Lloyd Webber thought he'd put one avenging diva behind him. Now another was after him. Dunaway called LuPone and asked for advice. "Sue him!" she said.*

After Lloyd Webber announced Dunaway was not up to the demands of the role, she held a press conference in her backyard. Looking every inch the glamorous movie star, she told reporters, "When I auditioned for Mr. Lloyd Webber I sang in my range. He cast me in that range, only later deciding to try to push me into a higher one. This is yet another capricious act by a capricious man."

The press lapped up yet another *Sunset Boulevard* feud. Lloyd Webber got clobbered. The *New York Times* described him as

* Miramontez secretly listened in on the call. "Patti egged her on," he said. "These two old warriors were commiserating and propping each other up."

having "a chilling temper, an aloof personality and, after so much power and money over the years, indifference to the sensitivities and needs of performers with fragile egos."[10]

Dunaway took LuPone's advice and sued Lloyd Webber for $6 million. They reached a settlement, yet another expense thrown on top of an increasingly expensive show. Looking back on the Dunaway episode, Lloyd Webber said, "I should have let her go onstage and see what happened. I wish I had."

Sunset Boulevard finally opened in New York at the Minskoff Theatre on November 17, 1994, with an advance sale of $37.5 million, the highest ever for a Broadway show. The critics adored Close, and, with a few exceptions, were much kinder to Lloyd Webber's work than they had been in the past. The musical was grossing nearly $800,000 week. It was indeed "The Female Phantom." But behind the scenes, there was concern. The dismissals of LuPone and Dunaway left the impression that only Glenn Close could play the part. Her contract would end in July. Would people still pay top dollar to see the show without her?

The test came in March when Close took a two-week vacation and her understudy, Karen Mason, went on. Jeremy Gerard, the theater reporter for *Variety*, gathered the grosses every week for publication. He checked *Sunset* and was surprised to see the gross was nearly the same for Mason as it had been for Close, about $730,000. It went up a little the next week. *Variety* printed the numbers.

And then Gerard got an anonymous fax. It contained the real numbers from the Minskoff box office. The gross had slipped by $155,000 each week Close was out. Tickets had been discounted for the understudy's run, but Lloyd Webber's company did not report the discounts. Really Useful inflated the figures so that *Sunset Boulevard* appeared to be a sellout even without Close.

Gerard ran the story under the headline SUNSET BULL-EVARD. Edgar Dobie, the head of Really Useful in New York, took the blame, though in an interview in 2018 he said he made the decision with the approval of the London office. Dobie offered to resign. Lloyd Webber, in a statement to the press, called the decision "idiotic" but refused to accept Dobie's resignation. He apologized for the inflated grosses and praised Karen Mason for receiving standing ovations at every performance.

A few days later Gerard got another anonymous fax. This one was a two-page, single-spaced letter to Andrew Lloyd Webber from Glenn Close.

"I am furious and insulted," she wrote. "I don't think it's an exaggeration to say that my performance turned 'Sunset Boulevard' around. I made it a hit. It has existed on my shoulders . . . and yet a representative of your company went out of their way and lied to try to make the public believe that my contribution to this show is nothing, that Karen's performance is equal to mine, and that my absence had absolutely no effect whatsoever on all the thousands of dollars that supposedly kept pouring into the box office. It sickens me to be treated with such disregard."

She concluded in high-diva dudgeon: "If I could leave 'Sunset' tomorrow, I would. If I could leave it in May when my contract says I can, believe me, I would. At this point, what is making me stay is my sense of obligation to all the people who are holding tickets until July 2."

Variety printed the letter, and the next day the tabloids splashed the latest *Sunset* feud across the front pages. BULLETS OVER BROADWAY, screamed the *Daily News*. Lloyd Webber's representatives said the composer was "distraught and shell shocked" by the letter. Lloyd Webber issued a statement: "I am at the end of my tether." Close expressed dismay that her private correspondence had become public. The press mobbed the stage door that night. Close sent her dresser to a costume store in Chinatown to get disguises. She and the cast left the theater wearing Groucho Marx glasses. *Sunset Boulevard* was in the news again.

The feud blew over, of course. Close and Lloyd Webber were pals at the Tony Awards in June. The field of new musicals was pathetic that season. *Sunset* had one rival—*Smokey Joe's Cafe*, a revue of songs by Jerry Leiber and Mike Stoller. Lloyd Webber privately joked, "We have to write a new musical fast, and it can't be very good."[11] *Sunset* received eleven Tony nominations in 1995, including Best Musical. Two of the nominations—Best Book and Best Score—were unopposed.

Sunset won Best Musical. Close won Best Actress. Overall the production picked up seven awards. Tickets for Close's final performances were impossible to come by. Grosses jumped to nearly $900,000 a week.

Another scandal put it in the headlines again a few months later. Barbara Walters profiled Lloyd Webber on the ABC news program *20/20*. She reported on the success of *Sunset Boulevard*. A few days later, working as the theater reporter for the *Daily News*, I was going over the show's financial papers at the New York State Attorney General's office (offerings for all Broadway shows are on file with the A.G.). The last page listed the investors.

"That's not supposed to be there," a member of the A.G.'s staff said. "Don't look at it." The staffer left the room to take a phone call. I looked at the list. One name jumped out at me, Barbara Walters. Next to her name was the amount of her investment, $100,000. She had not disclosed that investment to the viewers of *20/20*.

I called an ABC spokesman for comment. "Do you really think a hundred thousand dollars means that much to Barbara Walters?" the spokesman said, trying to shoot the story down. WALTERS ENTANGLED IN A WEB OF CONFLICT read the headline the next day.[12] Walters apologized on *20/20* that week.

* * *

Betty Buckley took over for Close in *Sunset Boulevard*. Then came Elaine Paige. Both actresses received rave reviews. Lloyd Webber launched *Sunset*s in Germany, Canada, and on tour across the United States. An Australian production featured an unknown actor by the name of Hugh Jackman as Joe Gillis.

Lloyd Webber also wrote a new show, *Whistle Down the Wind*, based on the 1961 British movie starring Hayley Mills. He planned to open it on Broadway in June 1997 after an out-of-town tryout in Washington, D.C. But the D.C. critics savaged the show, calling it "dull," "turgid," "bloated," and "bizarre." Lloyd Webber closed *Whistle* in Washington and scrapped plans for Broadway. As a gesture of goodwill, he returned $10 million to his investors.

Sunset was hemorrhaging money, too. Its weekly overhead on Broadway alone was $500,000. It hadn't done sellout business since Close's departure. The other productions were struggling as well. "Andrew had this shocking sit-down with his accountants, who said to him this show can never, ever break even," said Christopher Hampton.

Lloyd Webber announced he was closing the Broadway production on March 22, 1997, after 997 performances. Hampton begged him to keep it open one more week. "It would have been nice to have a show run a thousand performances on Broadway," he said. The London and Canadian productions also went down, as did the U.S. national tour. Australia packed it in, too, after just eight months.

None of the productions recouped. Frank Rich took a swipe at Lloyd Webber, dubbing *Sunset Boulevard* the "ultimate 'hit' flop, since it ran more than two years."[13]

Lloyd Webber went into a depression. "I was incredibly hurt by some of the things Patti had said, and by the way I was perceived," he said. "I very nearly put my whole company up for sale. The joy had gone out of it. I never wanted to go near a theater again."

He later came out of the depression and wrote more shows, including *The Beautiful Game* and *The Woman in White*. But he would not have another Broadway hit until *School of Rock* in 2015. The era of the British megamusical was indeed over.

CHAPTER THREE

508 GREENWICH, #4

In 1971, Julie Larson, a teenager living in White Plains, New York, bought Lloyd Webber and Tim Rice's album *Jesus Christ Superstar.* She played it over and over on the stereo in the living room. Her eleven-year-old brother, Jonathan, would sometimes wander by and listen. And then one day he sat at the family piano and played the entire score by ear. "That was the first time, I think, we realized Jon had real musical talent," Julie said.

Jonathan Larson was born February 4, 1960, in Mount Vernon, New York, to Nanette and Allan Larson, a direct-marketing executive. The family moved to White Plains shortly after Jonathan was born. It was a comfortable middle-class household. They spent summers on Cape Cod. The first show Jonathan ever saw was *The Wizard of Oz* at the Cape Playhouse. Julie, Jonathan, and family friends staged their own version on the beach.

Jonathan saw his first Broadway musical—*Hair*—when he was nine. He loved it, but "the reality was we could not afford a lot of Broadway shows," said Al Larson. "So we were big album buyers." Music filled their house. Julie played the piano and the clarinet. Al listened to live broadcasts from the Metropolitan Opera on Saturday afternoons. Folk and political songs by The

Weavers, Woody Guthrie, and Bob Dylan often were on the turntable. Julie and Jonathan listened to the latest Broadway cast recordings—*A Chorus Line*, *Annie*—and Jonathan played them on the piano. Their mother liked musicals by Stephen Sondheim. Her favorite was *Pacific Overtures.*

Jonathan saw Sondheim's *Sweeney Todd* in 1979, and the composer became an idol. But so did Billy Joel and Elton John. Larson loved rock and pop as much as musical theater, though musical theater often won out. Matthew O'Grady, his closest friend in high school, once asked him to get tickets to a Peter Frampton concert. Larson bought tickets to *Sweeney Todd* instead.

Larson took two years of piano lessons, but grew frustrated because his teacher insisted he play classical music. He preferred popular songs. Larson's friends called him "the piano man" because he loved Billy Joel and could not walk by a piano without playing it. He also loved the spotlight. He had a leading man's charisma, but a character actor's looks. Lanky, with big ears, a mop of black hair, and a winning smile, he played Motel the tailor in *Fiddler on the Roof* and Riff in *West Side Story* in summer theater. He got the Tommy Tune part one summer in a community theater production of *Seesaw.* He had a big dance number, "It's Not Where You Start." He couldn't dance, but that didn't matter. "He could sell it," his sister said.

Larson attended Adelphi University on Long Island on an acting scholarship. Jacques Burdick, who had studied under Robert Brustein at Yale, ran the theater department. The young actor's facility at the piano caught Burdick's attention. He was adapting the medieval Spanish poem *El Libro de Buen Amor* for the stage and asked Larson to write the score. Larson took to composing. Music poured out of him, but this time it was his. He wrote another show, a biting satire on the Moral Majority called

Sacrimmoralinority. Heavily influenced by Brecht, it was produced by the Adelphi theater department in 1981.

Despite his songwriting talent, Larson still wanted to be an actor. After graduation he went off to the Barn Theatre in Augusta, Michigan, to earn his Equity card. With friends he met at the Barn, including Marin Mazzie, who would go on to earn three Tony Award nominations, he moved to New York City in the fall of 1982 and formed a trio called J. Glitz. The trio performed in small clubs all over the city. Al and Nan Larson attended every show. Sometimes they were the only two people in the audience.

Like many struggling performers, Larson waited tables, ending up in a renovated railroad car called the Moondance Diner on Sixth Avenue between Grand and Canal Streets. He lived in a dingy four-story walk-up at 508 Greenwich Street, around the corner from New York's oldest bar—the Ear Inn, established in 1817. The neighborhood, south of the West Village, west of SoHo, was a no-man's-land. Larson and his friends called it Assho.

The apartment was ramshackle, but roomy. The bathtub was in the kitchen. A makeshift wall divided another room into two windowless bedrooms. The living room overlooked Greenwich Street. Larson kept his cheap Casio keyboard, computer, and television set in the living room. The buzzer was broken, so visitors had to call from a pay phone across the street and wait for Larson to throw a pouch containing the key out the window. The heat didn't always work in the winter (there was an illegal wood-burning stove), but in the summer Larson could climb out on the roof and watch the sun set over the Hudson River. Roommates—two, sometimes three—came and went, splitting the $1,050-a-month rent. Larson lived with close friends such as Ann Egan, an artist, and Jonathan Burkhart, an aspiring moviemaker. Other roommates he knew less well. One, a heroin addict, had to be thrown out.[1]

Every year around Christmas, Larson invited his friends to 508 Greenwich for what he and Egan dubbed a peasants' feast. Everybody brought a dish, drank plenty of beer and cheap wine, smoked pot, and talked about their various projects and dreams for the future. The peasant feast grew each year as Larson's circle of friends expanded. But you didn't have to be a close friend to be invited. Sometimes Larson or his roommates would extend the invitation to someone they met that day on the street.[2]

Making little headway as an actor, Larson began focusing on his music. He wrote a show based on *1984*, but couldn't get the rights from George Orwell's estate. He reworked the songs into an ambitious, futuristic musical called *Superbia*. The music was a pulsating mix of rock, new wave, techno, and Broadway. The show took aim at a society in which everyone was hooked on a corporate-controlled, mind-numbing entertainment culture. It had elements of *1984* and the movie *Network*. It was prescient, but sprawling and often incomprehensible. Larson developed it at the American Society of Composers, Authors and Publishers (ASCAP) and presented some of his songs to a panel of Broadway professionals, including Stephen Sondheim.

"I thought it was the most original and interesting piece I'd heard in any of the workshops I'd paneled on," Sondheim recalled. Larson asked Sondheim if they could talk in more detail about the show sometime. Sondheim invited him over to his elegant Turtle Bay town house. Larson arrived with a present: a huge blunt.

"I'd certainly seen—and smoked—joints before, but though I'd heard of them, I'd never seen a blunt," Sondheim said. Though the songs from *Superbia* impressed him, the plot did not. "It was unresolvable," he said.

But Larson persisted. He worked on the show for the next several years and got a workshop production at Playwrights Horizons, a leading nonprofit Off-Broadway theater. The workshop was not successful and Playwrights dropped the show. His friend Victoria Leacock produced a concert version at the Village Gate in Greenwich Village in the hope that a producer might pick it up. No one did. "He was devastated by that," said Julie Larson. "People told him it was too big for Off Broadway and too advanced for Broadway. And out of his frustration he went to work on his next show, which was just going to be him, a piano and a band, so nobody could tell him it's too big."

He called his new show *30/90.* Larson turned thirty in 1990 and was becoming anxious about his lack of success. Other friends were beginning to get ahead in their careers. He was still waiting tables at the Moondance Diner and getting around the city on his bicycle or in a beat-up Datsun 810 he'd bought from an ex-girlfriend.[3] He parked it on the street and left the doors unlocked hoping someone would steal it.[4] His sister and friends tried to get him work that paid, but for the most part he resisted their help.

Larson was on a mission. The Broadway of the 1980s depressed him. British pop operas such as *Les Misérables* and *The Phantom of the Opera* were for tourists and older people, he complained. Broadway had lost touch with his generation. He hoped to reclaim it by writing the first rock musical since *Hair* and *Jesus Christ Superstar.*

30/90 is a song cycle about a struggling composer trying to decide if he should continue writing music or take a job in advertising. One poignant song deals with the news that his best friend is HIV-positive. (Larson had recently learned that his friend Matt O'Grady had contracted the virus.) Retitled *Boho Days*, the show caught the attention of Robyn Goodman, artistic director of Second Stage, a small Off-Broadway theater company. The first time she met Larson he said, "I'm going to bring rock 'n' roll to Broadway."

"He wasn't arrogant," Goodman said. "He really meant it. He wanted to make Broadway contemporary. He talked about it all the time. He was obsessed, in a wonderful way." Goodman produced a couple of readings over a weekend at Second Stage. She thought the rock songs were terrific. The storytelling needed work. Larson was in the reading, and that was another problem. "I suggested we get an actor to play the part, so he could sit back and be the author and work on it," she said. "I also thought he needed to add some more characters." Larson disagreed. Goodman dropped the show. "He was very upset, but we had formed a bond," she said. "He was adorable. Big ears, lanky, long arms—so cute, and so talented. You just knew he was going to do something."

Jeffrey Seller, an aspiring twenty-five-year-old producer, went to a reading of *Boho Days*. When Larson came onstage and began singing about turning thirty and writing musicals no one wanted to produce, having an agent who didn't return his calls, and a girlfriend he should break up with but couldn't because he was afraid to be alone, Seller started to cry. "Here was this man telling his life story that I felt was my life story," he said, "and telling it in a musical vernacular that was giving me goose bumps." Seller went to a party after the show but was too shy to introduce himself to Larson. The next day he wrote him a letter:

"I saw your play, *Boho Days*, and was bowled over. Your work—music, lyrics, and spoken word—has an emotional power and resonance that I rarely experience in the theatre. You're also insightful, perceptive, and very funny. I'm writing because, like you, I also want to do great things in the theatre, but from the producing and directing side." Noting Larson's "predilection toward rock musicals," Seller outlined an idea for a show about an American family in crisis and the "dissolution" of the American dream, all told with a rock score. "From the looks of your impressive résumé," he wrote, unaware of a career going nowhere, "I figure you probably don't need to get involved with low men on the totem pole like me . . . but I'd love to get together and talk. I've got about a thousand ideas to share, and I'm sure you do too."

Seller booked touring shows in the office of Broadway producers Fran and Barry Weissler. They cornered the market on tightly budgeted musical revivals starring headliners from another era—*Zorba* with Anthony Quinn; *Cabaret* with Joel Grey; *Fiddler on the Roof* with Topol. Seller made the deals for those shows to tour the country. He was ambitious, opinionated, self-assured, and, by his own admission, arrogant.

"I was loudmouthed and rebellious," he said. He also wanted to work on his projects with artists his own age. A few weeks after he saw *Boho Days,* his boss called him into the conference room and told him he'd outgrown his job. It was time for him to move on. As she was handing him his two weeks severance, the secretary buzzed him over the intercom. "Jeffrey, Jonathan Larson is on the phone for you."

They met the next day at a bar near New York University. "I was on a mission to please myself," Seller said. "Jonathan, on the other hand, was on a mission to change the world. He did not believe the music on Broadway was our music. 'I am going to change that,' he said."

With *Boho Days,* now called *tick, tick . . . Boom!*, foundering, Larson turned his attention to another project he'd been working on—an adaptation of Puccini's *La Bohème* set in contemporary New York City. It was not his idea. Billy Aronson, a young playwright who loved the opera, brought the proposal to Playwrights Horizons in 1989. He was looking for a composer, so the theater put him in touch with Larson. They met on the roof of 508 Greenwich and talked about the show. The characters suffering from tuberculosis in the opera would have AIDS in the musical. Aronson wanted to set the show on the Upper West Side; Larson argued for the

East Village. An avid reader of the *New York Times*, he followed the riots in Tompkins Square Park in the summer of 1988. A group of squatters, drug dealers, artists, punks, and homeless people had commandeered the park. Some were protesting gentrification; others were just doing drugs. When the police tried to disperse them, a riot ensued. The *Times* reported on many instances of police brutality. The Tompkins Square riots, Larson thought, provided a dramatic background to a story about struggling artists trying to maintain a foothold in a city increasingly for the rich. From the beginning he wanted to call the show *Rent*. The title had a double meaning. The characters couldn't afford to pay rent, something Larson struggled with nearly every month. At the same time, their lives were being "rent" by AIDS, drugs, poverty, gentrification, and alienation.

Aronson and Larson worked on the show for about a year, writing a title song and two others—"Santa Fe" and "I Should Tell You." But their styles didn't mesh. Aronson, perhaps influenced by the TV series *thirtysomething*, gave the characters a yuppie spin. Larson wanted them to be more like himself and his friends, struggling artists frustrated they were not getting their due.[5]

Their collaboration stalled, and they both moved on to other projects. But within a year, three more of Larson's friends were diagnosed with AIDS. His friend Matt O'Grady joined a support group called Friends In Deed, which emphasized living with AIDS, not dying from it. Larson often attended meetings with O'Grady. The idea of dying people celebrating life, and facing death with dignity, touched him.

In October 1991, Larson wrote Aronson asking for permission to continue with *Rent* alone. Larson would credit Aronson's contributions should a production ever happen. Aronson agreed.

Larson threw himself into *Rent*. He'd worked out to the minute a schedule at the Moondance Diner that gave him enough shifts to pay the rent but still have time to write. He had notebooks and computer files full of scenes, characters, and lyrics. He wrote most of the score on a computerized eighty-eight-key Yamaha keyboard. It was a gift from his friend Jonathan Burkhart, who had started to earn some money. The keyboard gave him the freedom to explore all sorts of beats and styles—rock, pop, salsa, reggae, bebop, hip-hop. During a visit to Santa Monica to see his sister, he went to the public library and took out the English version of Henri Murger's *Scènes de la vie de bohème*, on which Puccini's opera is based. He sat in the backyard and "devoured it," Julie recalled.

Back in New York he called his friend Robyn Goodman to tell her about his new show. He sent her a tape of the title song. City Opera was doing a production of *Bohème* that season, so Goodman took him. Throughout the show he kept telling her what he was going to do. When Mimi, dying of tuberculosis came on, he whispered, "She's going to be on drugs." He made another change as well. In the opera, Mimi dies at the end. In his version, she would not. He had seen many of his friends with AIDS rally at times and told his sister, Julie, that Mimi "represents hope."

Larson wrote quickly, and couldn't wait to share songs with friends and family. If he finished a song at 2:00 a.m., he'd call his sister in Los Angeles. There was seldom a "hello." He would announce the title of the song and start playing it on his keyboard.

As he was working on the show, Larson would read and play it to friends at his apartment. Most were supportive, but one night two of his friends with AIDS erupted. They were dying and here was a show, influenced by Friends In Deed, emphasizing life and love. *You don't know what it is to have AIDS,* his friends said. *It's not all about love.* Their anger worked its way into a scene involving a support group for people living with AIDS, adding a bit of toughness, and reality, to this life-affirming show.[6]

* * *

In the summer of 1992, Larson was riding his bike down East Fourth Street when he noticed a new theater under construction. It was being built for the New York Theatre Workshop, which had outgrown its tiny theater on Perry Street in the West Village. Larson popped in and explored the space. He felt at home. A few days later he sent the script of *Rent* and a cassette of him playing and singing the score to Jim Nicola, the artistic director. Nicola was struck by a stage direction at the beginning of the script: "There should be a full Broadway orchestra in the pit and a rock band onstage." This show was ambitious, one that might match the ambitions of the New York Theatre Workshop. He also responded to the setting—the East Village, his new neighborhood. And he liked the score's combination of contemporary music and American musical theater. It reminded him of *Hair.* A song called "Light My Candle" impressed him. Mimi and Roger, a struggling musician, sing it when they first meet. "It was a really good pop song and a complete dramatic event," Nicola said. "It has a beginning, middle, and end. Puccini had an innate dramatic sense in his music. I thought Jonathan had that same gift."

One song, "Seasons of Love," did not impress him. "It felt like a fake big gospel number," he said. "It was totally inauthentic in the context of the show since there were no black characters." Nicola could see that Larson was trying to create a diverse array of characters, but most were generic, closely resembling their prototypes in *Bohème*. The script was diffuse, sprawling, muddled. And the structure was odd. The first act took place in one night, the second over the course of a year. Still, the show had promise, and Larson was a fresh voice.

Nicola invited Larson to join the Usual Suspects, a group of artists associated with the New York Theatre Workshop. In June 1993, Nicola let Larson do a reading of *Rent* at the theater. Jeffrey Seller, now working at a small booking agency called, appropriately, The Producing Office, attended with two friends. One of them, Peter

Holmes à Court, came from a rich Australian family that controlled the Stoll Moss Theatre group in London. Seller thought, *If this works Peter could be my money guy.* The opening number—"Rent"—was "fierce," Seller said. "And then the reading devolved into a collage of East Village life with absolutely no narrative spine. It lasted three hours." Holmes à Court bolted at intermission. Seller's other friend said, "Tell Jonathan he should start working on his next piece."

Seller had dinner with Larson a few days later. He was blunt about the reading. "What are you trying to do here? Are you just trying to write a concert, or are you trying to write a play? Because if you're writing a play, you have to flesh out a narrative." Larson was defensive and upset.

Nicola had his doubts about *Rent* as well. The script condescended to the homeless characters. "You can't put actors onstage and use them as a chorus of cute homeless people," Nicola said. "It's demeaning, it's insulting."[7] Larson bristled. Nicola was not prepared to take the next step and spend his limited resources on a workshop production. He told Larson he was free to take *Rent* elsewhere.

Larson's response to criticism was to grow defensive, sulk away, and go back to work, taking into account the criticism that had upset him. He reworked *Rent* to the point that in the spring of 1994—and with the support of Stephen Sondheim—he won a Richard Rodgers Fellowship of $45,000. That was enough money to pay for a workshop at Nicola's theater. The show needed a strong director. Nicola approached Michael Greif, who had just won rave reviews for his revival of *Machinal* at the Public Theater. Greif was precise, disciplined, and, when necessary, tough. He also understood how to structure a show, something *Rent* needed. Nicola sent him the script and a tape of the score.

"Some of his songs were fantastic and some of his songs were not," Greif said. "But enough of the songs were fantastic that I thought, I'm very excited to have a meeting with him." At that first meeting, Larson told him, "I'm writing this because I'm coping with my friends' illnesses." The script was a mess, but to Greif something was "deeply passionate and sorrowful" about the show.[8] He agreed to stage the workshop.

As they prepared for the workshop, Nicola and Greif pushed Larson to make his East Village characters more specific, more authentic. Larson understood the frustrated artist—he was one—but his portraits of ethnic minorities and the homeless remained vague. He had a handle on the character Mark, a would-be filmmaker who came from a nice middle-class family in Westchester—clearly autobiographical. Mark was emerging as the narrator, giving the show a spine. Roger, Mark's roommate, was a struggling songwriter with HIV. He came with a heavy dose of self-pity. The characters of Mimi, an exotic dancer, and Angel, a transvestite, "suggested Latino, but it was just an idea," Nicola said. Collins, a philosopher and Angel's lover, was white. Maureen, Mark's girlfriend and a not especially talented performance artist, was straight. In this early draft, she left Mark for another man. Missing from Larson's collage of East Village types, Nicola thought, were lesbians. So Larson made a change: Maureen now left Mark for another woman, Joanne, a lawyer from an upper-class black family.

Casting would go a long way to deepening Larson's characters. Wendy Ettinger, the casting director, sought out authentic East Village artists rather than musical theater kids with degrees from Carnegie Mellon. She posted casting notices in clubs, performance spaces, bars, and restaurants. One performer who came to her attention was Daphne Rubin-Vega. Born in Panama City, she lived in Greenwich Village and worked as a singer, comedian, and actress. She was rehearsing with the comedy group El Barrio USA when her purple beeper went off with a message to call her agent. Casting was underway for a new rock musical based on *La Bohème*, the agent told her. She wasn't interested in doing musicals—she thought of herself as a rock singer—but her father loved the opera, so she decided to give it a shot. The clothes she wore to the audition she bought on the street—a T-shirt, a Catholic schoolgirl skirt, ripped fishnet stockings. She sang "Roxanne" and did "my version of 'Flashdance.'" After the audition she was given a tape of a song from the show called "Out Tonight." Go home and work on it, she was told.

Greif and Nicola thought she was terrific. They loved her sultry voice and ferocious sexuality. But Larson was "horrified by her," Nicola said. He wrote Mimi with a friend of his in mind, a trained musical theater performer who had played Maria in a tour of *West Side Story*. Her voice was stronger than Rubin-Vega's. It was the essence of Broadway. East Village raw it was not. "I have written some of the best songs for the American musical theater ever and I want them sung really well," Larson said. "She can't sing them."[9]

Rubin-Vega listened to the tape of "Out Tonight." The singer was a white soprano, who was, in fact, Larson's friend. Rubin-Vega was not impressed. "Out Tonight" reminded her of The Who's "Baba O'Riley," and here it was being sung by a soprano. Rubin-Vega thought, *Fucking let me take this shit down and own it.* Which is what she did at her callback. She got the part, though Larson remained wary.

Anthony Rapp landed the role of Mark. He'd been on Broadway in John Guare's *Six Degrees of Separation*. But his career had hit a lull. He was working at Starbucks when he got the call for *Rent*. He captured Mark's neurotic energy and fear of failure.

Joining the creative team were two people who would play crucial roles in shaping the sound and look of *Rent*. Tim Weil, a versatile musician from the rock and pop worlds, became the music director. He could take Larson's melodies and turn them into fully realized rock, pop, reggae, or hip-hop songs. He and Larson became close collaborators. They were about the same age and at the same point in their careers, both working at what they loved, but unable to make a living at it. Larson's drive impressed Weil.

If a song didn't work, he'd throw it out, go home, and come back with a new one. Larson's growing desperation also struck him. "He was trying to do this show, and he was just barely scraping by," Weil said. "He was under a lot of stress." In many late-night conversations over beer, Larson said that if *Rent* didn't work he was going to have to do something else with his life. "He really thought this was his last shot," Weil said.

Angela Wendt joined the workshop as the costume designer. There was no money for a set designer, so she did that, too. (Greif would bring on set designer Paul Manley for the full production.) Her budget for the *Rent* sets and costumes was $500. The set became the back brick wall of the theater, scaffolding already in place for renovations, and a few tables and chairs. Wendt rummaged through vintage-clothing stores in the East Village for costumes. She bought clothes at Daffy's and Century 21, discount stores. She drew inspiration from designers Jean Paul Gaultier, Rei Kawakubo, and Leigh Bowery. She also picked through cast members' closets. Rubin-Vega's yielded Mimi's shiny turquoise leggings for "Out Tonight." Wendt found a vintage Santa Claus suit for Angel to wear in Act I, which takes place on December 24. Act II begins on New Year's Eve. Collins and Angel attend a party dressed as James Bond and Pussy Galore. The Pussy Galore costume stumped Wendt, but one morning in her bathroom she saw it: a shower curtain. The resourceful Angel could turn it into a coat. Wendt made the belt out of shower curtain rings, giving the costume a loopy 1970s look.*

Larson was hardly a fashionista. He wore what he could afford—jeans, T-shirts, ratty old sneakers. But he had big ambitions for his show. He told Wendt, "I want *Rent* to become the next fashion influence."

* The original Pussy Galore shower curtain coat is now in the Smithsonian National Museum of American History.

Rehearsals for the workshop began in October 1994. The plot was still scattershot so Greif decided to stage the show more like a concert than a theater piece.

"It wasn't clear all the time what the fuck was going on," Rubin-Vega said. She had a song called "Valentine's Day" with the lyric: "Beat her till she's black and blue and grey, draw a little heart, / Draw a little arrow, draw a little blood, v-v-v-valentine's day." The song bled into "Without You," sung by Mark and Joanne about Maureen. The connections were unclear. "It was mishy-mashy," Rubin-Vega said. But she felt the show "was talking to me. I had never felt represented in the theater, so to have that feeling of inclusion was special."

Jeffrey Seller, Larson's friend and aspiring producer, attended the first performance of the workshop. He brought Kevin McCollum, who had started The Producing Office where Seller was working. Before the show started, Seller said to McCollum, "This is either going to be brilliant or a piece of shit."

McCollum had no idea what was going on for the first twenty minutes. And then Mimi and Roger sang "Light My Candle." McCollum turned to Seller and whispered, "This is the best piece of musical storytelling I have seen in a long time."

McCollum met Larson at intermission. With a flourish, he took his Chemical Bank checkbook out of his coat pocket. "This is wonderful," he said. Larson smiled and said, "Do you want to see the second act?" Tim Weil invited his friend Lonny Price, a Broadway actor who would go on to become a respected director, to the workshop. They met outside the theater during intermission. "Don't ever leave this show," Price told him. "You're doing *A Chorus Line*."*

Not everyone was as enthusiastic. A staffer from Fran and Barry Weissler's office reported that the show was "a piece of

* When Weil told Larson what Price said, Larson responded, "Yeah. Show me the check."

shit."[10] The New York Theatre Workshop conducted audience surveys. While they were generally positive, a consistent thread was: Why don't these people just get a job?*

The budget for a full-scale production of *Rent* was $250,000. Seller and McCollum were prepared to put up half in exchange for the right to produce the show commercially. Before Nicola accepted the offer, he met with his board of directors. *A Chorus Line* was on his mind. Michael Bennett created that show at the Public Theater. The Public took it to Broadway and made millions of dollars. Several people on Nicola's board could easily write a check so that the New York Theatre Workshop would be the sole producer of *Rent*. Nicola made his pitch: "There are no sure things in the theater. I can't sit here and lie to you and say this show is going to be a hit and if we come up with the money it will be great for us. I can't say that. But I can say that of all the projects I've been involved with I'd bet on this one." The board turned him down.

Seller and McCollum became Nicola's partners. The only trouble was they didn't have $100,000. Seller had no money. McCollum had about $60,000 in the bank, but he had just bought out his partner in The Producing Office, and his finances were tight. He wasn't even taking a salary. But they knew somebody with plenty of money: Allan S. Gordon, who with his brother Edward ran one of the city's largest real estate empires. Gordon also had six seats on the New York Stock Exchange. He was eccentric, a billionaire who took the Madison Avenue bus home from work. To him, most people were "schmucks." But he liked McCollum, and had bailed him out on a stage version of *The Brady Bunch* that ran out of money on tour. Seller and McCollum took Gordon to see *Rent*. He became their partner, putting up $62,500. Seller and McCollum raised the rest from friends and investors.

* Al Larson thought the character Roger was "a bum guy." He wrote to his son, "This is not a hero for your story."

On October 21, 1995, Larson quit work at the Moondance Diner. He had worked there nearly ten years.

After the workshop, Nicola and Greif met with Larson. His songs were terrific, they said. His script was not. They gave him two choices: he could either commit to working with a writer or they would hire a dramaturge to teach him about playwriting. He opted for a dramaturge. Nicola recruited Lynn Thomson, who taught drama at New York University. That summer at Dartmouth College, where the New York Theatre Workshop did a two-week residency, she and Larson sifted through all the critical notes from Greif, Nicola, Seller, and McCollum. A fundamental problem remained: Larson's characters lacked specificity. They were mouthpieces for his jumble of thoughts on death, art, gentrification, and poverty. Thomson told him he had written "cartoons." She was going to teach him how to write a play.[11] With her help Larson reworked the show. He wrote new songs—"Tango: Maureen," "Happy New Year," "What You Own." He turned a song called "Right Brain" into "One Song Glory," which made Roger's struggle to write a decent song before he dies a poignant moment in the show.

Thomson would eventually become persona non grata on the *Rent* team. After the show became a Broadway hit, she sued Larson's estate claiming coauthorship and seeking 16 percent of the royalties. A judge rejected her claims, but she reached an out-of-court settlement. Sarah Schulman, a writer and activist, also claimed credit for parts of *Rent*. In 1990, she published a novel called *People in Trouble*, about an affair she had with a married woman. It was set in the East Village. Larson read it as he was developing the relationship between Maureen and Joanne. Schulman later claimed Larson lifted characters and events from her novel, though she never sued.

The people who helped Larson develop *Rent* have little patience with such claims. “Let me be very clear about this: There was a beautiful almost real-life sculpture there to begin with,” said Greif. “A lot of people chipped away at it—the nose went through eighty-eight incarnations. But Jonathan came in with a musical that he, and he alone, wrote.”

The New York Theatre Workshop scheduled the premiere of *Rent* for February 1996. Anthony Rapp, who played Mark in the workshop, got the part for the full-scale production. But Rubin-Vega had to audition again for Mimi. Larson wanted her to sing “Without You,” which he had taken from Mark and Joanne and given to Mimi and Roger. “What do I need to do to get this part?” Rubin-Vega asked Larson. “Sing the song and make me cry,” he said. After her audition she packed her things and left the theater. Nicola followed her out onto the street. “You don’t have to go home and wait by the phone,” he said. “You got the part.”

The show’s new casting director, Bernie Telsey, haunted clubs and performance spaces looking for non-Broadway performers. Idina Menzel, who wanted to be a rock star but was working as a bar mitzvah singer, auditioned with “When a Man Loves a Woman,” which she sang like, well, a rock star. She was cast as Maureen. For the role of Joanne, the producers cast Fredi Walker, an actress who worked off-off Broadway in shoestring productions. Wilson Jermaine Heredia, a struggling actor working as a dispatcher of emergency maintenance crews, got the part of Angel because he “sang like an angel,” Telsey said.[12] Collins, the philosopher, was hard to cast. Telsey was auditioning white actors and then one day decided to bring in Jesse L. Martin, a black actor. Larson had worked with him at the Moondance Diner. He got the part. Taye Diggs, another black actor, was cast as Benny, the landlord. Adam Pascal, a rock singer who had just left his band,

tried out for Roger. He auditioned with his eyes closed because rock singers sang with their eyes closed. Told to keep his eyes open, he auditioned again. He got the part.

Larson's deadline for rewrites was September 1995. But he was hard up for money and that spring took a job writing the score for *J. P. Morgan Saves the Nation*, a site-specific avant-garde musical that took place on the steps of the Federal Hall National Memorial on Wall Street. The *New York Times* called Larson's score "peppy."

Larson turned in the rewritten *Rent* in October, just two months before rehearsals were to begin. He was exhausted, broke, and upset. Two of his close friends had died of AIDS. And the rewrites were not good. He had deepened the characters, but added so many new twists and turns that the plot was difficult to follow. "We had a crisis on our hands," Seller said. Nicola thought about canceling the show. Seller put together a list of tough notes. Nicola showed them to Larson and he "had a freak out," said Seller. Larson called his idol, Stephen Sondheim, for help. Sondheim told him: You've chosen your collaborators, and now you have to collaborate. If not "then be Wagner and get a king of Bavaria to support you so you can do it yourself."[13] A few days later Larson had dinner with Seller. "I am going to do this," he said.

On the eve of rehearsals, Larson hosted a peasant feast for his cast. Pascal showed up wearing overalls and a pirate shirt underneath. Rubin-Vega, who was "dressed as a fucking elf," thought he looked adorable. *Oh, God,* she thought, *I'm going to fall for this guy.* Larson spoke to the cast. They were representing his friends, many of whom weren't there because of AIDS, he said. And then he cried.

Seller attended the first read through of *Rent*. He had not seen the rewrites, and was apprehensive. When it was over, he told Larson, "You did it. You got all the pieces in their right place."

One piece was missing, a song for Maureen and Joanne to illustrate their combustible relationship. Larson called the missing piece the "Maureen-Joanne Comedy Boffo Song." He made several attempts, but they often came across as "bickery songs," said Greif.

Rehearsals ran smoothly, but tension erupted as the show closed in on its first preview—January 26. Larson attended every rehearsal, standing at the back of the house reading the *New York Times*, his bushy black hair sprouting over the top of the paper. His presence unnerved some of the actors. As Weil put it, "When you do a Steve Sondheim show, Steve is there, but then he goes away for periods because he knows if Steve Sondheim is in the room it changes the dynamics." Greif took Larson aside one morning and told him to go away. The actors needed room to breathe.

"I have to come back this afternoon," he said.

"No you don't," said Greif. "Just go away and do what you have to do."

He came back after lunch with his tape recorder and a cassette of himself performing a song he called "Take Me or Leave Me." Weil heard the catchy first notes and then Larson, as Maureen, sang, "Every single day, I walk down the street / I hear people say 'baby so sweet.'" *Holy fucking shit*, Weil thought. *He's done it.* The song caught the fraught relationship. It was specific and character driven. And it was tailored to the actors' voices—Menzel's belt, Walker's old-time gospel style. When the song was over, Weil recalled, Larson flashed "that shit-eating grin" that always crossed his face when he pulled something off.

As *Rent* neared its premiere, Richard Kornberg and Don Summa, the press agents for the New York Theatre Workshop, began plotting their strategy. A new American rock musical was noteworthy, but who had ever heard of Jonathan Larson? Summa asked Larson if there were any places he'd like to be interviewed. Larson said he'd like to be on a radio show about new music that he listened to at night. It was on a small, alternative radio station. *Fine,* Summa thought, *but that's not going to sell a lot of tickets.* A story in the *New York Times* would. As it happened, February 1, 1996, marked the one hundredth anniversary of the world premiere of *La Bohème* in Turin, Italy. Summa pitched a story idea to Anthony Tommasini, the *New York Times*' opera critic. Why not write about *Rent* and peg it to the anniversary of the famous opera that inspired it? The pitch worked. Tommasini agreed to interview Larson after the final dress rehearsal.

On Sunday, January 21, the company took a dinner break from a long day of grueling technical rehearsals. The cast invited Larson to join them, but he had to meet Greif and Nicola at a diner around the corner. Back at rehearsal, Larson watched the cast run songs from the second act. He got up to go to the lobby. A sharp pain lashed his chest. He couldn't breathe. "You better call 911; I think I'm having a heart attack," he told a member of the theater's staff. He went back into the theater and stretched out on the floor. The actors were performing "What You Own." He heard them sing his lyric, "Dying in America / At the end of the millennium . . ."[14]

Rubin-Vega was backstage with other cast members when Fredi Walker told them Larson had just gone to the hospital in an ambulance. "His head was spinning, and he was feeling faint," she said. They held a little prayer vigil. Pascal came bounding in and said, "Oh, my God. You guys are so fucking dramatic. It's not like the dude's dying or anything."[15]

Doctors at Cabrini Medical Center gave Larson an electrocardiogram. One doctor noted: "No cardiac disease . . . just finished producing a play . . . increased stress."[16] The doctor diagnosed food poisoning, pumped Larson's stomach, and sent him home. He skipped rehearsals the next day, telling Greif and Nicola he thought he had the flu. "Don't worry about it," Greif said. "It's tech, it's boring. It's a good time for you to miss."

On the night of January 23, Larson had stabbing chest pains again. Friends took him to St. Vincent's Hospital in the West Village. He was diagnosed with the flu and sent home.

The next day was the final dress rehearsal. Larson wasn't feeling well, but there was no way he was going to miss it. Greif greeted him at the theater and thought he looked "bundled, fluey." Summa thought he looked green. Rubin-Vega asked him how he was feeling. "Okay," he said. "It was probably something I ate."

"Well, that's what you get for not coming to dinner with us," she said.

The cast ran through the show that night from start to finish for the first time without stopping. Larson winced at problems with the sound system, but it was a good performance. When Angel came on wearing his Santa Claus outfit, Larson grabbed Wendt and whispered, "I just love it." The audience gave it a standing ovation. Larson and Greif posed for photos for the *New York Times*, and then Larson met Tommasini in the box office. It was the only quiet place to do an interview.

As he was leaving the theater that night, Summa caught sight of Larson peering over the ledge of the box office window. He looked distracted, tired, nervous—but excited and alive. The *New York Times* was interviewing him.

CHAPTER FOUR

LA VIE BROADWAY

Jeffrey Seller took some time picking out his clothes the morning of Thursday, January 25. The first preview of *Rent* was that night, and he wanted to look good. He had an appointment with his psychoanalyst and then headed to The Producing Office. When he arrived, nobody said hello. Nobody even looked at him. A colleague took him aside. "Jeffrey, I have to tell you something. Jonathan Larson died last night."

Larson arrived at his apartment, alone, around 12:30 a.m. on January 25. He found a note from his roommate Brian Carmody, who had been at the dress rehearsal, congratulating him and inviting him to the Ear Inn for a celebratory drink. Not feeling well, Larson put a pot of water on the stove for tea, and then collapsed. Carmody came home at 3:30 and found him on the kitchen floor. He called 911, but it was too late. Larson, thirty-five, was dead. An autopsy revealed he died of an "aortic dissection"—a tear in his main blood vessel, undetected both times he went to the emergency room.

Jim Nicola heard of Larson's death from his stage manager at 7:30 that morning. He told his staff to call the actors and crew with the news and ask them to come to the theater. He could not reach Michael Greif, but they had a meeting scheduled with Larson that morning at the Time Cafe. Greif sat down and Nicola gave him the news. The director went to the theater to see his actors. Nobody spoke. And then "there was a wail, an intense peal of grief," said Daphne Rubin-Vega. It was Tim Weil, the music director who had become one of Larson's good friends.

Press agents Richard Kornberg and Don Summa phoned theater reporters with the news. Veteran *New York Times* theater critic Mel Gussow cobbled together an obituary, calling *Rent* "the composer's first major effort in New York." But not every reporter bit. When Richard Kornberg called me at the *Daily News,* I said, "I'm sorry to hear that, but I can't give you much space. Nobody's ever heard of Jonathan Larson."

Nicola canceled the first preview of *Rent.* Greif thought it best to have a simple reading of the show for Larson's friends and family. Al and Nan Larson learned of their son's death in New Mexico and got on a plane to New York. When they arrived, they went to the theater for the reading. "I'm not sure my parents were up for that," Julie Larson said. "But they went."

"What do I remember?" Al Larson said many years later. "A snowstorm. There was a lot of snow in front of the theater."

The actors read through the first act sitting behind a table. There were no microphones, costumes, blocking, or props. "I wanted them to live in Jonathan's words and music and not worry about staging they hadn't done and costume changes they hadn't made," Greif said. "I wanted it to be pure." But when the cast came to "La Vie Boheme," the rousing Act I finale, they could not sit still. Rubin-Vega thought, *Shit, if I was dead I would want you to fucking get on that table.* So she did—and the rest of the cast joined her. Backstage at intermission Greif told the cast to put on their microphones and costumes. "We're going to do the second act full on," he said.

At the end of the show, there was a long silence. Somebody called out, "Thank you, Jonathan Larson." The audience stood and applauded. Al Larson told Seller and McCollum, "You must do this show." He and his wife met the cast. "You have to make this a hit," Al told them.[1]

The core artistic team—Nicola, Greif, Weil, and dramaturge Lynn Thomson—met the next morning to discuss the future of the show. They talked about canceling it altogether but rejected the idea. Larson, they knew, would want *Rent* to open. But the show was still a work in progress. "There were holes in the storytelling," Nicola said. They considered hiring a writer, but in the end decided to let *Rent* stand largely as it was. They would make any cuts or changes themselves.

Previews began, and audiences were enthusiastic. But many Broadway insiders, hearing the show might move to a larger theater, were skeptical. Seller remembered looks in their eyes that said, *I'm sorry your friend died and I'm sorry your show isn't very good.*

Editors at the *New York Times* knew they had a great story. They had Larson's final words as well as the last photograph ever taken of him. On Sunday, February 11—two days before opening night—the paper published Tommasini's article on Larson in the Arts & Leisure section. Stephen Sondheim was quoted praising Larson's attempt to blend rock music with theater music. "He was on his way to finding a real synthesis," Sondheim said. Tommasini described Larson as "lanky" and "wistful." His closing paragraph moved many readers who'd never heard of Jonathan Larson or *Rent*. "On the last night of his life, Mr. Larson talked of something he had learned from a friend with AIDS: 'It's not how many years you live, but how you fulfill the time you spend here. That's sort of the point of the show.'"[2]

Three days later *New York Times* theater critic Ben Brantley called *Rent* an "exhilarating, landmark rock opera" and an antidote to the "synthetic . . . herd of Broadway musical revivals and revues." Brantley concluded: "People who complain about the demise of the American musical have simply been looking in the wrong places. Well done, Mr. Larson."[3]

Veteran critic Clive Barnes, writing in the *New York Post*, had reservations about the script—an "amorphous, jokey, radical-chic muddle"—but praised the music and lyrics, "neatly situated between rap and Cole Porter." The forerunner of *Rent*, Barnes wrote, was *Hair.* He predicted that *Rent* would be just as successful. Howard Kissel of the *Daily News* offered measured praise: "*Rent* is distinguished by its promise and invigorating energy rather than its understanding of Art and Life. *La Boheme* leaves you sad. *Rent* leaves you frazzled." *Variety* called the show "the most sensational musical in maybe a decade."

Rent became the hottest ticket in town. Celebrities such as Tom Cruise and *Vogue* editor Anna Wintour clamored to get in. The month-long run sold out the day the reviews appeared. The show was extended another month, and those tickets were gone as soon as they went on sale. Surely *Rent* would move to a larger theater, but where? Before Larson died, there had been discussions of moving it to offbeat spaces in the East Village. But now the conversation came down to Off Broadway or Broadway. Those pushing for Off Broadway didn't think a show about East Village drug addicts would appeal to the older, white, upper-middle class Broadway crowd. As for younger theatergoers to whom the show might have great appeal—well, they couldn't afford Broadway prices.

But Seller knew Larson wanted *Rent* to be on Broadway. Emanuel Azenberg, hired to be the show's general manager and consigliere, wasn't so sure. A veteran producer whose credits included

Neil Simon's *Broadway Bound* and *Lost in Yonkers*, Azenberg didn't get *Rent*, but his teenage daughter loved it. And there was no denying its success. "It sold out in five minutes down there," he said. He thought it was an Off-Broadway show, but it had momentum, perhaps enough to make it on Broadway. And Broadway was where the money was. Richard Kornberg also pushed for Broadway. "Off Broadway is just not as cool as Broadway," he said. "The only musical you ever thought of as an Off-Broadway show was *The Fantasticks*, and it played a 149-seat stupid little theater!"

Broadway won the day. Now the hunt was on for a theater. The producers met with the Shubert Organization, Broadway's largest and most powerful landlord. Gerald Schoenfeld, the chairman, suggested *Rent* open on Broadway in the summer after the Tony Awards. That way it would not have to compete with the show the Shuberts thought would be the major hit of the spring—*Big*, based on the Tom Hanks movie. The Shuberts were investors in *Big*, and it was playing in their flagship theater, the Shubert. Schoenfeld told Seller and McCollum a cautionary tale about the rivalry between *The Phantom of the Opera* and *Chess* in 1988. *Phantom* was such a big hit it overwhelmed *Chess*, which the Shuberts produced. *Big*, Schoenfeld said, was this season's *Phantom*. *Rent* would do well to stay out of its way.

"With all due respect Mr. Schoenfeld, *Big* is no *Phantom*, and *Rent* is no *Chess*," Seller said.* Schoenfeld offered them the Belasco, a small, undesirable theater east of Times Square that usually housed straight plays.

Jujamcyn Theaters, Broadway's smallest landlord, pursued *Rent* aggressively. The redevelopment of Times Square was underway

* Schoenfeld may have thought *Big* was a winner, but those working on the show during its Detroit tryout that month had doubts. "We weren't happy with how things were going," said Richard Maltby Jr., the lyricist. "So when the reviews for *Rent* came out we knew that was the ball game."

and many of the old theaters along West Forty-Second Street were empty and decrepit, waiting to be turned into something else. Jujamcyn chief Rocco Landesman offered to buy one of them—the Selwyn—and renovate it for *Rent.* Renovations would be completed in six weeks, he said. Seller and McCollum were tempted. But Azenberg straightened them out: "Are you out of your fucking mind? They will never make it in six weeks. And the theater only has 1,050 seats!"

Jimmy Nederlander offered his most dilapidated theater—the Nederlander (named after his father, D.T.) on West Forty-First Street between Seventh and Eighth Avenues. The cleanup of Times Square had yet to touch the block. It was barren during the day and scary at night. The Nederlander had been empty for nearly three years, but Jimmy told Azenberg he was fixing it up. "He put a million dollars into it to make it a reasonable slum," Azenberg said.

Al, Nan, and Julie Larson took a tour one day of the various theaters on offer for *Rent.* Jonathan Burkhart, one of Larson's closest friends, accompanied them. The Nederlander was the last stop. Burkhart remembered that one summer afternoon in 1992 he and Larson broke into the empty theater. Larson jumped onstage, sang a few notes, and clapped. He said he wished someone would give him a theater like the Nederlander so he could perform one of his shows. A theater like this should never be empty, Larson said.[4]

Seller and McCollum were beginning to think the run-down theater might be a good fit for *Rent.* "It was the perfect way to thread the needle of being on Broadway and not being on Broadway at the same time," Seller said. "We could still be Downtown but be Uptown."

In the end it was the deal that did the trick. Jimmy Nederlander needed *Rent.* Azenberg drew up the terms: there would be no rent until the show recouped. Nederlander would also give the show 50 percent of the interest on advance ticket sales—unheard of since theater owners rarely shared the interest on the advance with anyone. The theater had 1,232 seats—about 200 more than the Belasco on offer from the Shuberts. *Rent* was guaranteed to sell out at least a year, Azenberg thought. Those extra seats would mean another $4 million at the box office.

As soon as the deal was done, McCollum called up the Nederlanders and told them to "stop painting the theater—we like it the way it is!" The designers of the show explored ways to make the theater part of the *Rent* experience. "We wanted it to have a nightclub feel," McCollum said. Hand-painted urban murals, the kind found all over the East Village, were plastered on the outside of the theater. Workmen installed fake leopard carpeting inside. Even the ushers got in on the act. Instead of wearing the traditional white shirt, black tie, and vest, they wore jeans and T-shirts.

Azenberg drew up the budget. *Rent* would cost $2.8 million, with another $700,000 held in reserve should the show struggle to attract the traditional Broadway crowd in its first few months. Angela Wendt, whose costume budget for the first workshop was $500, now had $120,000, though that was a bit much for Azenberg.

"The costumes are schmatta!" he said.

"Well, now they're designer schmatta," McCollum replied.[5]

At $3.5 million, *Rent* was the cheapest musical on Broadway that spring. *Victor/Victoria*, starring Julie Andrews, came in at $15 million. *Big*, the new *Phantom*, had a budget of $10 million.

When word got out that *Rent* was headed to Broadway, cynics pounced. Gossip columnists ran items, always from anonymous sources, doubting the show's prospects. As one producer told the *Daily News*, "Like it or not, Broadway is mainstream. This is a show for people in their 20s and we lost them a long time ago."[6] But Seller and McCollum were undeterred. "I felt very passionately that if this show cannot run on Broadway then I can't work on Broadway because this is my aesthetic," Seller said.

The *New York Post* led the charge against *Rent* on Broadway. Columnist Ward Morehouse III never failed to point out how dirty and dangerous West Forty-First Street was. He rang up the press office asking about "concerns" theatergoers had about the neighborhood. An exasperated Don Summa snapped, "Ward, it's *Rent*. We can do it on Mars and people will come."

The press strategy was simple: never let a day go by without a mention of *Rent* somewhere. Summa and Kornberg had a lot to work with. Larson's death generated stories all over the world. Kornberg was careful not to exploit the tragedy. "Everything was about celebrating his life," Kornberg said. What Kornberg could exploit was the cast—young, attractive, unknown, and ripe for discovery. He scored a major coup: *Rent* would appear on the cover of *Newsweek* right after opening on Broadway. The magazine, which had a weekly circulation of 3.5 million, had not featured a Broadway show on its cover since *A Chorus Line* in 1975. The editors chose Adam Pascal and Daphne Rubin-Vega for the cover photo. Their sizzling onstage romance was sizzling offstage as well. But they, like the rest of the cast, were exhausted. In the three weeks between the final performance of *Rent* at the New York Theatre Workshop and the first performance at the Nederlander, the actors rehearsed almost every day while doing dozens of photo shoots and interviews.

Kornberg and Summa made sure everybody in the cast got attention. Nothing tears apart an ensemble faster than when the spotlight shines on only a few. *Cosmopolitan* requested three actresses for a photo shoot. Summa offered Rubin-Vega, Idina Menzel, and Fredi Walker. *Cosmo* rejected Walker. The magazine sold less well when it featured black people, an editor told Summa. "Either you do it with Fredi or you don't do it all," Summa said. The magazine relented. *Cosmo* needed *Rent* more than *Rent* needed *Cosmo*.

Wendt's Lower East Side costumes generated press and a marketing opportunity. Kal Ruttenstein, the fashion director of Bloomingdale's, loved the show and wanted to create a line of clothing inspired by Wendt's designs. He also offered to put *Rent* displays in all of Bloomingdale's windows along Lexington Avenue. Some people on the show resisted the offer. *Rent* celebrated Lower East Side bohemia. Bloomingdale's epitomized Upper East Side affluence. To go there would be to sell out. But *Rent* was in the business of selling tickets. As Nancy Coyne, who oversaw advertising, pointed out, "You're going to buy a billboard in Times Square to advertise the show. So why wouldn't you want free windows at Bloomingdale's?"*

Kornberg used the media to spur an investigation into Larson's death. Al and Nan Larson were upset that the New York State Department of Health seemed uninterested in examining Larson's emergency-room visits. Kornberg lined up an article about the botched diagnosis in the *New York Observer* and, through his contacts at ABC, a feature on *Primetime Live.* The pressure worked. The Health Department launched an investigation, concluding that both Cabrini and St. Vincent's had erred by not running a CAT scan or MRI on Larson. Cabrini paid a $10,000 fine. St. Vincent's paid $6,000.†[7]

Since *Rent* was not a typical Broadway show, Seller and McCollum thought it needed a different kind of advertising campaign—something that would convey its youth, energy, and contemporary

* One person not privy to discussions about the Bloomingdale's deal was Angela Wendt. "I read about it in the papers," she said. She didn't think much of the line of clothing her designs inspired. "But the windows were good," she said.

† The underlying cause of the tear in Larson's aorta was Marfan syndrome. Though difficult to detect in someone in his thirties, it can be treated. The Larsons established the Jonathan Larson Fund to bring attention to the ailment.

edge. A few days after *Rent* opened downtown, Seller's friend Tom King, a reporter for the *Wall Street Journal*, came to see it. King brought his friend David Geffen, the record and movie producer. Geffen loved the show, though during intermission he told Seller everything that was wrong with it. But he wanted to produce the cast album and offered to help Seller. "I need help with the logo," Seller told him. A few days later Drew Hodges, a thirty-three-year-old graphic designer who had done logos for Geffen Records, appeared at a *Rent* advertising meeting. Hodges was not a "theater freak—I was more the guy who went to the Stones at Madison Square Garden."

Hodges went to *Rent* that night. He loved the show, but thought for all the talk about "rock 'n' roll," *Rent* was a musical. He wrote a letter to Seller and McCollum urging them to back off the rock angle. Don't sell it as an Iggy Pop concert, he said. Sell it as "the musical that brings rock back to Broadway."[8] Seller and McCollum, Broadway babies like Larson, agreed. They hired Hodges to design their logo and work on the ad campaign. Hodges told them to cut back on advertising. "Everybody is talking about your show," he said. "They're all telling each other what kind of show *they* think it is. Don't give them too much information. Don't tell them what the show is about. Let them decide."

That became the driving idea behind the way *Rent* was sold and marketed. Was it an opera, a musical, a rock 'n' roll concert, or a rock opera? The logo, the marketing, the advertising would never answer those questions. "What we needed was the un-ad, something that said so little it would seem wildly confident, and that the ticket-buying public would fill in all the rest of the story-telling," Hodges wrote in his book *On Broadway: From* Rent *to Revolution*.[9]

The first ad for *Rent* that appeared in the *New York Times* featured the title of the show in stencils "you buy at the hard-ware store," Hodges said. There were no photographs, just white space. The text—phone number, theater, Larson's and Greif's names—was typewritten, giving the ad a gritty, homemade feel, as if the characters in *Rent* had done it themselves. The word *musical* appeared nowhere. The first billboard that went up in Times Square also avoided the word *musical*.

They experimented in other ways as well. *Rent* was the first Broadway show to advertise heavily in subway cars. An older Broadway producer told Hodges that was a waste of money. "People who go to Broadway don't take the subway," he said. "They take taxis."[10] But *Rent* wasn't after the typical Broadway audience. Its younger audience rode the subway to work every day. Seller, McCollum, and Hodges irked the old guard even further by adding a line to the subway ads: "Don't you hate the word 'musical'?" The strategy worked. The first day tickets went on sale the box office took in $750,000. Within a few weeks, *Rent* had an advance of $10 million.

Hodges played around with other images for the show. He wanted to harness the energy of the young cast. He hired Amy Guip, who worked for *Rolling Stone*, to photograph them. The shoot cost $18,000, much to the dismay of the accounting department. Guip photographed the actors individually in costume and then solarized, or tinted, the negatives. She and Hodges assembled the photos in a *Brady Bunch* grid around the stenciled *Rent* logo. That now iconic image became the poster for the show and the cover of the cast recording. The grid had an advantage: it could be pulled apart and the portraits of the actors placed on sides of buses, in the subway, and on the front of the Nederlander Theatre.

Not everything about the look of *Rent* was by design. Sometimes a happy accident occurred. One day Hodges got a call from McCollum. "Oh my God," he said, "have you seen the marquee at the Nederlander? It's a total disaster." Hodges rushed to the theater to check it out. The marquee was supposed to be the stenciled black *Rent* logo on a white background. But King Displays, which made the marquee, had put the logo on a clear piece of

Plexiglass by mistake. You could see the light bulbs and inner electrical gear of the marquee. It looked shabby and unfinished. But as Hodges and McCollum stared at the naked bulbs, they realized the marquee was perfect. "It was a deconstruction—the un-*Rent*," said Hodges. "It was using the decrepitness of the theater in a good way."

On April 9, 1996, six days before the first preview of *Rent* on Broadway, McCollum interrupted a rehearsal at the Nederlander to tell the cast and crew that Jonathan Larson had won the Pulitzer Prize for Drama. Al Larson told the *New York Times* he still thought of Jonathan as a little boy. *Rent*, he said "was like him bringing home his first report card [with] all As."[11]

Rent opened at the Nederlander on April 29, 1996. The press covered it as if it were the premiere of a Hollywood blockbuster. The first-night crowd included Sigourney Weaver, Michelle Pfeiffer, George Clooney, and Isabella Rossellini. Before the show started the cast came onstage. Anthony Rapp said, "We dedicate this and every performance of *Rent* to Jonathan Larson." The audience stood and cheered.

The critics cheered, too, though some reviews were more mixed than they'd been the first time around. Brantley, in the *New York Times*, thought the larger theater overwhelmed the show. He complained about the awkwardness of the second act and pointed out some clunkers in the lyrics. But he emphasized that Larson's was an "original talent and a flame of youth that the mummified world of Broadway musicals so needs."[12]

Now there was no doubt: *Rent* was going to be Broadway's biggest hit since *Phantom*. But with a top ticket price of a "whopping" $67.50, as Brantley put it, Seller and McCollum feared it was out of reach of the young audience they were trying to attract. *Rent* was about people who could not afford to see a Broadway show. Larson himself could not afford a ticket at that price. Seller noticed that *Miss Saigon* offered student rush tickets at $20 in the last three rows of Broadway Theatre. *Why not flip it,* he thought. Offer $20 tickets for students in the first two rows of the Nederlander. They would be rebellious and raucous and their enthusiasm would work its way to the last row of the balcony. The older crowd, skeptical of a new rock musical, would have a hard time resisting the exuberance of the kids in front.

It was an instant hit. Young people began camping out for days in front of the theater for tickets. The demand was so great that the sleeping bag line stretched down the block. It was another opportunity for press. Newspapers ran photos and interviewed the camped-out *Rent*-heads, as they were dubbed. The Nederlanders hired security guards to tamp down drug and alcohol use. Sex, though, was another issue. One guard admitted to looking the other way as a young couple had sex in a Coleman tent.[13] As the number of *Rent*-heads grew, the producers, fearing the line of sleeping bags was making an already seedy block look even seedier, instituted a lottery system. Fans showed up during the day, wrote their names on index cards, and gave them to a collector. At 6:00 p.m., someone from the box office would pick the cards out of a hat and announce the lucky winners over a megaphone.*

A week after opening night, *Rent* picked up ten Tony Award nominations, including Best Musical, Best Book, and Best Score. Acting nominations went to Adam Pascal, Wilson Jermaine Heredia, Daphne Rubin-Vega, and Idina Menzel. But the nominators snubbed costume designer Angela Wendt. Many came from the

* The lottery system has since become a staple on Broadway, though with today's ticket prices hitting $495, it's become a fig leaf against charges that Broadway has priced itself out of the reach of many theatergoers.

era of glamorous gowns by Cecil Beaton, Raoul Pene Du Bois, and Theoni V. Aldredge. A coat made from a shower curtain was hardly worthy of a Tony. Wendt experienced more Broadway snobbery when she appeared on an American Theatre Wing panel about costume design. The moderator, Isabelle Stevenson, a grand dame of the theater who lived on Park Avenue, asked where Wendt found some of her costumes. When she said Daffy's and the Salvation Army, Stevenson "almost fainted," Wendt recalled, laughing.

Rent's closest competitor was another musical that came from Off Broadway—*Bring in 'da Noise, Bring in 'da Funk.* Conceived by George C. Wolfe and starring Savion Glover, it chronicled the struggle of blacks in America through rap, tap, and the blues. It received nine nominations. In a pointed jab at the commercial theater, the nominators failed to give a Best Musical nod to *Victor/Victoria* and *Big*, the season's two most expensive productions. They nominated instead two little shows that were no longer running—*Swinging on a Star* and *Chronicle of a Death Foretold. Victor/Victoria* received one nomination for its star Julie Andrews. After the Wednesday matinee performance that week, Andrews told the audience (and a phalanx of reporters standing at the back of the theater) that she was declining the nomination, preferring instead "to stand with the egregiously overlooked" cast and creative team, including her husband, director Blake Edwards. It was a deliciously melodramatic gesture that eclipsed, at least for one day, the *Rent* juggernaut.

Heading into the Tony Awards on June 2, the *Rent* team had much to celebrate. The show was certain to win Best Musical as well as several other awards. But behind the scenes, a nasty fight was brewing. The *Wall Street Journal* ran a front-page profile of Seller and McCollum, portraying them as young producers shaking up Broadway with one of the "great home-run bets in show-business history."[14] Their portraits ran with the article, a distinction normally reserved for world leaders, business tycoons, and showbiz celebrities. The *Journal* mentioned Allan Gordon, calling him a Wall Street financier. But its focus was Seller and McCollum. They got the portrait. He did not. Gordon was furious.

"He called the *Journal* and threatened to sue them," Richard Kornberg recalled. "We had to take the story out of the press kit—and it was a major cover story!"

"Allan did not have practical day-to-day dealings with *Rent* and the story clarified that and I think that embarrassed him," said Seller. "I was sorry he was upset, but I didn't write the story, so why was he complaining to me?"

Gordon was convinced Seller and McCollum orchestrated the story behind his back with the help of Seller's friend Tom King, the *Journal* reporter. Seller and McCollum denied it, but he didn't believe them. As they prepared for the Tony Awards, word came from CBS that due to time constraints only one of them could speak should *Rent* win Best Musical. Seller, who was closest to Larson, thought he should do it. Gordon told him, "If you don't let me speak, I'll push you off the stage."[15]

When the curtain rose on the fiftieth annual Tony Awards at the Majestic Theatre, the audience saw the back of someone wearing one of Julie Andrews's costumes from *Victor/Victoria*. The person turned around. It was Nathan Lane, the host. "Come on, you really thought she was going to show up?" he asked.

Rent won awards for book and score. Julie Larson accepted both. "My brother, Jonathan, loved musical theater, and he dreamed of creating a youthful, passionate piece that would bring a new generation to the theater," she said. "The dream became *Rent*." Wilson Jermaine Heredia won featured actor in a musical, but *Bring in 'da Noise, Bring in 'da Funk* won Tonys for direction

(Wolfe), choreography (Glover), lighting (Jules Fisher and Peggy Eisenhauer), and featured actress (Ann Duquesnay).

Andrew Lloyd Webber, the previous year's winner for *Sunset Boulevard*, presented the award for Best Musical. To no one's surprise, it went to *Rent*. Seller spoke, but so too did McCollum, Gordon, and Jim Nicola. Nobody got pushed off the stage.

Later that night everybody wound up at Angela Wendt's apartment on the Lower East Side. Not being nominated, she did not attend the Tonys. But she threw the party for the show that won.

Rent ran twelve years on Broadway, grossing nearly $300 million. It brought a new generation of writers to the theater—Robert Lopez, who wrote *Avenue Q* and *The Book of Mormon*; Benj Pasek and Justin Paul, the creators of *Dear Evan Hansen*; Tom Kitt and Brian Yorkey, who won the Pulitzer Prize for *Next to Normal*; and Lin-Manuel Miranda, whose *Hamilton* now seems destined to run forever. Miranda once estimated he'd seen *Rent* thirty times.

Twenty-four years after Jonathan Larson's death, his family continues to get letters from people all over the world whose lives have been shaped by *Rent*—letters from gay kids who came out because of the show; from parents who accepted their son's or daughter's sexuality because of the show; from aspiring writers pursuing careers in the theater because of the show; from suicidal teenagers who chose life because of the show. "It's still remarkable to me that this little thing my punky brother did has touched so many people," said Julie Larson, adding with a laugh, "because, you know, he was just my punky younger brother."

CHAPTER FIVE

THE GAMBLER

Emanuel Azenberg was right to reject Jujamcyn Theaters president Rocco Landesman's offer to buy the decaying Selwyn Theatre and restore it in six weeks for *Rent*. Trying to restore a theater in such a short period of time was, as Azenberg put it, "insane." It would also have been a big gamble as there was no guarantee *Rent* would run long enough to justify the expense. But Landesman was a gambler and his play for *Rent* was just the kind of risk that turned a money-losing theater chain into a Broadway powerhouse.

Jujamcyn is an odd name for a theater company. "It sounds like an antibiotic," Landesman said. The company began in 1957 when William McKnight, the chairman of Minnesota Mining and Manufacturing, bought the St. James Theatre from the Shuberts, who were forced to sell it after losing an antitrust suit. McKnight bought the Martin Beck, located in no-man's-land west of Eighth Avenue on Forty-Fifth Street, in 1966. He combined the names of his grandchildren—Julie, James, and Cynthia—to form the name Jujamcyn. McKnight's daughter, Virginia, was married to James H. Binger, CEO of the Honeywell Corporation. Binger loved the theater and took over the St. James and the Martin Beck when

McKnight died in 1978. He expanded the chain in the early 1980s, acquiring the Ritz, the ANTA (which he renamed the Virginia after his wife), and the Eugene O'Neill.

With only five theaters, Jujamcyn was a distant third to Broadway's two other landlords—the Shuberts, who controlled seventeen theaters, and James M. Nederlander, who owned ten. But Binger had more money than they did, and he let it be known that he would buy any theater that came on the market. As a Broadway insider told the *New York Times*, "Binger and his wife, with their Honeywell and 3M money, could buy the Shuberts and the Nederlanders and never know it. Small change to them."[1]

Binger lived in Minneapolis and had other interests besides the theater, including breeding Kentucky Derby winners at his Tartan Farms in Ocala, Florida. He left the day-to-day running of Jujamcyn to Richard Wolff, a longtime box office treasurer and theater executive. Predictions that Jujamcyn would become a rival to the Shuberts and the Nederlanders never materialized. While the Shuberts and the Nederlanders fought for every show, Jujamcyn was lucky to get the scraps. The chain's bookings in the early 1980s were few and unimpressive. The St. James had Tommy Tune's popular *My One and Only*, but the Martin Beck got *The Rink*, a flop by John Kander and Fred Ebb, while the Virginia had an indifferent revival of *On Your Toes*. The O'Neill had a show that became a legend, *Moose Murders*, a mystery farce that opened and closed on the same night. It would become the gold standard of Broadway flops. "From now on there will always be two groups of theatergoers in this world: Those who have seen 'Moose Murders' and those who have not," Frank Rich wrote.[2]

In 1985, most of Jujamcyn's theaters were empty. So when Rocco Landesman, a fledgling producer with a new musical based on *Huckleberry Finn*, called Dick Wolff to see if a theater was available, Wolff offered him the O'Neill. Landesman took it because the Shuberts and the Nederlanders never returned his calls.

* * *

Rocco Landesman grew up around show business. His father, Fred, a painter, antiques dealer, investor, and poker player, co-owned the Crystal Palace, a popular cabaret in the Gaslight Square district of St. Louis. All the big acts of the 1950s and '60s played the Palace: Lenny Bruce, the Smothers Brothers, Mike Nichols and Elaine May, Barbra Streisand. Dinners at the Landesmans' were lively, with Fred leading discussions on politics, art, philosophy, and sports. Fred pressed an important lesson on his son—go your own way, on your own terms. His father also taught him that life can be painfully short. Fred Landesman battled cancer for twenty-five years, dying when Rocco was in his twenties.

Landesman packed a lot into his student years at the University of Wisconsin. He took writing classes from Isaac Bashevis Singer, joined the drama department, and became the arts editor of the student newspaper. He developed his father's love of gambling, playing poker and betting on the horses. He went on to study drama criticism at Yale under Robert Brustein. They became close friends, and after Landesman graduated, Brustein gave him a teaching job and made him editor of *yale/theatre*. Landesman also befriended Jerzy Kosinski, who was teaching at Yale. A 1982 article in the *Village Voice* revealed that Kosinski relied on unacknowledged collaborators to help write his novels. Landesman was one of them. He had a hand in *Being There* and *The Devil Tree*. "We would reshape paragraphs, and rewrite and reorder sentences. I would call it heavy editing," he said.[3]

At Yale, Landesman met his wife, Heidi Ettinger, who was studying set design. The slow pace of academic life did not suit him so he and Heidi moved to Brooklyn, and Landesman turned his attention to managing a mutual fund and raising racehorses. His wife designed sets for Broadway and Off-Broadway shows.

And then he got a call from Edward Strong, one of his former students at Yale. Strong was part of a group of producers that included Michael David, another Yale graduate who had helped run the Chelsea Theater Center; Des McAnuff, a young director; and Sherman Warner, a producer. They formed their group, which they called the Dodgers, one day in a car parked in Brooklyn. Their mantra: "We will produce only shows we want to see in a manner that doesn't embarrass our children." They went on to produce critically acclaimed work at the Brooklyn Academy of Music and the Public Theater. But they weren't making any money, supplementing the occasional paycheck with unemployment.

They wanted to become commercial producers, but couldn't afford to rent an office. Landesman gave them $40,000 to set up shop at 1501 Broadway, a hub of commercial producers. He was now a Dodger. With Landesman on board, the Dodgers produced an Off-Broadway musical called *Pump Boys and Dinettes.* It moved to Broadway in 1982 and became their first commercial hit.

That same year, Landesman and Heidi caught Roger Miller at the Lone Star Cafe. Best known for his hit single "King of the Road," Miller was Landesman's favorite songwriter. Landesman wondered if he could write a musical. His wife suggested an adaptation of Landesman's favorite book, *Huckleberry Finn.* Landesman pitched the idea to Miller. "I might as well have been peddling junk," Landesman recalled. "Roger had no idea what I was talking about." Miller, in fact, had never seen a musical. He would later say, "Rocco made me an offer I couldn't understand." Landesman persisted. Finally, Miller agreed to meet him after a concert in Reno. Miller was stoned. And he had not written a song in ten years. "If you've got some songs in your trunk, we can use those," Landesman suggested. Landesman made regular visits to Santa Fe, where Miller lived. They drank a lot as Landesman coaxed songs out of him. They were good songs. They captured the characters and flavor of Twain's Mississippi. Landesman commissioned William Hauptman, a friend from Yale, to write a script. Hauptman had never written a musical before, but his script was solid enough that Landesman showed it to his old teacher, Robert Brustein, now running the American Repertory Theater at Harvard. Brustein agreed to produce the show, called *Big River*, at his theater. Landesman asked fellow Dodger Des McAnuff to direct.

At A.R.T., *Big River* was a play with a few songs. It needed further development. Landesman took it to the La Jolla Playhouse in California, where McAnuff had become artistic director. Audiences loved it, and the reviews were favorable but for one. Jack Viertel of the *Los Angeles Herald Examiner* thought the show was too sunny and lacked the guts to confront the thorny issue of race. The review stung, but Landesman agreed with many of its points. He used it to improve the show.

In his book *The Season: A Candid Look at Broadway*, William Goldman notes that Broadway insiders gauge the potential of every new show "by weighing the skill and the track record of the production's chief creative people."[4] Goldman wrote the book in 1969, so back then a show produced by Harold Prince or David Merrick was going to sell tickets as soon as the box office opened. A play by Neil Simon and directed by Mike Nichols was going to sell a lot of tickets. Anything starring Angela Lansbury, George C. Scott, or Sammy Davis Jr. had to be taken seriously, sight unseen. It was by no means a foolproof method—Goldman's book abounds with flops that looked good on paper—but the pedigree of the creators counted.

Big River had no pedigree. As Landesman put it, "It was by a composer who had never seen a Broadway show. Des McAnuff had never directed a Broadway show. William Hauptman had never written a Broadway show. And Heidi and I had not produced a show at summer camp, much less on Broadway. The only person in the show who had ever been on Broadway was René Auberjonois [playing the Duke]." Which is why the Shuberts and the Nederlanders never returned Landesman's calls.

Big River opened April 25, 1985. There were several favorable reviews. The mighty Frank Rich, alas, tried to like it but could not: "If all of 'Big River' were up to its high water marks, the season might even have found the exciting new musical it desperately craves. . . . But there are too many times . . . when the imaginative flow of 'Big River' slows to a trickle, and the show loses its promising way."[5] John Simon, in *New York*, did not help matters by panning Miller's country score: "This stuff is to my idea of show music what hog calling is to poetry."[6]

But *Big River* had a powerful champion in Walter Kerr. He rode to the rescue in the Sunday *New York Times*, calling it a "warm, beguiling, and intelligent musical," and demanding that other reviewers stop referring to it as a "show you can take the whole family to." *Big River*, Kerr concluded, was a "current rarity, a musical you can bring yourself to."[7]

"That review saved the show," Landesman said. It came out the day of the Tony Awards, and in a pathetically weak season—the show's rivals were the flops *Grind*, *Leader of the Pack*, and *Quilters*—*Big River* won seven Tonys, including Best Musical.

Thrilled to have a hit in one of his theaters, James Binger invited Landesman to Belmont Park. They started spending afternoons together at the track, Binger betting ten dollars on a horse, Landesman a thousand—"an inverse proportion to our net worth," said Landesman.

Landesman told Binger about another show he and Heidi were producing, Stephen Sondheim's *Into the Woods*. Every producer on Broadway wanted the new Sondheim show. The Landesmans got it because they'd been at Yale with James Lapine, who was writing the book and directing. The Shuberts and the Nederlanders offered desirable theaters and substantial investments, but Landesman was loyal to Binger. He gave Binger *Into the Woods* for the Martin Beck, which had been dark for more than a year.

The theater was available because Jujamcyn had lost Andrew Lloyd Webber's *The Phantom of the Opera*. Dick Wolff thought he had a deal for the show, but the wily Shuberts outmaneuvered him. They convinced Lloyd Webber that *Phantom* would be better off, and make much more money, in one of their largest theaters, the Majestic. Binger was not happy. And he was not happy that Jujamcyn, with three empty theaters, was losing $2 million a year.

In June 1987, he invited Landesman to lunch. "How would you like to run Jujamcyn?" Binger asked.

"Sure," Landesman said. "I'd like it a lot."

"When do you want to start?"

"The day after Labor Day," Landesman said.

A few days later, the *New York Times* announced Landesman's appointment. Wolff, the paper reported, would be seeking "independent producing opportunities."[8]

Landesman showed up for work on September 1, 1987. He had no idea what he would be paid as he had never bothered to negotiate a salary.*

The first person Landesman hired at Jujamcyn was Jack Viertel, who panned *Big River*. "Your review of *Big River* was bad, but it was smart, and I think you're smart. Come to New York and I'll seduce you," Landesman told him. Viertel became Jujamcyn's creative director.

* After Jujamcyn had been profitable for several years, Landesman asked Binger for equity in the company. Binger didn't like partners, but said that at his death Landesman could buy the company at book value. They shook hands on it. When Binger died in 2004, Landesman got Jujamcyn.

Landesman and Viertel realized that to fill Jujamcyn's theaters the company would have to start spreading money around. It would have to become a producer. Landesman secured a pledge from Binger to invest up to $1 million in musicals and $250,000 in plays. The first show Landesman put into one of Jujamcyn's theaters, along with a $500,000 investment, was *Carrie.* Based on Stephen King's novel, it was already in the works before Landesman took over, but "we went with it," he said. It featured a song and dance number about slaughtering a pig. It closed after five performances. "This is the biggest flop in the world history of the theater, going all the way back to Aristophanes," Landesman told *Time*, a crack that did not endear him to the writers but earned him a reputation for speaking frankly and colorfully.[9]

The next show was *M. Butterfly*, which ran nearly two years at the O'Neill.

Landesman and Viertel, the new kids in Shubert Alley, wanted to meet the old guard to learn the business. Arthur Cantor, who'd worked on Broadway since the 1940s as a press agent and a producer, came by their offices one day. Cantor was famously cheap, specializing in one-person shows. Asked once why he never did a two-character play, he replied, "I don't do spectacle." Landesman and Viertel asked him what he'd learned from his years in the theater. "This business is completely baffling," he said. "It's just baffling. You never know what's going to work, and what's not going to work. You don't know, you just don't know. Welcome to the business, but you're walking into a world that can't be understood." After he left, Landesman and Viertel looked at each other and laughed. "This business isn't baffling," they said. "We can figure it out."

Their first inkling that Cantor was onto something came with their latest booking, *City of Angels*, a musical comedy set in the 1940s about a screenwriter and his relationship with the fictional detective he created. Cy Coleman wrote the music. Larry Gelbart, the creator of the TV show *M*A*S*H*, wrote the book. The show was complicated. Scenes set in real life took place in color, while those from the film were in black and white. Landesman and Viertel attended the first preview at the Virginia Theatre. The show ran three hours. The audience had no idea what was going on. Over drinks at Gallaghers Steakhouse across the street, Landesman said, "Well, it's not our funeral. It's just a flop. Let's not worry about it. It's only a flop."

A week later, they returned to a show that was well on its way to becoming a hit. Michael Blakemore, the director, had pulled it together. It was tight and fun and the audience had no trouble switching between the real and reel worlds. *City of Angels* received raves and won the Tony for Best Musical.

Landesman and Viertel got away with another one they thought would be a disaster—Tommy Tune's *Grand Hotel*. The show was in such trouble in Boston that Tune insisted the opening party be held on a boat in the harbor so nobody could get hold of the reviews. Then he fired the writers and brought in his friends Maury Yeston and Peter Stone to fix the show. *Grand Hotel* opened to generally favorable reviews in New York, won five Tonys, and filled the Martin Beck for more than two years.

For years, Bernie Jacobs and Jerry Schoenfeld of the Shuberts had dominated Broadway. Both were over seventy. Their longtime rival, Jimmy Nederlander, also in his seventies, was recovering from a stroke. Landesman, thirty-nine, brought youth and color to the business. He wore tweed coats, jeans, and cowboy boots. He always had $10,000 in his pocket because "you might meet someone and decide you want to spend the rest of your life in Argentina."[10] He'd bet on anything, anywhere, anytime. "If you were walking down the street with Rocco and there was a cockroach, he'd bet you if it was about to go right or left," a producer once said.

Producers meeting him in his office above the St. James Theatre (an office that once belonged to another colorful producer, David Merrick) were surprised to meet his constant companion, Mr. Dirt, so named because he had dirt everywhere, even under his fingernails. A bookie, Mr. Dirt worked full-time for Landesman, gathering information about horses, trainers, and jockeys. The computer on Landesman's desk flashed stock market prices throughout the day.

Landesman courted controversy. A few months into the job, he wrote an essay for the *New York Times* attacking Lincoln Center Theater, a nonprofit then enjoying a run of success with Broadway shows such as *Anything Goes*, *Sarafina!*, and David Mamet's *Speed-the-Plow*, starring Madonna. Landesman thought Lincoln Center had strayed from producing risky work to pursue Broadway box office returns and Tony Award glory. He noted that Jujamcyn took huge risks with its own money while Lincoln Center received funding from the government, corporations, and foundations. And because of its nonprofit status, Lincoln Center paid actors and stagehands lower wages than commercial producers. Landesman acknowledged his involvement in the nonprofit theater (he had developed *Big River* at such an institution), but knocked Lincoln Center for being "the ultimate '80s hit: it has succeeded at being successful."[11]

The rebuke stung. Attacks on Landesman filled the Letters to the Editor page. Paul Libin, who ran the nonprofit Circle in the Square Theatre, fired off a blistering one. Landesman, who knew Libin only slightly, invited him to dinner. Libin impressed him with his knowledge of the theater. He knew the ins and outs of every theatrical contract, many of which he had negotiated. He could run a box office. He would even climb into a duct to fix the air-conditioning in his theater. Landesman invited Libin to his Brooklyn brownstone for a nightcap and offered him a job. Libin dithered. A few days later Landesman showed up in his office and said, "Either you're coming with me or you've got to find somebody like yourself who will." Libin replied, "There's nobody like me." He took the job.

Landesman further angered Lincoln Center by swiping its star director Jerry Zaks, whose run of hits included *Anything Goes* and John Guare's *Six Degrees of Separation*. Landesman gave Zaks an office and salary to develop plays and musicals to fill Jujamcyn's theaters.

His team in place, Landesman outlined his strategy to save Jujamcyn. When Viertel asked him how they planned to compete against the Shuberts and the Nederlanders he said, "We're not." The Shuberts had London sown up. They had relationships with Andrew Lloyd Webber, Cameron Mackintosh, and playwright Peter Shaffer, who'd given them two smashes—*Equus* and *Amadeus*. The Nederlanders—or the "Neanderthals," as some of Landesman's friends called them—had a deal with the Royal Shakespeare Company. They also booked low-rent revivals at the tail end of a national tour. Jujamcyn would go after work by Americans, new plays and musicals, many of which could be developed in partnership with nonprofit theaters around the country.

They didn't always get the shows they sought. They wanted Wendy Wasserstein's Off-Broadway hit *The Heidi Chronicles*, and were sure they'd get it since it was named for Wassertein's best friend, Heidi Landesman. But then they showed her the Ritz, which was covered in scaffolding because a condominium tower was being built next door. The inside of the theater had not been painted in years. She went with the Shuberts, who gave her the Plymouth, one of their best playhouses.

(Wasserstein was also close to Bernie Jacobs, who had spotted her talent early on and cultivated a relationship. "Bernie was way ahead of us, as he always was," Viertel said.)

To be competitive, Jujamcyn had to start restoring its theaters. Viertel found the original plans for the Ritz in the Shubert archives, and the company spent $2 million restoring the theater.

Landesman renamed it the Walter Kerr, after the critic who had saved *Big River.* The Kerr's first tenant was August Wilson's *The Piano Lesson*, the fourth play in what would become his celebrated *Pittsburgh Cycle.* Wilson had written two Broadway hits, *Ma Rainey's Black Bottom* and *Fences*, which won the Tony Award and the Pulitzer Prize in 1987. His last play, *Joe Turner's Come and Gone*, received raves, but did not recoup. Viertel had seen the premiere of *The Piano Lesson* at the Yale Repertory Theatre and developed a relationship with Wilson. He admired the play, but thought it had flaws. "I wrote him enthusiastic letters, but I also had questions," Viertel said. "Like, who gets the piano, and how does the play end?"

Wilson never answered Viertel's letters, but whenever he was in New York he would meet Viertel at the Polish Tea Room, the coffee shop in the Edison Hotel that was popular with theater people. "He still didn't answer my questions," Viertel said. "He never told me what he was going to do. He would tell me about his next play. But then a new draft would emerge and sometimes I felt some of the things I had raised actually caused him to think something through. I've learned that in trying to help writers you're much better off asking questions than making suggestions. It's not your play. It's their play."

The Piano Lesson won the 1990 Pulitzer Prize for Drama and was nominated for the Tony Award for Best Play. Landesman and Viertel made a commitment to Wilson: Jujamcyn would produce any play he wrote.

None, including *The Piano Lesson*, would ever make money on Broadway. But that did not matter. Jujamcyn wanted to be associated with significant American works. "If you don't do an August Wilson play, then why are you here? No one is going to remember the ledger," Landesman said. "I can't remember how much money we made. But you do remember that you produced every August Wilson play that matters."

* * *

Jujamcyn's commitment to American works would soon pay off. The company had its eye on two shows. One would remind a Broadway dominated by British spectacles of the joys of American musical comedy. The other would become one of the most celebrated plays of the twentieth century.

CHAPTER SIX

I GOT THE HORSE RIGHT HERE

Musical comedy, "the most glorious words in the English language," as Julian Marsh says in *42nd Street*, is America's contribution to the theatrical arts. From Italy came grand opera, with its tears and fat sopranos. From Vienna came operetta, with its patter and Champagne. From America came *The Black Crook*, a lively mixture of songs, drama, and dance. Scholars consider it to be the first musical. It opened at Niblo's Garden on Broadway and Prince Street in 1866, ran sixteen months, and toured the country for forty years.

Edward Harrigan and Tony Hart brought New York's immigrant culture to the musical stage with their enormously popular series of shows about an Irish social club called the Mulligan Guards. Their characters were "the street-cleaners and contractors, the grocery men, the shysters, the politicians, the washerwomen, the servant girls, the truckmen, the policeman, the risen Irishman and Irishwoman of contemporary New York," wrote critic William Dean Howells. Harrigan and Hart wrote character songs and songs that propelled the plot. Victor Herbert, classically trained but a populist at heart, added elegance with his tuneful operettas *Babes in Toyland*, *Mlle. Modiste*, and *The Red*

Mill. George M. Cohan invented the idea of Broadway with one song: "Give My Regards to Broadway" from *Little Johnny Jones* in 1904. Then along came Irving Berlin, Jerome Kern, George and Ira Gershwin, Richard Rodgers, Larry Hart, and Cole Porter. Their shows of the 1920s and '30s were sophisticated and witty, but with the exception of Kern's *Show Boat*, only the songs—not the scripts—have endured.

Richard Rodgers and Oscar Hammerstein II pulled it all together in 1943 with *Oklahoma!* The American musical comedy, with elements of drama, dominated Broadway for the next three decades: *Finian's Rainbow; On the Town; Annie Get Your Gun; Kiss Me, Kate; South Pacific; The Pajama Game; My Fair Lady; How to Succeed in Business Without Really Trying; Gypsy; Fiddler on the Roof; Hello, Dolly!*

Hal Prince and Stephen Sondheim, trained in musical comedy, took the form in another direction in the 1970s with tougher, darker (though still witty) musicals such as *Company, Follies,* and *Sweeney Todd.* Bob Fosse brought cynicism and black humor to *Chicago,* while Michael Bennett caught the spirit of showbiz—its triumphs and heartaches—in a musical set in contemporary times, *A Chorus Line.*

The two outstanding musical comedies of the early 1980s, *42nd Street* and Jerry Herman's *La Cage aux Folles,* were throwbacks to another era. Tastes were changing, and AIDS was ravaging the theater world, claiming top talents (Michael Bennett, Charles Ludlam, Alvin Ailey) as well as countless chorus kids who might have become the next Michael Bennett. The British fueled Broadway with *Cats, Les Misérables,* and *Phantom,* but those shows were not known for their sparkling dialogue, witty lyrics, or—*Cats'* anthropomorphic choreography notwithstanding—dancing. The American musical was on the wane. Tommy Tune kept the tradition of the Broadway director-choreographer going with *Nine* and *My One and Only,* but he was, as Frank Rich wrote, "the only game in town in his field."[1]

Then in 1990, Roger Horchow sold his catalog business, the Horchow Collection, to Neiman Marcus for $117 million. He now had the money and time to produce a musical by George Gershwin. Horchow had been a Gershwin fan since the age of six when, in bed one night at his house in Cincinnati, he heard someone playing the piano downstairs. It did not sound like his mother's usual Bach and Chopin. This music was jaunty, rhythmic, and catchy. Horchow crept downstairs and saw a tall, handsome man at the piano. It was Gershwin. He'd given a concert that night, and at the stage door afterward Horchow's mother asked him for an autograph. Gershwin mentioned he was on his way to Chicago, but the train wasn't leaving until 1:00 a.m. "Come to my house," his mother said. "I live near the station."

As an adult, Horchow collected everything he could find connected to Gershwin. And now, with $117 million in the bank, he wanted to produce a revival of *Girl Crazy*, which Gershwin wrote with his brother Ira. Its standards included "Embraceable You," "But Not for Me," and "I Got Rhythm." His producing partner, Elizabeth Williams, suggested he read the script. "It was awful," he said. The only solution was to create a new show around a Gershwin score. Horchow hired Mike Ockrent, who staged the hit musical *Me and My Girl*, to direct. Ken Ludwig, who wrote the popular Broadway farce *Lend Me a Tenor*, signed on to write a new script. Susan Stroman, a young choreographer who won raves for her work on the John Kander and Fred Ebb revue *And the World Goes 'Round*, joined the team. So, too, did costume designer William Ivey Long, who won the Tony for *Nine*, and set designer Robin Wagner, whose many credits included *A Chorus Line* and *Dreamgirls*.

"I wanted the show to be the best it could be, and I didn't care if I lost all my money," Horchow said. "I did not want to look back and say, 'If only we'd done this.'" In the end, he wound up spending $7.5 million, making *Crazy for You*—"the new Gershwin musical comedy," as it was billed—almost as expensive as *The Phantom of the Opera*. It was a hit from the moment it played its first tryout performance in Washington, D.C. Though the music was from another era—and the "new" script was set in the 1930s—the entire production felt fresh. Stroman's dances, which made ingenious use of props, stopped the show. Chorus girls tap-danced out of a fancy car in "I Can't Be Bothered Now." They stretched long strings of rope the length of their bodies to become basses in "Slap That Bass." In "I Got Rhythm," a bunch of bumpkins in a dusty Nevada town kicked up a joyous racket with tin roofing, mining picks, washboards, and prospector's pans.

Crazy for You lifted Broadway's spirits when it opened at the Shubert Theatre on February 19, 1992. As Frank Rich wrote, "When future historians try to find the exact moment at which Broadway finally rose up to grab the musical back from the British, they just may conclude that the revolution began last night." *Crazy for You* "uncorked the American musical's classic blend of music, laughter, dancing, sentiment, and showmanship with a freshness and confidence rarely seen during the 'Cats' decade."[2] Meow, indeed.

While Roger Horchow was putting together his "new" Gershwin musical, Michael David was trying to get the rights to what many theater people believe to be the great musical comedy, *Guys and Dolls*.

The short stories of Damon Runyon are to New York what the short stories of Colette are to Paris. Set in the Times Square of the 1920s and '30s, usually after the sun has gone down or is about to come up, they feature gangsters, gamblers, bootleggers, and chorus girls with names that jump off the page: Rusty Charley, Handsome Jack, Midgie Muldoon, Joe the Joker, Rosa Midnight. Broadway producers Cy Feuer and Ernest Martin thought the stories could make a musical and acquired the rights in 1946, a few years after Runyon's death. They hired Frank Loesser to write the score and Jo Swerling to do the book. Abe Burrows, a comedy writer working in radio, came on to revise Swerling's book. The director was George S. Kaufman.

Guys and Dolls was based on two stories, "The Idyll of Miss Sarah Brown," about a gambler named Sky Masterson who falls in love with a missionary, and "Blood Pressure," about a floating crap game run by Nathan Detroit. To give Detroit a love interest, Kaufman created Miss Adelaide, a stripper at the Hot Box nightclub. In an early draft, Adelaide caught a cold from stripping. Burrows changed it to a "psychosomatic symptom" brought on by Detroit's aversion to marriage. "Adelaide's Lament," one of the great comedy songs, was born.[3]

Guys and Dolls opened on November 24, 1950, to rapturous reviews. "Here is New York's own musical comedy—as bright as a dime in a subway grating, as smart as a sidewalk pigeon, as professional as Joe DiMaggio, as enchanting as the skyline, as new as the paper you're holding," John Chapman wrote in the *Daily News*. Almost every song became a standard—"Guys and Dolls," "Fugue for Tinhorns," "I'll Know," "A Bushel and a Peck," "I've Never Been in Love Before," "Luck Be a Lady." *Guys and Dolls* won five Tony Awards, including Best Musical, and ran 1,200 performances. Hollywood bought the rights for $1 million but made a disappointing movie starring a miscast Frank Sinatra as Nathan Detroit and an indifferent Marlon Brando as Sky Masterson.

The musical became a staple of high school and amateur theater but was revived only once on Broadway—in 1976 with an all-black cast. Producers pursued the rights for years, but Jo Sullivan Loesser, Frank's widow, held them close. She knew their value and was reluctant to take a chance on anything less than a production that would equal or exceed the original.

Michael David first saw *Guys and Dolls* as a teenager at a summer playhouse in Traverse City, Michigan, and loved it. He and his fellow Dodgers came up with a novel approach to the show. "We looked around and saw that revivals on Broadway were the ends or beginning of tours, usually with a TV star," David said. He thought they were "bus-and-truck," meaning cut-rate versions of the originals. The Dodgers imagined a *Guys and Dolls* that would feel brand new. "We didn't use the word *revival*," David said. "The idea was to resurrect a classic from scratch."

David began wooing the widow Loesser over meetings at her apartment and lunches at the Russian Tea Room. They were an odd pair—Loesser, Upper East Side elegant; David, with his baseball cap, jeans, and long bushy beard looking by his own admission "wild and wooly." But they got along, and served together on the Tony Award administration committee. Loesser thought the show needed stars and suggested Mandy Patinkin and Bernadette Peters. But the Dodgers wanted fresh faces—"younger than anyone who had done the show before," David said. Loesser liked the idea, but what swayed her was David's behavior on the Tony committee. "I liked the things he stood for," she told *New York*. "And I guess what I *really* liked is that he always voted for the same things I voted for."[4]

She gave the Dodgers the rights to the show for an advance of $25,000. David was thrilled, but became uneasy as soon as people started congratulating him and saying, "It's my favorite show." That phrase, David knew, was code for "Don't fuck it up."

Jujamcyn slotted *Guys and Dolls* for the Martin Beck Theatre. Jerry Zaks, the company's new in-house creative consultant, was the ideal choice to direct a show the Dodgers wanted to "resurrect from scratch" for the simple reason that he knew so little about it. "I had no interest in musicals as a kid whatsoever," Zaks said. "I was into rock 'n' roll. I wanted to be Sam Cooke."

The son of Holocaust survivors, Zaks grew up in New Jersey and studied pre-med at Dartmouth "because I was a nice Jewish boy." One winter night during his sophomore year he took a blind date to see the school production of *Wonderful Town*. "It was funny, it was melodic, it was filled with light and laughter and joy, and it changed my life," he said. He left the show wanting to become an actor. When he told his parents he wanted to get his MFA in theater at Smith College (the women's college admitted men to its graduate programs), "they thought I'd lost my mind. To them, theater was for gypsies, whores, and thieves. Period."

After Smith, Zaks studied acting in New York and got a job as a replacement Kenickie on Broadway in *Grease*. He joined a touring production of *Fiddler on the Roof* as Motel the tailor. The tour starred Zero Mostel as Tevye. Mostel liked Zaks and gave him lessons in comedy, often during the performance.

One night Zaks's parents met Mostel backstage. "Is my boy going to be all right in this fakakta business?" his father asked in Yiddish. "Listen to me," Mostel replied in Yiddish. "He's going to be more than all right."

Zaks eventually turned to directing. He staged plays by Christopher Durang and an acclaimed revival of John Guare's *The House of Blue Leaves* for Lincoln Center, followed by *Anything Goes*, *The Front Page*, and *Six Degrees of Separation*. He developed an approach to comedy that he called "seriously silly." What it boils down to is that the characters in a comedy do not know they're in a comedy. "Their lives are at stake," Zaks said. "For us, it's nah—we have permission to enjoy the shenanigans. For them it's life and death."

The first person Zaks brought to *Guys and Dolls* was Tony Walton, who had designed the sets for Zaks's Lincoln Center hits. One afternoon at Walton's house in Sag Harbor, Zaks thumbed through a book of Walton's illustrations. The primary colors jumped out at him. *Guys and Dolls*, he told Walton, "is going to look like this." William Ivey Long joined the team and began sketching costumes with exaggerated lapels, ties, fedoras, and buttons. His colors were vivid and luminous.

The original creators of *Guys and Dolls* tailored it for the stage mechanics of the 1940s. A scene would be played, a painted drop would come down, the sets would be changed, and then the drop would go up on a new scene. Zaks wanted a more fluid staging. But he couldn't crack it. He asked Cy Feuer, the original producer, for advice. "Listen to me," Feuer said. "There is something so structurally sound about this show that if you defy it or deny it, it will bite you in the ass." The trick, Zaks realized, was to modernize old-fashioned staging. So instead of painted drops, Walton created a series of sepia scrims portraying a scene. The scrims would bleed away to the same scene, now in vibrant colors. The scrims, in other words, came to life.

Zaks auditioned several choreographers, giving them the task of creating one dance for the show. Christopher Chadman submitted a seven-minute "Runyonland" that had buoyancy, musicality, and athleticism. He got the job. His "Runyonland" would open the show.

As for his cast, Zaks had in mind from the start Peter Gallagher as Sky. The actor had the right combination of masculinity and sensitivity and was gaining some name recognition from the movie *Sex, Lies, and Videotape*. To play Sarah Brown, Zaks cast an old friend, Carolyn Mignini, with whom he had appeared on Broadway in *Tintypes* in 1980. She was older than Gallagher, but Zaks thought a May-December relationship could work. Faith Prince, a quirky redhead who had been the only bright spot in the 1991 flop *Nick & Nora*, landed Adelaide from the moment she sang "A person can develop a cold" with a Marilyn Monroe squeak in her voice. Nathan Lane auditioned for Nathan Detroit. He had everyone in the room falling down with laughter. But after he left, several people said, "He's not Jewish." They thought Nathan

Detroit was Jewish because Sam Levene played him in the original production. Zaks auditioned Lane a second time. Once again everybody doubled over with laughter. But he still wasn't Jewish, they said. Zaks overruled the objection. "If he had to perform a circumcision onstage then we might have had issues. But where is it written that Nathan Detroit is Jewish?"*

For the denizens of Runyonland, Zaks cast a bunch of character actors of all shapes and sizes—Ernie Sabella, Ruth Williamson, J. K. Simmons, Herschel Sparber, John Carpenter. Zaks cast against type for the role of Nicely-Nicely Johnson, originally played by short, fat, bald Stubby Kaye. Zaks gave the part to his friend Walter Bobbie, who was tall and slim and had plenty of hair. "Every fat tenor on Broadway was furious with me," Bobbie said.

As Zaks was pulling together his cast, David was pulling together the money. The cost of a typical Broadway revival in 1992 was around $2 million. But this *Guys and Dolls* was being conceived as a new show. William Ivey Long's costume budget was $700,000. Tony Walton's sets came in at $875,000. At a total coast of $5.5 million, *Guys and Dolls* was going to be the most expensive revival in Broadway history. But raising money was not difficult. Roger Berlind, who had made a fortune on Wall Street, showed up at David's office one day, took out his checkbook, and wrote a check for $1 million.

On the first day of rehearsals, Zaks told the actors not to say anything, good or bad, about one another's performances. They

* Lane wasn't the only non-Jewish actor to play Nathan Detroit. Frank Sinatra, who preferred meatballs to matzo balls, played the part in the movie. When Sam Goldwyn told Frank Loesser that Sinatra was doing the movie, Loesser said, "That's great. He'll be wonderful as Sky Masterson."

"No, he's playing Nathan Detroit," Goldwyn said.

"I was hoping Sam Levene could do it," Loesser said. "He's the person we wrote it for."

"Oh, Sam Levene," Goldwyn said. "No—too Jewish."

were not even to discuss the show among themselves. "If you have an idea, bring it to me," Zaks said. "Don't talk to anyone else."

"Jerry's rules fall somewhere between direction and Riker's Island," said Lane. But Lane and Prince violated Zaks's rule. They had a duet—"Sue Me"—they felt could be more than just a throwaway comic number. Zaks was busy with so many other things they worked on the number in secret, terrified he'd find out.

Rehearsals seemed to be going well for everybody but Bobbie. He could not get laughs. "The part was all based on Stubby's personality and his look," Bobbie said. "So Nicely always came in eating a sandwich and drinking, and none of that stuff made sense to me." Nicely makes one entrance carrying a bag of groceries. Kaye always got a laugh because he was fat. But nobody laughed at the tall and thin Walter Bobbie. He tried everything, including having sausage links fall out of the bag. And still no laughs. The day before the cast moved into the Martin Beck, Zaks took Bobbie aside and asked him if he was worried he was going to be fired. Bobbie was. Zaks suggested he wear a fat suit, but Bobbie didn't think that would help. "If what I'm doing doesn't work, it doesn't work," he said, dejectedly. His costume didn't help. Wearing a straw boater and white shoes, "I looked like I was in *The Music Man*."

There is a rule on Broadway: Nobody knows how good (or bad) a show is until it plays its first performance in front of a *paying* audience. Ignore their reaction at your peril. As it happened, the first performance of *Guys and Dolls* played well. Jack Viertel, standing at the back of the Martin Beck, thought, *We've got a huge hit*. But the next day "there was a lull," he said, "and that lull lasted a long time." The show was not landing. Audiences were restless. People were leaving at intermission. One investor withdrew her money. Watching a Wednesday matinee play to a half-empty theater, Viertel felt ill. The house manager, who'd been around since *Oklahoma!*, put his arm around him and said, "This show is going to be a smash. But you've got to have a strong stomach to stay in this business."

Zaks called the company together after a performance for what they thought was going to be a pep talk and "laid into us," Lane said. "He said we weren't really trying. And I thought, *If I try any harder, I'll start hemorrhaging.*" And then Zaks said, "Nathan and Faith are going to do 'Sue Me.' They have the style that this show has to have, and I want you all to sit here and watch it."

"We were shivering, ready to cut our throats," Ivey Long recalled. "And then we watched those brilliant clowns with their brilliant timing sing a love song between two misfits and we were moved." In secret, Lane and Prince had turned a throwaway comic song into a touching duet about two people, who despite their differences, can't live without each other. "It was not a cartoon," Ivey Long said. The rest of the cast had been pushing too hard for the laughs. They were silly, not "seriously silly." Even Zaks, who coined the phrase, had lost sight of it. Lane and Prince got him and everybody else back on track.

Michael David put his finger on another problem. In notes to Zaks after an early preview, he wrote of Carolyn Mignini: "No sexual tension, no dramatic tension. If no heat then how about funny? What do we get instead of youth, sexiness? What does Sky fall in love with—and can we, too?" Mignini, he concluded, was "stiff as a board." *Guys and Dolls* was floundering because there was no chemistry between its leads.

Zaks knew that was a problem, and he spent chunks of rehearsal time trying to create chemistry between the leads. Mignini was such a close friend that he had to help her "to get whatever was not happening." Then one night he pretended to buy a ticket and look at the show as if he had never seen it. He knew it wasn't working. The audience was giving it "polite attention, which is awful." He saw all the problems he had neglected due to the time he'd spent working with Mignini. And then at her curtain call he heard something he'd never heard in a Broadway theater: somebody booed. "It was chilling, but it was the stamp," he said. Zaks knew he had to fire his friend.

He rehearsed her understudy—Josie de Guzman—in secret for a week so she'd be ready to go on as soon as Mignini was gone. After a Wednesday-night performance, he steeled himself to enter Mignini's dressing room, but she'd already left the theater. He called her later that night and, his heart pounding, fired her. He put down the phone and it rang. It was Mignini's husband imploring him to give her another chance. Zaks refused.*

The next night, de Guzman went on. She was talented, young, and appealing. The unlikely romance between Sky and Sarah took off. Now Zaks could concentrate on the other problems. Chadman's brilliant seven-minute "Runyonland" dance that opened the show was too long. The audience was impatient for the story to begin. He told Chadman, "I have to cut it and go right to 'I got the horse right here.'" Chadman begged for a chance to tighten the dance. A few days later he came in with a two-and-a-half-minute "Runyonland" that launched the show like a rocket.

Zaks looked at Bobbie's performance and made a simple decision. Cut the grocery bag scene. Bobbie wasn't fat, so it wasn't funny. Bobbie also got a new costume—a plaid suit, a bow tie, a newsboy cap. And he had developed a rapport with his fellow gamblers, especially J. K. Simmons. Audiences loved their back-and-forth. Bobbie knew he'd stepped out of the shadow of Stubby Kaye the night he stopped the show with "Sit Down, You're Rockin' the Boat." A few nights before the opening, Zaks ducked out of the theater to get some air. Chadman was standing on the

* Walter Bobbie admitted he was relieved to learn Mignini had been fired. "Honestly, selfishly, I thought, *I'm safe*, because I knew they couldn't fire two people," he said.

sidewalk. They looked at each other and sobbed. "Because we'd been through so much," Zaks said.

Guys and Dolls opened April 14, 1992. At around 9:50 that night, John Barlow, a junior press agent on the show, slipped into the lobby of the *New York Times* on West Forty-Third Street to get the first edition of the paper. On the front page below the fold was a picture of Faith Prince and Nathan Lane as Miss Adelaide and Nathan Detroit. Barlow tore down the street screaming, "It's on the cover! It's on the cover!" Frank Rich came through with a review that buys country houses: "This is an enchanting rebirth of the show that defines Broadway dazzle." Everybody came in for praise, though Rich had one tiny quibble. "He mentioned I wasn't Jewish," Lane said.

The next day the line to buy tickets stretched down West Forty-Fifth Street to Ninth Avenue. By close of business, *Guys and Dolls* had taken in $396,709.50, shattering by more than $35,000 the single-day record set by *Phantom* in 1988.[5]

Faith Prince became an overnight sensation, while Nathan Lane was on his way to becoming one of Broadway's great stars. The revival also buoyed a city that, in the early 1990s, was still in the doldrums. The cleanup of Times Square was barely underway, David Dinkins's administration was adrift, there had been rioting in Crown Heights, and crime was spiking due to a raging crack epidemic. Adrian Bryan-Brown, the lead press agent for *Guys and Dolls*, remembered stepping on crack vials littered outside the Martin Beck. But inside, audiences were transported to a Times Square that was joyous, bright, and hopeful. It was, of course, only a musical. But as Ross Wetzsteon wrote in *New York*, "Perhaps the transfixed theatergoers at the Martin Beck feel they're hearing the faint first note of the overture to their own hopes that their sinful city can find a kind of rebirth."[6]

CHAPTER SEVEN

WINGING IT

One morning in March 1992, Jack Viertel opened his *New York Times*, turned to Frank Rich's "Critic's Notebook" from London, and read a rave for a play at the National Theatre called *Angels in America* by Tony Kushner. Viertel had heard about the play—it had been in development at the Mark Taper Forum while he was in Los Angeles—but he had no idea it was this good. Within forty-eight hours, Viertel was at the National in London taking in Kushner's three-and-a-half hour epic about AIDS, the Reagan era, Mormons, and Roy Cohn. Viertel was impressed, but the end puzzled him. An angel crashed through the roof and told a young man dying of AIDS, "The Great Work begins: The Messenger has arrived." Viertel thought, *And then what happens?* Kushner was at work on a second part, but it was nowhere near ready to be staged. That didn't matter. Part One—*Millennium Approaches*—was "a masterpiece," Viertel said. It was just the kind of play—ambitious, political, angry—that would make Jujamcyn's reputation. It was also the kind of play that a Broadway drifting toward intellectual irrelevance needed.

Critics have been carping about the lack of serious plays on Broadway since, well, Broadway began. Brooks Atkinson, in his invaluable book *Broadway*, noted that a foreigner surveying the light fare on the Great White Way in 1905 predicted "there will be no dramatic art in America for another twenty years."[1] By the 1920s, however, serious American plays were gaining a foothold amid the frivolity. Audiences recognized Eugene O'Neill's talent in *Beyond the Horizon*, produced at the Morosco Theatre in 1920. For the next fourteen years, O'Neill towered above his contemporaries with works such as *Desire Under the Elms*, *Mourning Becomes Electra*, *The Hairy Ape*, and *Strange Interlude*. In 1936, he became the first American playwright to win the Nobel Prize for Literature.

American plays enjoyed a good run in the 1930s as critics and audiences applauded dramas by Clifford Odets (*Waiting for Lefty*), Lillian Hellman (*Watch on the Rhine*), Thornton Wilder (*Our Town*), Robert Sherwood (*Abe Lincoln in Illinois*), and William Saroyan (*The Time of Your Life*), as well as the comedies of George S. Kaufman and Moss Hart (*You Can't Take It with You*, *The Man Who Came to Dinner*). During World War II, musicals overshadowed plays, probably because audiences wanted a few hours of fun in a world gone mad. As Robert Sherwood said, "The American theater is today bristling with potential talent in all departments save one: playwriting."[2]

That fear would not last long. In 1945, audiences were sobbing at the end of Tennessee Williams's *The Glass Menagerie*. Two years later, they were shocked, and many angered, by the suicide of a businessman who cut corners (with deadly results) in *All My Sons*, Arthur Miller's blistering attack on the war machine. Williams and Miller charged into the late '40s and '50s with masterpieces of American drama—*A Streetcar Named Desire*, *Death of a Salesman*, *Cat on a Hot Tin Roof*, *The Crucible*. Just a rung below them was William Inge, who wrote movingly of alcoholism and infidelity in *Come Back, Little Sheba*; *Picnic*; and *The Dark at the Top of the Stairs*. The great man, O'Neill, was fading, but before he died in

1953 he gave Broadway *The Iceman Cometh.* Three years after his death, his widow, Carlotta Monterey, defying his wishes that his most personal play never be published or produced, attended the November 7 Broadway opening of *Long Day's Journey into Night.*

Still, the critics clamored for more serious drama. "Except for Williams, Miller, and a few others, the spoken drama was beside the point," Atkinson wrote, adding that Broadway "is a holiday promenade not equipped to cope with intellectual problems."[3] Edward Albee joined O'Neill, Williams, and Miller in the front pew of American drama in 1962 with his scorcher *Who's Afraid of Virginia Woolf?*, followed by *The Ballad of the Sad Café* (a touching adaptation of Carson McCullers's novella), *Tiny Alice* (haunting and mysterious though underappreciated at the time), *A Delicate Balance* (magnificent but also underappreciated at the time), and *Everything in the Garden* (tabloid sensational but entertaining). British writer Harold Pinter arrived on Broadway in the 1960s with his enigmatic and unsettling plays: *The Caretaker, The Birthday Party,* and *The Homecoming* (the only box office hit among the three). Critics praised director Peter Brook's production of *Marat/Sade,* about the assassination of Jean-Paul Marat in an insane asylum during the French Revolution. Culture vultures lined up for hours outside the Martin Beck for tickets. The decade's biggest box office draw, though, was Neil Simon, racking up hit after hit with *Come Blow Your Horn, Barefoot in the Park, The Odd Couple,* and *Plaza Suite.*

By the 1970s, with Broadway mired in financial troubles and Times Square engulfed by squalor, the action shifted to Off Broadway and nonprofit theaters, especially Joe Papp's Public Theater. The plays that won the Pulitzer Prize in the first half of the '70s, as Atkinson pointedly noted, were all produced Off Broadway. Broadway hits such as *That Championship Season, Sticks and Bones,* and *Gemini* originated in nonprofit theaters. That trend continued into the 1980s. Plays by David Mamet and August Wilson opened on Broadway only after successful runs at nonprofits outside New York. But for the most part, the street's straight-play houses stood empty for months at a time.

The one bright spot was Neil Simon, who after stumbling in the early '80s with a couple of flops, gave his producer Emanuel Azenberg thirty pages of a play he called *The War of the Rosens*. He based it on the summer of 1937 when his family shared a small cottage in the Rockaways with relatives. He switched the setting to Brighton Beach and named his autobiographical younger self Eugene Jerome.

The play, now called *Brighton Beach Memoirs*, starred Elizabeth Franz, Joyce Van Patten, and, as Eugene, Matthew Broderick. Azenberg offered it to the Shuberts, but they thought it was "episodic." Azenberg walked across Times Square to Jimmy Nederlander's office above the Palace Theatre. "You want Neil's new play?" he asked. "In a minute," Nederlander said. *Brighton Beach Memoirs* opened at the Alvin Theatre and ran three years. Nederlander was so thrilled to have it he renamed the theater the Neil Simon. Frank Rich gave the play a mixed review, but enjoyed it enough to hope there would be a sequel. Simon took up the suggestion and wrote *Biloxi Blues*, about his experiences in the army. Broderick once again played Eugene, and Simon had another box office hit.

He capped his autobiographical cycle with *Broadway Bound*, about his early days writing comedy sketches for radio while his parents' marriage crumbled. The first act went over well at an early reading. The mother—Kate, played by Linda Lavin—emerged as a compelling character. But she receded in the second act as Simon introduced a new character, Eugene's girlfriend. A scene between Eugene and the girlfriend in the second act dragged. Azenberg looked down at his script and began counting pages. Simon slipped him a note: "Don't worry, I know how to fix it." At dinner that night Azenberg told him, "I miss the mother in the second act." "Give me two weeks," Simon said. Two days later he showed up at rehearsals with a new draft. The girlfriend was gone, replaced by a scene between Kate and Eugene in which she reminisces about the one thrilling night of her life, the night George Raft asked her to dance. Frank Rich called the scene "the indisputable peak" of the play. Lavin won the Tony Award for Best Actress. *Broadway Bound* ran two years.*

Simon's next play, *Louis the Gangster,* was about a gangster, his mentally impaired sister, and their mother, a formidable German Jewish immigrant incapable of affection. Simon thought Irene Worth could play the mother. Born in Nebraska, Worth was living in London when Azenberg and Simon went to see her. "Everything she said was in a British accent," Azenberg recalled. "It was 'darling this,' and 'darling that.' Finally we said, 'Can you be a German Jew?' She dropped the British accent and started speaking like a German." Retitled *Lost in Yonkers,* the play won Simon's first—and only—Pulitzer Prize in 1991. Worth, Kevin Spacey, and Mercedes Ruehl won Tonys for their performances, and *Lost in Yonkers* beat out John Guare's *Six Degrees of Separation* for Best Play.

Yonkers and *Six Degrees* notwithstanding, it was a dreary season for plays on Broadway. Fear was spreading once again that the American play was becoming an endangered species. In his annual summation of the theater season, Frank Rich blasted the Tony Awards for ignoring Off Broadway, where new American plays such as Jon Robin Baitz's *The Substance of Fire* and Spalding Gray's *Monster in a Box* were thriving. "The Tony Awards seem almost beside the point . . . when no one on Broadway seems to have a clue as to what will fill its vacant stages," Rich wrote.[4]

* A year later Simon and Azenberg developed a musical based on the songs of George Gershwin. The show began with the stage direction: "Curtain opens and there's fog all over the stage." Jason Alexander, at a reading, entered and began singing "A Foggy Day in London Town." Simon slipped Azenberg a note: "Worry. I don't know how to fix it."

* * *

There were no vacant stages at the Public Theater in 1991. New York's leading nonprofit—the closet thing to a national theater in America—produced challenging plays, some great, many interesting, several tedious. The Public had high hopes in January 1991 for *A Bright Room Called Day*, a new play by Tony Kushner that drew parallels between the rise of Nazi Germany and the Reagan revolution.

A Bright Room Called Day was an angry play. Kushner, recently out of New York University's graduate program in directing, started writing it in 1984, "a very black time" in his life.[5] His best friend from his undergraduate days at Columbia University suffered brain damage in a car accident. A theater group he was involved in fell apart. A close relative died. And Reagan won reelection. "The desolate political sphere mirrored in an exact and ugly way an equally desolate personal sphere," he said.[6] That desolation produced a tiresome screed that many critics dismissed as predictable lefty agitprop. "A Bright Room Called Cliché," said the *Daily News*. Frank Rich killed it with one word: "Fatuous."

Kushner was wounded, but he didn't have much time to dwell on the attacks. He was under a tight deadline to finish the sprawling *Angels in America* in time for its world premiere at the Eureka Theatre in San Francisco that spring. Part One (*Millennium Approaches*) was in pretty good shape. Part Two (*Perestroika*) barely existed. Kushner wanted to postpone the premiere, but Eureka's lawyers threatened to sue him if he didn't deliver a script.[7]

A dream Kushner had in 1985 about a friend who had recently died of AIDS inspired the play. His friend was lying in bed, the ceiling caved in, and an angel appeared. Kushner wrote a long poem about the dream. He called it "Angels in America." He read it a few times and then squirreled it away. As he told the authors of the book *The World Only Spins Forward: The Ascent of* Angels in America, "No one will ever see it."

Angels in America, the play, came about as a commission from the Eureka Theatre. Oskar Eustis, the theater's artistic director and Kushner's good friend, was miffed that he'd lost the rights to *The Normal Heart*, Larry Kramer's furious play about the AIDS crisis, to the Berkeley Repertory Theatre. He wanted his own AIDS play, and secured an NEA grant of $50,000 to produce it. Kushner received $10,000 to write a two-hour play about "five gay men and an angel" that would, like plays by his hero Bertolt Brecht, have songs.[8] The play expanded beyond two hours. Characters poured out of Kushner—Joe, a closeted Mormon lawyer and his drug-addicted wife, Harper; Prior, an AIDS patient whose healthy lover Louis leaves him; the ghost of Ethel Rosenberg; Belize, a transvestite and nurse to AIDS patients; and Roy Cohn, the rapacious Republican lawyer who died of AIDS in 1986. Cohn was a delicious villain. Kushner rendered his cleverness and charisma so vividly that the character nearly hijacked the play.

The draft he gave Eustis in 1988 was 240 pages with no end in sight.[9] The first reading of *Millennium Approaches* took place at the New York Theatre Workshop in the fall of 1988. Kushner stood in the lobby and apologized to people for the play's length. Leave anytime you want, he told them. They stayed. Jim Nicola, the artistic director, offered to produce the play, but Kushner had made a commitment to Eureka. The theater was struggling and needed a boost from a high-profile production.[10] But Kushner was still writing. The theater might have dropped the whole thing but for Gordon Davidson, the wily head of the Center Theatre Group in Los Angeles. He made a deal with Eureka: his theater would develop the play—with Eustis overseeing readings and workshops—but Eureka would stage the world premiere. As Kushner struggled to finish his epic, a friend suggested that *Millennium Approaches* could stand on its own. Why not stage it and then write a second play to continue the story? Davidson's theater put $80,000 into a workshop production of *Millennium Approaches* that generated considerable buzz among theater insiders in 1990. Scouts for the National Theatre in London attended and offered to do a full-scale production in 1992, directed by Declan Donnellan.

Kushner, meanwhile, was scrambling to finish the first draft of Part Two for Eureka's world premiere. He holed up in a cabin in the Russian River Valley in California and wrote seven hundred pages in ten days. They were unwieldy and bizarre. In one draft, the play ended with all the characters standing around the Empire State Building and then being blown up by an atomic bomb. The world premiere of *Angels in America* at the Eureka turned out to be a staged production of Part One and a reading of Part Two. Even unfinished, the play was a hit. Some who saw it say Part One was terrific, Part Two terrible. Others say it was the best production of all because it was so raw. Eureka spent $250,000 on the play. That was too much for the cash-strapped theater. It had a sensation on its hands, but it couldn't do anything with it. Not long after the opening of *Angels*, Eureka went out of business.

Kushner turned his attention to *Millennium Approaches* at the National Theatre. Fretting about everything from the set to the blocking, he made a pest of himself, as he admitted to the *Times*. He took a break to go back to New York, wrote fifty pages of notes on the plane and faxed them to Donnellan the next day.[11] He returned a few weeks later for previews and the opening and this time liked what he saw. So did the London critics. "Sprawling and over-written as it may be, it is a play of epic energy that gets American drama not just out of the closet but, thank God, out of the living-room as well," Michael Billington wrote in the *Guardian*. Frank Rich came to see the production a few months later and his rave kicked off a battle for the play in New York.

Jujamcyn was in the mix but so, too, was the Public Theater, now being led by JoAnne Akalaitis, who had been appointed artistic director after the death of Joe Papp in 1991. The Shuberts were moving in as well. "It was going to be all-out trench warfare," said Rocco Landesman.

Gordon Davidson picked up both parts of *Angels in America* for the Mark Taper Forum, where it was codirected by Oskar Eustis and Tony Taccone. Everybody jockeying for the show in New York attended the opening. And they were let down. "It was not a great production," said Viertel. "And I did not know what to make of the second part. It was not cohesive. But I came away thinking, *We've got to do this.*" Frank Rich summed up the Broadway crowd's reaction in his review. The play, especially the first part, was "miraculous," but the staging was "stodgy" and *Perestroika* "embryonic." Rich praised cast members Ron Leibman (Cohn) and Stephen Spinella (Prior) and thought Joe Mantello (Louis) "shows a lot of promise," but he gave the back of his hand to some of the other actors.[12] Rich kept the focus on the brilliance of Kushner's writing, but his review made it clear that this production was not good enough for New York.

The Public Theater, which was confident it would get the play, was not in the running long. Davidson told Kushner *Angels* had to go to Broadway, which for all its faults was still the center of the American theater. The Shuberts offered Kushner his pick of their playhouses along West Forty-Fifth Street, the most desirable block in Times Square. If he wanted a theater that already had a play in it, they would move that play somewhere else. Bernie Jacobs, a master manipulator of people, tried to woo Kushner with stories about his father-son relationship with Michael Bennett, whose death from AIDS had devastated Jacobs.[13]

While the Shuberts had five great theaters to offer Kushner, Rocco Landesman had one, the Walter Kerr. Now refurbished, it was a gem. But it was several blocks north of Forty-Fifth Street with all its eye-catching Broadway marquees. Meeting with Kushner, Landesman said, "Tell us what you want. Tell us the one thing you must have to do this play with us."

"I want an absolute promise that you'll do *Perestroika* when it's ready," Kushner said.

"Done," Landesman said. "I don't know how we'll do it, but we'll do it." And then he added, "Everybody wants this show, but you're going to be a playwright for a long time. You're going to have other shows that people aren't going to be falling all over themselves to produce. We do every play August Wilson writes. We don't ask if it's going to be commercial. We do them because we have a commitment to August. We'll make that commitment to you. If you have another play and people don't think it should be on Broadway, we will be there for you." Kushner went with Jujamcyn.*

It was clear to everybody that the show needed a new director. Margo Lion, a producer aligned with Jujamcyn, suggested George C. Wolfe, who had staged the acclaimed musical *Jelly's Last Jam*, which Jujamcyn had backed. "We had a lot of faith in George," said Viertel, "though he was a handful. But it was a great idea. And when Margo introduced Tony and George to each other they got along like a house afire, though they both are very mercurial, difficult personalities."

Kushner agreed to let Wolfe direct, which meant dumping his friend Eustis, who had commissioned *Angels*. It was a wrenching decision, and some involved in the show thought Kushner, for all his talk of morality and social justice, had sold out his friend for the lure of Broadway. Some accused him of bowing and scraping to the mighty Frank Rich. But Kushner always said he knew the

* Kushner would call in the chit for his musical *Caroline, or Change*, which opened at the Public in 2003. Jujamcyn moved it to the Eugene O'Neill Theatre, where it flopped.

production in Los Angeles was not good enough. "I needed to take care of the play. All of those decisions had been made long before Frank came and reviewed it."[14]

Where he would not budge—and where he clashed with Wolfe—was over the cast. He wanted the actors from Los Angeles. "He was loyal to them, but not as loyal to the rest of the production," Viertel said. Wolfe knew he could find better actors in New York. In the end, they reached a compromise. Some of the actors, mainly those Rich praised, came to New York. The rest of the cast would be replaced.

Jujamcyn's plan was to open *Millennium Approaches* first, go into rehearsal for *Perestroika*, open it six months later, and play the two shows in repertory. When the number crunchers worked out the budget they were aghast. "The budget for this thing is going to be eighty billion dollars," one of them said. "How are you going to do this?" But Jujamcyn had given its word to produce both parts.

The opening of *Millennium Approaches* on May 4, 1993, dispelled any misgivings the company may have had. The play jumped off the theatrical pages of the newspapers. It was being discussed everywhere from network television to the *New York Review of Books*. Frank Rich led the way proclaiming it "the most thrilling American play in years."[15] Most of the other critics followed suit, though the notoriously tough, and skeptical, John Simon withheld judgment until he could see both parts: "The good [news] is that for all its three and a half hours, the play doesn't ever bore you; the bad is that it is unfinished and that it is hard to see how Kushner—or anyone—could pull such far-flung ambitions, such heterogeneous though homosexual strands together into one tightly knit, ravel proof whole."[16] *Millennium* won the Pulitzer Prize and four Tony Awards, including Best Play. Tickets were nearly impossible to find.

Now it was time to put *Perestroika* together. Rehearsals began in the summer, which meant scaling back the number of weekly performances of *Millennium* to four from eight so the actors wouldn't have meltdowns. The original budget of $2.2 million was creeping up to $3 million, making *Angels* the most expensive play in Broadway history. And people still had doubts about the soundness of *Perestroika*, which opened, after some expensive delays, in rep with *Millennium* on November 23, 1993. Rich kept the hype flowing, calling the second part a "true millennial work of art." But *Angels* fatigue was setting in. Simon found much to like in the play, but concluded: "The fact remains that *Angels in America*—and especially Part Two, from which we expect a resolution—goes nowhere."[17] Others were less kind. Andrew Sullivan, the openly gay editor of the *New Republic*, sniped: "The script itself never ascended . . . above a West Village version of Neil Simon."

Perestroika was not the box office hit *Millenium* had been. *Angels* chugged on for another year, but the heat was gone. "Part One would have been quite a big financial success," said Landesman. "But in fact the whole show barely recouped." Recoupment was not the point, however. *Angels in America* fulfilled its main purpose: it established Jujamcyn Theaters, the perennial number three landlord, as the driving producing force on Broadway. Viertel recalled sitting in a rehearsal of *Angels* and listening to Wolfe complain about the Walter Kerr. The shallow stage inhibited some bold, dramatic entrances he was trying to create. Exasperated, he snapped: "Why are we doing this show at the Walter Kerr?" Viertel replied, "George, we're doing it at the Walter Kerr because it is the rock upon which Jujamcyn's reputation will be founded."

CHAPTER EIGHT

WHO'S AFRAID OF EDWARD ALBEE?

Second acts in the American theater are rare. Writers have a good run and then tastes change, talent wobbles, and critics become disappointed or even hostile. Eugene O'Neill found favor again with the original Broadway production of *Long Day's Journey into Night*, but it opened three years after his death. Arthur Miller never had another hit new play after *The Price* in 1968. There were successful revivals of *The Crucible* and *Death of a Salesman*, of course, but critics dismissed *The Creation of the World and Other Business*, *The American Clock*, and *Broken Glass*. In the 1990s, Miller spent much of his time in London, where his plays were much better received. He did have a comeback in the late 1990s, but that was due to the terrific revival of *Death of a Salesman* starring Brian Dennehy.

For Tennessee Williams, the decline was slow, sad, drenched in alcohol, addled by drugs. He often came to the theater stoned. John Lahr, his biographer, recalled seeing him at a revival of *Camino Real* in 1970. "Tennessee had to be literally lifted into his seat. He was legless. Afterwards he came backstage to see everybody, and it was very hard to understand that there was such a discrepancy between the perfect self of the writing and the imperfect author of the writing."[1]

In the 1970s, Williams wrote one flop after another. His last Broadway play—*Clothes for a Summer Hotel* in 1980—ran just fifteen performances. Critic Walter Kerr called it "dismaying." Williams was found dead in his suite at the Hotel Elysée in New York on February 25, 1983. He choked to death on a bottle cap.

Edward Albee's fall was brutal. He won a Pulitzer for *Seascape* in 1975, but the play ran just sixty-five performances. After that came two more flops and then the play that made him a pariah on Broadway, *The Man Who Had Three Arms*. The play was an attack on critics. "He used the word *cunt* about eight minutes into the play and lost the audience," said playwright Terrence McNally, Albee's onetime lover and friend. "And of course the only woman critic we could think of was Edith Oliver [from the *New Yorker*], and she was always good to him, so why was he calling her a cunt? But I think he just wanted to use that word to hit the critics." They responded in kind. Frank Rich called the play "a temper tantrum in two acts." It closed a week after opening.

Albee continued to write, but nobody on Broadway would touch his plays. He took teaching posts at the University of Houston and Johns Hopkins. Royalties came in from *The Zoo Story* and *Who's Afraid of Virginia Woolf?* and while he lived frugally (his one extravagance was art) money became tight after a battle with the IRS. At one point he had to sell a Henry Moore sculpture he'd bought in the 1960s. He was also confronting years of alcoholism. In the 1970s, he would go on benders and lash out at everyone, friend or foe. He once showed up drunk at a play, shouted at the actors, and stormed out of the theater. With the help of his lover Jonathan Thomas he managed to curb the drinking, giving it up when he was diagnosed with diabetes. Every now and then, though, a remnant of the past would come back: "I'd take down a book from the shelf and sometimes find an old sticky glass of scotch I'd hidden from Jonathan. What can I say? I started drinking at eleven in the morning."[2]

If he resented his exile by New York critics and producers, he never showed it, at least publicly. "New York and I, well, we don't seem to be getting along quite as well as we should," he told the *Daily News* in 1993. "What I would love to do with my next play is . . . have it submitted for production, produced and received under a pseudonym. It would be difficult, but maybe we could get away with it. We'll see," he added.[3]

Sometime in the late '70s, Albee began reconciling with his mother, Frances (Frankie, as everyone called her). "She was like one of those famous cartoons in the *New Yorker* of over-privileged Park Avenue matrons," McNally said. "Gloves, hat with a veil—formidable and very unfriendly." Frankie and her husband, Reed Albee, whose father was the famous vaudeville producer and theater owner Edward Franklin Albee, adopted Albee eighteen days after he was born on March 12, 1928. He had a privileged upbringing in Larchmont and Palm Beach, where the Albees lived next door to the Kennedys. But his childhood was not happy. His father spoke to him rarely, and he and his mother loathed each other. "Just you wait until you are eighteen, and I'll have you out of here so fast it will make your head spin," she once said to him.[4] Albee left home for good at twenty after a fight with his parents about his homosexuality. He never spoke to his father again and cut off his mother for twenty years. They responded by disinheriting him. After he became famous, Frankie warmed up to him a little, calling him, "My boy Edward, who wrote *Who's Afraid of Virginia Woolf*?"[5] But they remained wary of each other, and she never accepted his homosexuality. In the 1980s, as her health began to deteriorate, he visited her in her apartment above the Westchester Country Club. She slipped into a coma in March 1989 and died later that spring in the hospital. She was ninety-two. "Nobody was in the room except the chauffeur and the maid," Albee told his biographer Mel Gussow. "Final irony."[6]

A year after Frankie died, Albee began writing a play about a rich, tough old lady, full of the prejudices of her day, but a survivor. As with all of his plays, he didn't plot it out. He heard the woman in his head talking to him as he took long walks on the beach in Montauk and then wrote down what she said. He knew the woman was his mother, but he resisted settling scores. "When I got to writing the play my anger about my adoptive mother was still there, but I added something—a little pity," he said.[7] In addition to the old woman, called A in the play, he added two more women—B, a fifty-two-year-old caretaker, and C, a twenty-six-year-old lawyer, tidying up the old lady's accounts. He called the play *Three Tall Women.*

He wrote the first act quickly. Nobody in New York was much interested in anything he was up to, so he gave it to the English Theatre in Vienna, which had produced some of his plays. Albee asked a friend, Myra Carter, to play A. Carter was a respected regional theater actress. She appeared in revivals of *All Over* and *A Delicate Balance.* But she was unknown in New York. The actor James Coco once told Terrence McNally, "There's a great actress in the regionals named Myra Carter, and for the life of me I cannot understand why no one in New York has ever heard of her."[8]

Carter was a genuine eccentric. As a young woman, she'd been married to a Wall Street banker but left when he wanted to have children. "That's what the bourgeoisie do—they procreate!" she used to say. For years she lived in a tiny apartment above a pizza parlor on Christopher Street in Greenwich Village. She lived in genteel poverty surrounded by art, including, as she said, a few "things Andy gave me." Andy was Andy Warhol, an old friend. Back in the 1960s, she used to take him for rides around the city on her Harley-Davidson.

Carter didn't have high hopes for Albee's new play. "He's out of vogue," she repeatedly said. But she liked it, though there was a problem. The second act did not exist. Nevertheless, off they went to Vienna in 1991 to do *Three Tall Women*. As the cast rehearsed the first act, Albee retreated to his hotel room to write the second. He came up with a twist that still makes audiences gasp. The old woman has a stroke at the end of Act I. At the start of Act II, she's lying in bed in a coma. B and C are talking about her. And then the old woman enters from the wings to join the conversation. The woman in bed is a dummy. A, B, and C are now the same woman, at three different stages of her life.

Three Tall Women ran nearly three hours in Vienna, but Albee's friends from New York who saw it were impressed. Beyond that small group of people, however, nobody cared. Albee was "out of vogue." A small theater in Woodstock agreed to produce the play in the summer of 1992. Albee and the director, Lawrence Sacharow, kept Carter on as A. They auditioned several young women for C, including a tall and strikingly beautiful blonde named Jordan Baker. She was mourning her brother, who had just died of AIDS, when her agent called to tell her about a part in a new play. "Listen, it's by Edward Albee, and nobody's really interested in him anymore," the agent said. "But here's the deal: you get to go to Woodstock and they'll put you up in a lovely cabin and you'll have some time to rest."

At the audition, Jordan noticed her competition—a slender, pretty girl in four-inch high heels. Jordan was wearing flats, and began to wonder if she was tall enough for a play called *Three Tall Women*. She sat next to an older, tall, gangly actress she did not know. As the girl in the high heels clicked her way into the rehearsal room, the older actress turned to Baker and said, "Darling, I think this one is yours."

The actress was Marian Seldes, a grande dame of theater who had been cast as B and was reading with the women auditioning for C. Seldes, whose every gesture was theatrical, called everyone "darling." She and Albee were old friends, having worked together on *Tiny Alice* and *All Over.* She'd also appeared in *Equus* and *Deathtrap,* and was famous for never missing a performance no matter how long the run. She was married to Garson Kanin, the celebrated director and playwright. They were theatrical royalty, but a mismatched pair: Seldes, slender, tall, elegant; Kanin, short, bald, bearded.

Seldes's prediction about Baker turned out to be true. Baker auditioned that day in a dark little room for Albee himself, reading a scene that "was a little jewel," and got the part of C.

On the first day of rehearsal in Woodstock the actresses sat around a table and read the play. It was more than three hours long, but elegantly written. A's final monologue, about death, touched Baker. Death was all around her. Her brother had died of AIDS and she'd just learned that her agent was HIV positive. Albee, too, was surrounded by death while writing the play—not only his mother but also his longtime producer, Richard Barr, who died of AIDS; and his close friend, Howard Moss, a poet, who had a heart attack. Carter read the last lines of the play: "So. There it is. You asked after all. That's the happiest moment. When it's all done. When we stop. When we can stop." She closed her script, turned to Albee and said, "This will be your next fucking Pulitzer."

Rehearsals went smoothly until Sacharow decided Baker and Seldes should move around in the first act as if they were walking underwater. "Marian was into it, but Myra was sitting in the chair watching us and thinking, *What is this bullshit?*" Baker said. Albee watched the rehearsal and when it was over pulled Sacharow aside for a quiet word. The director then said to the cast, "Ladies, you're all excused for the afternoon." The next day at rehearsal he said, "Okay, we're going to start from the beginning.

We're going to erase everything I told you, and we're just going to play it straight."

That's how Albee worked—quietly but forcefully. Tantrums, grand gestures, dramatic statements were not his way. "He was the least theatrical theater person I've ever met," said Terrence McNally. He didn't hesitate to give actors notes, but they were never about their performances. They were about his words. Every line had to be said as written. He listened to his plays during rehearsals as if they "were radio plays," McNally said. He once pulled Baker aside and said, "Jordan, page four, third line. There's a comma."

Seldes was not prone to histrionics either. She was a pro who did what she was asked exceptionally well. She invited Baker over to her cottage for dinner and introduced her to Kanin. Baker had studied his plays in school, but had no idea he was still alive. She was overwhelmed and "started to tear up." Seldes turned to Kanin and said, "Darling, I think she knows who you are!"

Carter could be volatile, a combination of stubbornness and insecurity. She had the major part, and, even though she had done it in Vienna, it was a mountain to climb. At the top of the first act she had to cry, a cry that, as the stage directions say, "concludes with rage and self-loathing at having to cry. It takes a while."

"What the fuck is this?" Carter complained. "I have to fucking weep, then a double weep, then a deep weep. What the fuck am I doing?"

"She was crazy," Baker said. "But after a while I understood. I think there was fear. Every night she'd have to pull herself up for it. She would probably slap me right now, but I think there was fear."

Albee pared the play down to two hours. Local critics gave it good notices, but when Albee's agents shopped it to New York producers, including the Shuberts and Lincoln Center Theater, nobody wanted it. Finally the script landed on the desk of Doug

Aibel, who ran the tiny nonprofit Vineyard Theatre in Union Square. He liked it and agreed to produce it in January 1994 with the three actresses. Baker was surprised she still had the part. She thought a name actress like Elizabeth McGovern would replace her in New York. McGovern, after all, had played Seldes's daughter in the Pulitzer Prize–winning play *Painting Churches*. "She would have been a good fit, and she was tall," Baker said. "I told Marian that, and she said, 'Darling, the part's too small.' "

If nobody was paying much attention to *Three Tall Women* in Woodstock, everybody took notice when the reviews for the Vineyard's production came out. Some critics had reservations here and there, but all recognized the return of a great playwright. Even John Simon, who once called Albee the "execrated perpetrator of *The Man Who Had Three Arms*," was impressed: "If someone had told me how good . . . *Three Tall Women* is, I wouldn't have believed him; I hardly believed my own eyes and ears." Carter, he wrote, "is A-1 in my book." Seldes "gives the performance of her lifetime." Baker "more or less holds her own." He concluded: "These three [women] are not a crowd; they are a company."

Producers who once shunned Albee now circled the play for a commercial transfer. Elizabeth I. McCann had an in as she was good friends with Seldes. McCann had seen the play in Woodstock and was not impressed. She liked it better at the Vineyard. She especially liked that it was sold out. McCann met Albee at his loft on Harrison Street in Tribeca. She'd never met the great playwright before and was nervous. The first thing she noticed was a vast collection of African art he had amassed from his travels in the 1960s and '70s. There were drums, spears, sculpted wooden heads, witch doctor ceremonial masks—"all that stuff *staring* at you," said McCann.

They chatted about nothing for a while, and then Albee said, "You want to move my play?"

"Yes," said McCann.

"Three weeks from the day it closes I want it to reopen."

"That's not a lot of time, Edward. How about five weeks?"

"Four."

"Okay."

"He rightly believed, and I think it's true, that if a play is hot you can't fool around," said McCann.

McCann had no trouble raising money. Steve Roth, the billionaire real estate developer, read a rave for the play in the *Wall Street Journal*. His wife, Daryl, was beginning a career as a producer. She'd had some small hits Off Broadway and a big flop on Broadway—*Nick & Nora*. After reading the rave, Steve Roth said, "If you're going to lose money in the theater, then you should lose it on something like this." Daryl Roth was in for a third of *Three Tall Women*.

The question now was whether to move the play to Broadway or to a commercial Off-Broadway theater. Albee vetoed Broadway. As he told Baker one night over dinner, "They won't do to me what they did to Tennessee."

On April 12, just a few days before *Three Tall Women* was to reopen at the Promenade Theatre on the Upper West Side, Albee won the 1994 Pulitzer Prize for Drama. "I suppose I will be very warm and cuddly and pleased with myself for a while," he told the *New York Times*. About his years in the wilderness, he said, "There is not always a great relationship between popularity and excellence. If you know that, you can never be owned by public opinion or critical response. You just have to make the assumption you're doing good work and go on doing it. Of course, there are the little dolls you stick pins in privately."[9] A month later "those little dolls you stick pins in" gave Albee the Drama Critics Circle Award for Best American Play. He edged out Tony Kushner's *Perestroika*.

* * *

Three Tall Women returned its $300,000 investment in four weeks and settled in for a year-and-a-half run at the Promenade. Jordan Baker got to spend a lot of time with two great but very eccentric actresses. The three were directed to take their bows together, but Seldes and Carter would wait a couple of beats so Baker went out first. Then Seldes would come on to take a little private bow, followed by Carter. The "young one," as they called Baker, had to know her place in the lineup.

One night a pipe burst in the middle of the first act and water came down "like Niagara Falls," said Baker. People scrambled out of their seats. "Oh, my God!" Baker said and turned to Seldes and Carter, who were still in character. Baker ran offstage. Seldes escorted Carter into the wings. Then she wheeled on Baker: "Don't you ever, ever break character! They won't believe us when we go back on again."

Carter's performance was attracting attention. McCann got a call from Carter's agent asking if she would let her out of the show to go to Los Angeles for a few weeks to shoot an episode of *Frasier*. Sure, McCann said. Carter confronted her that night at the theater.

"Do you know what you're doing?" she demanded.

"What are you talking about?" McCann asked.

"You're letting me go to California!" Carter snapped.

"Well, your agent asked," McCann said.

"You think my agent knows what he's doing? I don't want to go. Do you know what shape this show will be in when that cow of an understudy plays my part for three weeks? I'll have so much work to do when I get back!"

Carter ended up going to Los Angeles, but disappeared on arrival. NBC put her in a fancy hotel that used plastic card keys. She hated plastic keys so she checked into an old hotel that had real keys. Nutty though she was, the cast of *Frasier* adored her. "It was like Laurette Taylor had landed in their lap," said McCann.

They came to see her in the play and sent her flowers before the show. She exploded. "The stage manager has standing orders never to tell me who's in the house!"

Her antics amused Albee—until the day she found out that Maggie Smith had been cast as A in the London production. Albee came to the theater a few days later. Carter saw him and screamed, "Why don't you just kill me? After all I've done for you. Went to Vienna. Went to the Vineyard. Came to the Promenade. Night after night after night. The weeping, the weeping, the weeping. And then you stab me in the heart like this? You star fucker!" Albee heard her out, said nothing, and left the theater.

The success of *Three Tall Women* launched Albee's comeback—a word that always made him chuckle. "I don't know why people call it a 'comeback' because I never went anywhere," he told interviewers. It was one of his stock answers to questions he heard again and again. Another was his response to the question, What is your play about? "It's about one hour and forty-five minutes," he'd say.

While *Three Tall Women* was running at the Promenade, Lincoln Center decided to revive *A Delicate Balance* on Broadway. Director Gerald Gutierrez and André Bishop, the head of Lincoln Center, cast Rosemary Harris and George Grizzard as Agnes and Tobias, an upper-class couple living in Connecticut with their adult, troubled daughter (Mary Beth Hurt). To play the part of Claire, Agnes's alcoholic sister, Bishop courted Elaine Stritch, whose career had slumped due in part to alcoholism. She was sober now, but most of the work she got was performing her signature song—"The Ladies Who Lunch" from Stephen Sondheim's *Company*—at fundraisers. "I'm the queen of the benefits," she said.

Bishop met Stritch at the Regency Hotel on Park Avenue and Sixty-First Street where she was living. "Let's get something to eat," she said and then charged up Madison Avenue with Bishop trying to keep pace. They wound up at the bar at the Carlyle Hotel on Seventy-Sixth Street. Stritch had coffee. Bishop offered her the part of Claire. "I don't want to play that part," she said. "It's so boring. It's so obvious. Who wouldn't want to see me play Claire, the drunk? I want to play Agnes. Now that would be interesting." Bishop told her Rosemary Harris already had the part. "I don't know how much was real or how much she was playing me, but eventually I got her to agree to play Claire," Bishop said.

Gutierrez and designer John Lee Beatty wanted to update *A Delicate Balance* by changing the setting from a New England manor house to a modern house made of stone and glass. "As the play gets darker and scarier, you could see the fog rolling in—you'd be able to see the fear through the glass," Bishop said. Beatty designed a model of the house. "It was absolutely beautiful," Bishop said. "We showed it to Edward. He looked at it for five seconds and said, 'Sorry. No.'" Albee knew his characters. They lived in a colonial house, not a mid-century modern.

Rehearsals began, and that's when things started to get "insane," said Bishop. Stritch was a handful, fretting about her diabetes, dropping her pants to give herself a shot of insulin, stopping in the middle of a scene to call out for orange juice. She needed a lot of attention, and Gutierrez gave it to her because he knew why she needed it. "She was playing a character who had habits she had struggled mightily to give up," Bishop said. "She was playing an alcoholic, having stopped drinking. And she was playing a chain smoker, having stopped smoking. It was brave of her to play that role."

Harris and Grizzard didn't see it that way. They hated her antics and Gutierrez for indulging them.

Stritch had a list of demands, including the star dressing room on the first floor. Which meant cast member Elizabeth Wilson, who had a broken hip, had to climb two flights of stairs every night to her dressing room. When previews began, Stritch, wearing just a bra and panties, would run into the lobby of the theater minutes before the show began to make sure the box office staff hadn't stolen her house seats.

Nobody knows what set him off, but one night Grizzard snapped. When the curtain came down after a prolonged standing ovation, he slugged Stritch. She later went after him with her curling iron.

"The only time you were safe in that theater was when the curtain went up," said Bishop. "Nothing bad happened then, and they gave great performances, no question about it."

The revival of *A Delicate Balance* was a sensation, with critics now calling this once-neglected work a masterpiece. Grizzard, Harris, and Stritch were nominated for Tonys (Grizzard won), and the production won Best Revival of a Play. Lincoln Center could have extended its run, but the war raging backstage was taking its toll. "The stage manager practically had a nervous breakdown, and I thought I was going to have one, too," Bishop said. The closing notice went up. Albee, amused by all the backstage nonsense but floating above it, didn't seem to mind. His return to Broadway had been a triumph. The critics had not done to him what they had done to Tennessee.

Albee went on to write several more plays, including *The Goat, or Who Is Sylvia?* It opened on Broadway in 2002 and proved that, at seventy-four, he still had the power to shock audiences. The play is about a successful architect who at age fifty falls in love with a goat. When his wife finds out, their calm, cool upper-class life explodes.

Albee gave the script to Elizabeth McCann. She thought the play was elegant, witty, troubling—a dark drawing-room comedy. "It's not about bestiality," she said. "It's about the boundaries of love." Albee thought it should be produced Off Broadway. McCann disagreed. "If you go Off Broadway, it's like you're hiding it away as an experimental play. It's not a dirty little play, so it should be on Broadway."

The first preview at the Golden Theatre was raucous. Some theatergoers walked out. Others burst out laughing. When Mercedes Ruehl, as the wife, carried the dead goat onstage, there were gales of laughter. The laughter sometimes bothered Albee, but he enjoyed the walkouts. "It meant he had gotten under their skin," said Sam Rudy, the show's press agent. Albee's main concern was the goat. It was not quite the Abyssinian goat he had in mind. After lugging different kinds of goats across the stage during previews, an exasperated Ruehl said one night, "Either the goat goes, or I go."

Some thought the play was Albee's most brilliant. But some of his old friends thought it was worse than *The Man Who Had Three Arms*. The play ran just ninety minutes, but post-performance discussions about it in theater district restaurants lasted hours. Two women leaving the theater one night saw a mounted policeman at the curb. One turned to the other and said, "Do you find that horse attractive?"[10]

The reviews were mixed, but there was no trashing of Albee as there once had been. He could no longer be dismissed with a cruel back of the hand. Albee promoted the play, appearing onstage after the show every now and then to be interviewed by friendly critics. Whenever the *New York Times* carried an ad for one of his talkbacks, *The Goat* sold out. As the Tony Awards rolled around that year, Sam Rudy would often run into voters. "You know, I really liked *The Goat*," they'd whisper. To which he would reply, "Why are you whispering?" In the end, they voted. *The Goat* won the 2002 Tony Award for Best Play. Albee praised his producers for "their outrageous faith that Broadway was ready to see a play about love."

His comeback never faltered. Critics praised new plays staged Off Broadway—*The Play About the Baby, Occupant*, about his friend, artist Louise Nevelson, and a terrific Broadway revival of *Who's Afraid of Virginia Woolf?* starring Kathleen Turner and Bill Irwin. In 2005, he received the Tony Award for Lifetime Achievement. And in 2008, at a fancy dinner at the Rainbow Room above Rockefeller Center, Mayor Michael Bloomberg designated March 12, Albee's eightieth birthday, "Edward Albee Day" in New York City.

A few days later, interviewing Albee in his Tribeca loft, I noticed that the Edward Albee Day proclamation was on the kitchen floor propped up against the wall. His Tony Awards and Pulitzer Prize citations were nowhere to be found amid the mass of African art he long collected. There were no posters of his thirty-one plays hanging on the walls.

"When I was young, I was always embarrassed to go into theater people's apartments and see all their posters on the walls," he said. "I decided that, if I ever got a poster or an award, I would never put it up."

He smiled.

"Well, maybe I'll put up *The Man Who Had Three Arms*."[11]

CHAPTER NINE

RAZZLE DAZZLE

After a long day of auditions for their new Broadway musical *Steel Pier* in the spring of 1996, John Kander and Fred Ebb headed to City Center to catch the first preview of *Chicago* at Encores! They hadn't given the production much thought. They hadn't even attended a rehearsal. City Center's Encores! produced concert versions of old shows, highlighting neglected scores. There was a full orchestra onstage, but the actors only rehearsed for a week, gave four performances over a weekend, wore tuxedoes or gowns, and carried scripts. "We were happy they were doing it, but we weren't that excited about a concert," Kander said. *Chicago,* which originally opened on Broadway in 1975, was in their past. *Steel Pier,* a Depression-era musical about a dance marathon in Atlantic City, was in their future.

Before the performance, they had coffee with John Mineo, a friend who'd been in a revival of their musical *Zorba the Greek*. One of Bob Fosse's favorite dancers, he was in the chorus of *Chicago*. As Mineo got up to leave for his half-hour call, Ebb asked, "So how is it?" He gave them a funny look and said, "Oh, I think you're going to like it."

* * *

Of all the shows they wrote, *Chicago* was Ebb's favorite "because there aren't any ballads in it," he said. Bob Fosse and his wife, Gwen Verdon, tried to get the rights to the 1926 stage play *Chicago* in the 1960s, but author Maurine Watkins turned them down. Her play was based on two women accused of murdering their lovers. Both were acquitted after sensational trials Watkins covered for the *Chicago Tribune*. In the intervening years, Watkins had become deeply religious, disavowing her racy, cynical play. But when she died in 1969, her estate realized there was money to be made from a musical directed by Bob Fosse and starring Gwen Verdon, and made a deal.

As Fosse analyzed the play, he became disenchanted. He could not figure out how to musicalize it. But Verdon wanted to do it. Her career had stalled. She needed a comeback. Guilty about cheating on her—they had recently separated—and worried about her precarious financial position, Fosse plugged away. He asked Ebb for help. Ebb liked the play's cynical take on the American justice system—the criminal as a celebrity. He began to think of the trial as a stage show. A vaudeville setting, he thought, might work. Fosse, who had worked in vaudeville as a kid, loved the idea.

Kander and Ebb got to work on the score. They met every morning at ten in Ebb's San Remo apartment on Central Park West. After half an hour of chitchat, Ebb would present a musical idea. They'd talk it through and then move to the piano. Kander might improvise a vamp, while Ebb threw out some lyrics. The first song they wrote was "All That Jazz." Ebb lifted the title from a chapter in Time-Life's *The Roaring Twenties*, which he was reading for research. The writing was "a joy," said Kander. Songs flowed: "Funny Honey" for Roxie; "All I Care About" for the slick lawyer Billy Flynn; "Mister Cellophane" for Amos, Roxie's sad-sack husband; and "When You're Good to Mama" for prison matron Mama Morton. As they were writing "Razzle Dazzle," Ebb said,

"Let's put two snaps in at the beginning. Bobby will love it." He did. He loved the entire score.

Chicago: A Musical Vaudeville began rehearsals on October 26, 1974. Three days later Fosse suffered a massive heart attack and underwent open-heart surgery. *Chicago* was postponed until the spring of 1975. When Fosse returned to the show, he was angry, frightened, and depressed. "He was much tougher on us, especially Fred," said Kander. "I later learned that depression often sets in after the particular operation he had."

Chicago had always been cynical, but it was also fun and buoyant. Fosse now wanted to make it bitter, brutal, and, at times, pornographic. He staged "Razzle Dazzle" as an orgy with choreography so explicit it belonged in a peep show.[1] During the show's tryout in Philadelphia, Fosse often lashed out at Ebb, blaming the show's problems on his book. Things got so ugly that Kander said to Ebb, "Why don't we get on a train and go back to New York. This isn't worth it. No show is worth dying for."[2] The reviews were so vicious that Fosse had to rethink his approach. He cut the orgy from "Razzle Dazzle" and asked Kander and Ebb for a new, more upbeat song to end the show. They went back to their hotel and wrote "Nowadays" so fast they "took the rest of the day off," Kander said.

Chicago opened to mixed reviews in New York in June 1975. It was eclipsed by *A Chorus Line*, which swept the Tony Awards that year. When Verdon fell ill, the show was in danger of closing at a loss of $800,000. But Liza Minnelli stepped in for a month and the box office exploded. When Verdon returned, the show was a solid hit, eventually running 936 performances.

Walter Bobbie, then a struggling actor several years away from his turn as Nicely-Nicely Johnson in the revival of *Guys and Dolls*, attended the opening night. He knew someone in the chorus and managed to snag a seat way up in the balcony. "I liked the score, but I wasn't smart enough to get all the vaudeville references," he said. "Honestly, I didn't know what the hell was going on."

Twenty years later, while in Maine filming the Stephen King movie *Thinner*, Bobbie picked the *Chicago* script out of a pile of shows he was thinking of staging at Encores!, where he'd become artistic director. He happened to be watching the O. J. Simpson trial and as he started to read the script he thought, *This feels like it just got written. Chicago* was no longer a satire of the judicial system. It was what America was watching every day on television.

The board of City Center did not want to do *Chicago*. The company's mission was to stage old, largely forgotten shows, not musicals from the 1970s. The first Encores! concert was *Fiorello!*—originally produced in 1959. Subsequent concerts included *Allegro* (1947), *Call Me Madam* (1950), and *DuBarry Was a Lady* (1939). The board felt it was time for a musical from the 1920s, preferably by George and Ira Gershwin. But Bobbie wanted to try something more contemporary, and *Chicago* did meet two Encores! requirements: its score was known only to musical theater buffs, and the show itself was seldom revived. The board reluctantly gave him the go-ahead.

Bobbie asked Ann Reinking to choreograph the concert. "I don't want to revive Bob's production," he told her. Reinking agreed, with a caveat: she would create new dances, but they would be in the style of Bob Fosse—shoulder rolls, toes pointing inward, pelvises thrusting forward, bowler hats, splayed hands, finger snaps. "It had to be that way," she said. "Bob was one of the main creators of the show." If anyone knew the "style of Bob Fosse," it was Reinking. She'd been in *Pippin*, *Dancin'* and *Sweet Charity* and replaced Verdon as Roxie in *Chicago*. She'd also been Fosse's lover for six years in the 1970s and played herself in his autobiographical movie *All That Jazz*.

Set designer Tony Walton, a member of the original production, offered to design the sets, but Bobbie turned him down. He wanted a fresh production with a new design team. Walton, ever the gentleman, understood. John Lee Beatty, best known for designing plays, got the job. William Ivey Long, who had given Bobbie a better hat in *Guys and Dolls*, signed on to do the costumes. Bobbie didn't want the actors in tuxedoes and evening gowns, the traditional Encores! look. "I want to do this show in Bob's two favorite colors—black and flesh," he told Long. "And I want the cast to look like dancers. I want sexy. I want underwear. I want to see legs, legs, legs." Long's costume budget was just $2,000.

Bobbie offered the role of Billy Flynn to James Naughton, a tall, handsome, slick actor whom Bobbie had admired since he saw him in *I Love My Wife* in 1977. Bebe Neuwirth, one of Broadway's best dancers and a veteran of three Fosse musicals, accepted the role of Velma, telling Bobbie when he made the offer, "This is the happiest day of my life." Marcia Lewis, a short, plump, adorable comic actress, auditioned for Mama Morton. "Marcia always had warmth," Bobbie said. "The thing about that part is that her name is Mama, not bitch or dyke. I wanted someone the girls [in jail] could trust." Lewis wore a red boa for the audition and sang a comic song called "The Middle Years." She was good, as always, but too cute. Bobbie took away the boa and said, "Can you sing the song again and this time think strong, tough powerful woman?" Lewis did—"and killed it," Bobbie said.

For the part of Amos, Bobbie wanted Joel Grey, who had won the Oscar as the Emcee in Fosse's *Cabaret*. But Grey was living in Los Angeles and didn't want to go back to New York to do a small part in a concert that only ran four performances. Besides, he couldn't see himself as Amos, an auto mechanic. Barney Martin, a big, lumbering actor, originally played the part. Grey was short and slight. "I'm not a big dumb mechanic," he told Bobbie. A few days later a friend told him he should reconsider, if only because

Amos had a great song—"Mister Cellophane." Grey looked at the part again, called Bobbie and said, "I'll do it if we can figure out a way to play him not as a dumb jerk, but as a guy who is so in love with Roxie he can only see the best in her."

Bobbie wanted Grey because the actor had a strong connection to the person City Center wanted for Roxie—Liza Minnelli. Grey and Minnelli reunited for the first time since *Cabaret* would grab the New York theater world's attention. But as negotiations began, Bobbie realized dealing with Minnelli was going to be a headache. He went to his boss at City Center and said, "We can't handle this. We're not equipped to deal with the security she needs. We're not equipped for all the perks she needs. We're not equipped to meet her scheduling demands." He paused, then added, "And here's the other thing, and it's the most selfish thing I'm going to say. This is my show and Ann's. I don't want it to be Liza's show, and that's what will happen if she's in it."

With only a few days to go before rehearsals, *Chicago* did not have a Roxie. Bobbie called Reinking and said, "You have to do it. You are the heir to Fosse's vocabulary and you are perfect for the show."

"I'm out of shape!" Reinking protested.

"Oh, Ann. You can bowl your way through four shows," Bobbie replied.

Reinking had just ten days to choreograph a show she was now starring in.

On the first day of rehearsal Bobbie addressed his cast, which included some of the sexiest dancers, male and female, ever assembled. "We're going to do this show like every perfume commercial we've been watching for the past five years," he said. "This is seduction. This is not, 'Fuck you.' This show does not start out with a 'fuck you.' It starts out with a 'Come on, babe.'" He laid down a rule: "Nobody is to touch themselves or anyone else. You can be as a hot as you want, but don't touch. What makes this show sexy is that people almost touch, but they never do. It's the anticipation that's sexy."

With only a $2,000 costume budget, Long told the actors to wear their own clothes, which he'd supplement, if need be, by miniskirts, bras, panties, and gypsy shawls he'd found in secondhand clothing stores along Fourteenth Street. In keeping with Bobbie's vision, Long developed costumes that were sexy but never raunchy. Caitlin Carter, a tall, smolderingly sexy blonde, set the tone. She came in one day wearing a black bra and panties. But her character walked around like a lady. Long added some black netting to the outfit. You could still see her underwear, but now there was a touch of class. Neuwirth wore her own Patricia Field black slip. Reinking wore a little black suit she'd picked up at Saks Fifth Avenue. Lewis found a black turtleneck and pantsuit in her closet. Naughton looked elegant in a rented Armani tuxedo (the only tuxedo in the show). Grey brought in a thin-lapelled suit he'd bought at Maxfield Bleu, a hip clothing store in Los Angeles. Long shortened the pants for the "Mister Cellophane" number.

Reinking, meanwhile, created new dances in the Fosse style. She remembered that in the original "Cell Block Tango" the "six merry murderesses of the Cook County jail" performed behind bars. But there was no money in the set budget for bars. So Reinking gave them chairs—because Fosse liked chair dances. The chairs became the murderesses' cells. The number evoked Minnelli dancing with a chair in "Mein Herr" from *Cabaret*.

Bobbie wanted to create a courtroom atmosphere, so Beatty designed a jury box for the onstage band. Bobbie remembered that Fosse had used a ladder in *Pippin*. He told Beatty he wanted ladders. "I've only got two," Beatty said. He fitted them on hinges on both sides of the stage so they could swing out. Neuwirth swung out on one at the top of the second act, greeting the audience with "Hello, suckers!" And in the show's one chilling moment, Hunyak, the Hungarian murderess, who knows just two words in English—"not guilty"—mounts the other as she is about to be hanged.

Bobbie was worried about Joel Grey. Having come in with a strong idea to make Amos sympathetic, he was now struggling to put his performance together. He tried props—a cane, a hat for "Mister Cellophane"—but nothing worked. At one point he told Bobbie he'd like to put some white makeup on his face, evoking the Emcee from *Cabaret*. Bobbie was horrified. Amos and the Emcee were worlds apart. Then Bobbie had an idea. He gave Grey a pair of white gloves to wear during the number. Grey put them on, and his hands came alive. Then he added a gentle sway, as if an almost imperceptible breeze buffeted his body. "Joel just unfolded," said Bobbie. "He knew what to do as soon as he got those gloves." Grey was on his way to making Amos the most pitiable—and human—character in *Chicago*.

But Bobbie still worried about the makeup. At the Wednesday-afternoon dress rehearsal, Bobbie dispatched Long to Grey's dressing room with a directive—"No makeup!"

"You know, Jerry Zaks always says no makeup for men," Long told Grey.

"But they want to see me in whiteface," Grey said.

"Well, I think Walter wants them to see your real face."

As they were talking, they heard the first notes of "All That Jazz," played by a muted trumpet, which opens the show. And then they heard something else. Long had heard it once before, while he was working on *Nine* at the 46th Street Theatre in 1982. The theater shared a wall with the Imperial next door, where *Dreamgirls* was playing. Every night when Jennifer Holliday sang "And I Am Telling You I'm Not Going" the sound penetrated the wall. It was the roar of an audience. They were roaring now—at the first notes of "All That Jazz." When the song finished, the audience stood and cheered. They stood and cheered for every number that afternoon.

At the start of the show's first public performance the next night, Grey and Naughton watched from the wings as Neuwirth stopped the show with "All That Jazz." Then Reinking stopped the show with "Funny Honey." Lewis stopped the show with "When You're Good to Mama." Naughton came out, sang "All I Care About" and stopped the show. Grey was "terrified." His number—spare and subtle—wasn't until the second act. Surely, he thought, the audience would settle down by then. He performed "Mister Cellophane," and stopped the show.

Kander and Ebb were stunned. "It was like a rock concert," Kander said. "And we had nothing to do with that night except that we were there and thinking, *Why can't this last forever?*" The next morning, word was out in the New York theater world: miss *Chicago* at Encores! and you'll regret it for the rest of your life. There were only three performances left.

Fran and Barry Weissler attended the Saturday matinee. They were close to Kander and Ebb, having produced touring revivals of *Zorba* and *Cabaret*. Reinking worked for them opposite Tommy Tune in a revival of *Bye Bye Birdie*. They'd heard how good the show was, but came to support their friends. The first act "blew us away," Barry Weissler recalled. During the intermission, a man suffered a heart attack. Marcia Lewis, a registered nurse, tried to revive him before paramedics arrived. Act II started forty-five minutes late. *A terrific show was over,* thought Weissler. *How do you pick the audience up after someone's probably died?* Then Neuwirth swung out on her ladder and said, "Hello, suckers!" The audience went wild. "The poor man was completely forgotten," Weissler said. "The show could play through death. It was something special."

That night Fran called Fred Ebb to congratulate him. "We know everyone in the world wants this show," she said, "but could you please just give us a tiny part of it? We don't even care if our names are on it." There was a pause. Then Ebb said, "You can have the whole show." Fran was stunned. "What do you mean?" she asked. "You have the show," Ebb said. "Nobody wants it." Kander and Ebb's agent, the powerful Sam Cohn, did offer *Chicago* to Broadway's top producers, including the Shuberts and the Nederlanders. But nobody wanted it because it was a concert. "There's no chandelier, there's no revolving barricade, there's no flying helicopter," a Shubert executive told Cohn. "Nobody's going to pay seventy-five dollars to see a concert."

Barry Weissler called Cohn to make a deal. The two men were not on good terms. The Weisslers wisely had bailed on the musical *Carrie* before it flopped. Cohn represented the show and never forgave them. He was also furious he couldn't get anybody to bid against them for *Chicago*. He demanded a high advance and high royalty payments. He had one more stipulation: they had to open the show before the end of the year or they would lose the rights.

The Weisslers drew up a budget for a Broadway production—$2.5 million, modest compared to the $10 million most shows cost. Rocco Landesman and Jujamcyn put up $1.25 million and gave the Weisslers the Martin Beck Theatre, "which got Sam off our backs," Barry said. The Weisslers set about raising their share of the money from their investor pool. But almost everybody they approached turned them down. They heard the same excuse over and over: nobody's going to pay Broadway prices for a concert version of an "old chestnut" that was never a big hit in the first place. The Weisslers scraped together $1.25 million from bonds, loans, and mortgages—"whatever we had available," Barry said. Then Landesman called and told them he had the chance to book Andrew Lloyd Webber's *Whistle Down the Wind* at the Martin Beck. His predecessor at Jujamcyn had been fired because he'd lost *The*

Phantom of the Opera to the Shuberts. Landesman could not afford to lose the next Lloyd Webber show. "I know we have an agreement, but I'm asking you as a friend to let me out of it," he said. The Weisslers did. Then Landesman told them Jujamcyn would not be investing in the show. It was a concert and not a good bet.

The Weisslers had to find another $1.25 million and a theater or else Sam Cohn could take away the rights. They went to Jimmy Nederlander and asked for the Richard Rodgers. "You can have it for nine weeks," he said, "because I've got *Steel Pier* coming in next season. That's the *new* Kander and Ebb show. You've got the old chestnut." He added, "Nine weeks is plenty. I don't think you'll last three. Nobody wants to see a concert on Broadway."

The Weisslers approached the Shuberts, asking if they could move the show to one of their theaters after their nine weeks were up at the Rodgers. The only possibility was the Shubert Theatre, though it was booked with *Big*, which Jerry Schoenfeld thought would be a hit. "It's a new show," he said, "and you have to admit yours is a chestnut."

"By now we had so many chestnuts we could roast them," Fran joked. But Schoenfeld made a deal. If in the unlikely event *Big* should falter, they could move to the Shubert. But they had to cover the $480,000 moving cost themselves.

The Weisslers had a theater—albeit for just nine weeks—but now they still had to come up with another $1.25 million. Once again they heard the words *chestnut* and *concert*. They had a hit revival of *Grease* on Broadway at the time and, over the years, had socked away a couple million dollars. They crawled into bed one night, looked at each other, and decided to violate the cardinal rule of show business. They would put their own money in the show. They'd be on the line for 75 percent of *Chicago*. Fran Weissler turned out the light and thought, *What have we done?*

CHAPTER TEN

THE FRAN AND BARRY SHOW

Many of Fran and Barry Weissler's producing colleagues came from money or had made their money in other businesses. They could afford to lose a few million here and there on Broadway. The Weisslers started with nothing, making their money by producing touring revivals with stars whose careers had begun to fade. They paid the stars handsomely, but kept costs low everywhere else. Most of their shows earned a profit, but the snobs looked down their noses at the Weisslers. One of the snobs called them "The Weisslers, of New Jersey."

Barry Weissler grew up in Jersey City, the son of working-poor immigrants from Russia and Poland. A D student in high school, he managed to get into Upsala College in East Orange. "It was an offshoot from a very fine college in Sweden," he said. "But here, not so fine." He played football, but was too small to be much good. His transcript wasn't good either—three Fs and three Ds. He got a letter from the dean saying he'd have to up his average to a C or leave school. Feeling "beat up, scared, and confused," Weissler wandered the campus one afternoon and stumbled into a theater where some students were rehearsing *Measure for Measure*. "I wasn't smart enough to know what it was, but I sat down and lo and behold for the first time in my life I felt comfortable," he said. "I watched rehearsals and never left." He joined the group and did everything from acting to painting the sets. He started reading plays and earned a reputation as a good character actor. He made the dean's list the next year. "The theater saved me," he said.

After college he went to Mexico, fell in love with bullfighting, and tried to be a matador. "I didn't make it," he said. Back in New York, he studied acting with Stella Adler. Nobody would hire him as an actor, so he decided to hire himself. He created a company he grandly called the National Shakespeare Company, directing and performing Shakespeare plays that toured small cities in the Northeast. In 1965, when he was twenty-six, his little troupe was performing *The Taming of the Shrew* in West Orange, New Jersey. He noticed an attractive woman working in the box office. They struck up a conversation after the show. Her name was Fran Weller. She was a thirty-seven-year-old New Jersey housewife with two children. She was working in the box office as a favor to a friend.

She was leaving her husband when she met Barry. She was not attracted to him at first. "He was short compared to my husband. And he had no money. All he had was a dream of going to Broadway one day." They kept in touch. Barry was at odds with his business partner and he found that Fran gave him good advice. She enjoyed learning about the theater business. One day she said to Barry, "Let's go into business together."

With $1,500 they formed the National Theatre Company. Their plan was to put on plays in public schools. But then they found out they couldn't charge students to see the shows during the school day. She called her best friend, who happened to be Catholic, and "whined" about her problems. The friend gave her some advice: Play Catholic schools. They're private and can do whatever they want. You can charge admission.

Fran began calling Catholic schools to make appointments to sell their shows. The first nun she and Barry met was in charge of St. Aloysius High School in Jersey City. "We're terrified," Fran said. "Number one, we're Jewish. Number two, we're in love and I'm getting a divorce. And number three, we have no money." But the nun liked them and their proposal. She suggested they stage *The Somonyng of Everyman*, a fifteenth-century morality play. It was required reading, but difficult. It would be easier to teach, the nun suggested, if performed.

The Fran and Barry Weissler production of *Everyman*, directed by Barry, turned out to be popular on the Catholic-school circuit. The next year they toured two Chekhov one acts—*The Bear* and *A Marriage Proposal*. They needed a decent actor, so Barry called his friend from Stella Adler, Robert De Niro. "How much are you paying?" De Niro asked. "Sixty-five dollars a week," Barry said. "Fabulous! I'm only making fifty dollars now." Fran, Barry, and Bob De Niro toured in a station wagon (for the actors) and a U-Haul (for the sets).

From high schools, they expanded to colleges, producing one-person shows such as Leslie Nielsen in *Clarence Darrow* and Julie Harris in *The Belle of Amherst*. They landed a big get in James Earl Jones, who agreed to play Paul Robeson. They booked him around the country, collecting 20 percent deposits up front—more money than they had ever seen. And then Paul Robeson's son got hold of the play and objected to the portrayal of his father. He threatened protests. Jones did not want to be embroiled in controversy. He dropped out of the show, forcing the Weisslers to return the deposits on which they were living. "He owes you one," Jones's agent told them.

"Owes us one?" Fran said years later. "Just give me the money, please. It was a very, very bad year for us."

* * *

In the summer of 1981, a friend who worked at the American Shakespeare Theatre in Stratford, Connecticut, invited the Weisslers to see Christopher Plummer in *Henry IV, Part I*. At intermission they learned that the production of *Henry IV, Part II* had fallen through. Plummer was looking for something else. James Earl Jones owed them one. Why not pair him with Plummer in *Othello*? Stratford told the Weisslers if they could deliver Jones, the theater would pay for the production, and if it worked out, the Weisslers could tour it and bring it to Broadway. Jones agreed, but they had to secure Plummer, whom they did not know. After a performance, they went backstage to introduce themselves. Barry thought Fran should do the talking. She knocked on Plummer's dressing room door. When his dresser opened it, a terrified Fran said, "My name is Fran Weissler and I'd like to meet Christopher Plummer." The dresser eyed her up and down and said, "The curtain has just come down and he's still in makeup. I'll open the door when he's ready to see you."

The Weisslers waited . . . and waited. "Every actor walks out, every stagehand, every plumber, but not Christopher Plummer," Fran recalled. At last the dresser opened the door. More terrified than before, Fran walked in and saw Plummer sitting in a rattan peacock chair. He wore a satin smoking jacket, a cravat, and Royal Crest velvet loafers.

"Yes?" he said.

"My name is Fran Weissler, and I have James Earl Jones and my husband and I would like to produce *Othello* here and take it to Broadway with you playing Iago and him playing Othello, if you would allow us to do it," she stammered.

There was a long pause.

"What did you say your name was again?" Plummer purred.

"My name is Fran Weissler, and I have James Earl Jones and my husband—"

Plummer held up a hand. "Mrs. Weissler, a *professional* producer doesn't walk into the dressing room of an actor she wants to hire. A *professional* producer calls the actor's agent to find out if he's interested in doing the job. My agent is Lou Pitt at ICM in Los Angeles. Which by the way has a three-hour time difference. I suggest you call him and he'll tell you if there's any interest."

The next day, after several failed attempts, their nerves frayed, the Weisslers got Lou Pitt on the phone. "I spoke to Mr. Plummer last night," he said. "You know, there's a three-hour time difference here so he was able to call me after his show. I can tell you that Mr. Plummer would be delighted to play Iago to Mr. Jones's Othello. Goodbye."

Peter Coe, an Englishman who'd directed the musical *Oliver!*, staged *Othello*. He and Plummer were chummy, but Coe did not care for Jones. One afternoon Fran walked into the theater at Stratford and saw Jones sitting on a little stool onstage with his head down. Plummer was practicing his sword fighting. Coe stood at the foot of the stage pounding his hand to make a point. As she walked down the aisle, she heard a dejected Jones say, "Why don't I just say the line and you'll tell me if you like it or not."

"I don't think the line is your problem, Mr. Jones," Coe said. "Your problem, Mr. Jones, is that Mr. Plummer is mopping the floor with you. That is your problem, Mr. Jones." Plummer looked over and said, "Oh, don't be silly."

Fran approached Coe and said, "We have two great actors and a wonderful play, and we shouldn't let anything get in the way of that. So, Peter, if you could find it in your heart to tell James you didn't mean what you just said, we could go on with rehearsal."

Coe looked at her and said, "How many shows have you produced?"

"This is my first Broadway show," she said.

"That's right, and if you don't mind I'd like to repeat to Mr. Jones that Mr. Plummer is mopping the floor with him, so if I were Mr. Jones I would get my act together. Do you understand that, Miss First-time Producer?"

Fran was stunned. And then she steeled herself. "I may be a first-time producer, but I know one thing a producer can do that a director cannot," she said. "A producer can fire a director, and you're fired." Jones looked up. Plummer dropped his sword. Coe said nothing, picked up his belongings, and left.

As Fran left the theater, she saw the other actors sitting at a picnic table. As she passed them, they stood up and applauded. Nobody, it turned out, liked Peter Coe.

A few days later, the Weisslers were in Plummer's dressing room when the producer Robert Whitehead and his wife, the actress Zoe Caldwell, dropped in to say hello. It dawned on Fran that perhaps Caldwell could take over the show. She'd done plenty of Shakespeare and knew Plummer and Jones. Fran followed her into the parking lot and asked for her card. She called Caldwell the next day, explained their predicament, and offered her the job. "I'm not a director," she said. But she called back a few days later and said, "My husband, for whom I have the greatest respect, said I must do this. I can't let Shakespeare down and I can't let the actors down. I'll do it."

Othello toured several cities—and raked in a lot of money—before opening at the Winter Garden Theatre in February 1982. That same season, the Weisslers produced *Medea*, starring Caldwell in the title role and Judith Anderson as the Nurse. Both productions were nominated for Best Revival. The Weisslers spent weeks working on their speeches should they win. That night, the first time they'd ever attended the Tonys, Barry had his *Othello* speech in his left pocket and his *Medea* speech in his right pocket. Alexander H. Cohen, the all-powerful producer of the Tonys, had

Andrew Lloyd Webber arrives at the Broadway opening of *Aspects of Love* with his children Nicholas and Imogen and his second wife, Sarah Brightman. Lloyd Webber was at the height of his power, having written and produced *Cats* and *The Phantom of the Opera*. He was laying the groundwork for his next show, *Sunset Boulevard*. But there was concern about *Aspects*. Its score was lush and romantic, but the production was, as someone who worked on it said, "bloated" and "turgid."

2

Trevor Nunn, the director of *Cats*, *Les Misérables*, and *Aspects of Love*. The opening night party for *Aspects* was held at the Rainbow Room in Rockefeller Center. When Don Black, the show's lyricist, arrived, he took Nunn aside for a quiet word. Black was worried about what critic Frank Rich would say in the *New York Times*. "I'll be thrilled if he hates it," Black said. Rich destroyed it, and it closed after eight months.

3

Peter Brown (center, flanked by Michael Ball and Sarah Brightman). One of Andrew Lloyd Webber's oldest friends and confidants, Brown oversaw Lloyd Webber's public relations. As the composer started work on *Sunset Boulevard*, Brown courted Billy Wilder, who directed the movie. He knew Wilder had the sharpest tongue in Hollywood, and he did not want him taking aim at the musical version. Lloyd Webber wanted to show Wilder a videotape of a presentation he had put on at his country estate in England. But when he pushed the on button, nothing happened. He finally got it going, but there was no color. The video was in black and white. Lloyd Webber was beside himself. Wilder turned to Brown and said, "Tell Mr. Webber I like it in black and white."

4

Lana Turner arrives at the Los Angeles opening of *Sunset Boulevard* with her daughter, Cheryl Crane. Marvin Davis, the owner of 20th Century Fox, and his wife, Barbara, had bought out a preview performance for a charity. Every star in Hollywood was there. Peter Brown was furious. Nobody would come to opening night, he feared. Then a friend suggested he invite an old star that had not been seen in years. As Turner walked down the aisle, Brown's friend Nancy Reagan said, "There's Norma Desmond."

5

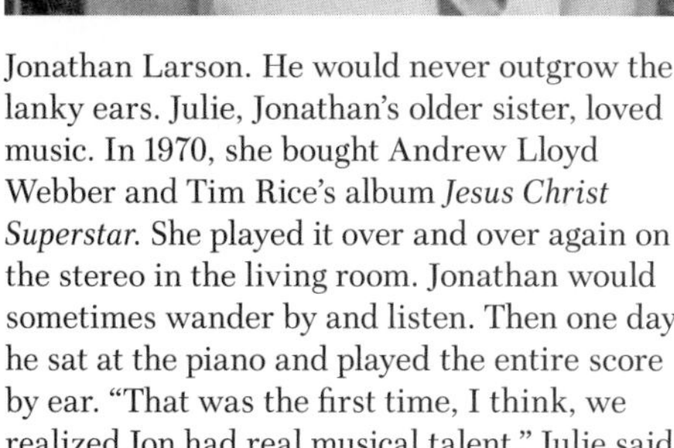

Jonathan Larson. He would never outgrow the lanky ears. Julie, Jonathan's older sister, loved music. In 1970, she bought Andrew Lloyd Webber and Tim Rice's album *Jesus Christ Superstar.* She played it over and over again on the stereo in the living room. Jonathan would sometimes wander by and listen. Then one day he sat at the piano and played the entire score by ear. "That was the first time, I think, we realized Jon had real musical talent," Julie said.

6

Jonathan Larson and his sister, Julie. When he was writing *Rent*, Jonathan would often call his sister in the middle of the night to play her a new song. There was seldom a "hello." He would announce the title of the song and start playing it on his keyboard. He'd take criticism "as long as it was frugal," Julie said. "It depended on the mood he was in."

7

Jonathan Larson (right) with his mother, Nan; sister, Julie; and father, Allan. When Larson moved to New York City in the fall of 1982 to become an actor, he and two friends formed a trio called J. Glitz. The trio performed in small clubs all over the city. Nan and Al rarely missed a gig. "There was one where we were literally the only ones in the audience," Al said.

8

Jeffrey Seller. An aspiring twenty-five-year-old producer, Seller was booking national tours in the offices of Fran and Barry Weissler when he attended a reading of Jonathan Larson's autobiographical musical *Boho Days*. "Here was this man telling his life story that I felt was my life story," Seller said. He wrote Larson a letter the next day: "I figure you probably don't need to get involved with low men on the totem like me, but I've got a thousand ideas to share, and I'm sure you do too."

9

Jeffrey Seller with his partner, Josh Lehrer. Ambitious, opinionated, and, by his own admission, arrogant, Seller was eager to break free of the Weissler office and work on his own projects. One day his boss called him into the conference room and told him he'd outgrown his job. As she was handing him his two weeks' severance, the secretary buzzed him over the intercom: "Jeffrey, Jonathan Larson is on the phone for you."

10

Jonathan Larson with his nephews, Matthew (in overalls) and Dylan. A few days before Christmas 1995, Larson flew to New Mexico to see his family. He almost didn't go, since there was still so much work to be done on *Rent* before its January premiere at the New York Theatre Workshop. But he wanted to take his nephew to the movie *Toy Story*. "He was a bundle of nerves," his sister Julie said. "So proud and terrified."

11

The author talking to Kevin McCollum; his wife, Lynette Perry; and Allan S. Gordon (right). McCollum joined Jeffrey Seller as a producer of *Rent*. But neither had much money. Gordon had plenty. He was an eccentric billionaire who took the Madison Avenue bus home from work. He put up half the money for the New York Theatre Workshop production. Tensions flared, though, when the show moved to Broadway and Seller and McCollum got most of the publicity. Just before the Tony Awards, Gordon told Seller: "If you don't let me speak, I'll push you off the stage."

12

Rocco Landesman (left) with Meryl Streep, Jujamcyn Theaters creative director Jack Viertel, James H. Binger, and Second Stage founders Carole Rothman and Robyn Goodman. Binger, the CEO of Honeywell, owned Jujamcyn Theaters. Landesman and his wife, Heidi, produced *Big River* at one of Binger's theaters. Landesman and Binger started hanging out at the racetrack. "How would you like to run Jujamcyn?" Binger asked Landesman in the summer of 1987. "Sure," Landesman replied. "I'd like it a lot."

13

James H. Binger with playwright August Wilson. Under Rocco Landesman, Jujamcyn produced all of Wilson's plays, starting with *The Piano Lesson* in 1990. Jack Viertel, Jujamcyn's creative director, was close to Wilson and acted as his informal dramaturge. "I've learned that in trying to help writers you're much better off asking questions than making suggestions," Viertel said. "It's not your play. It's their play."

14

Bernard B. Jacobs, the powerful president of the Shubert Organization, and his wife, Betty. Jacobs was fading in the 1990s (he died in 1996), but he was still a canny operator. Jujamcyn wanted to produce Wendy Wasserstein's *The Heidi Chronicles*. The play was, after all, named for one of her closest friends, Heidi Landesman. But Jacobs had long ago cultivated a relationship with Wasserstein. He scooped up the play by offering her one of his best theaters. "Bernie was way ahead of us, as he always was," Jack Viertel said.

15

Rocco Landesman with *Playbill* publisher Arthur Birsh (center) and Paul Libin. As he was putting his team together at Jujamcyn, Landesman heard that Libin, who ran Circle in the Square, knew more about the nuts and bolts of the theater business than just about anybody in Times Square. Landesman took him to dinner and offered him a job. Libin dithered. Landesman charged into his office one day and said, "Either you're coming with me or you've got to find somebody like yourself who will." Libin replied: "There's nobody like me." He took the job.

16

Heidi Landesman and Michael David. The Landesmans and David were part of a producing company called the Dodgers. Their mantra was: "We will produce only shows we want to see in a manner that doesn't embarrass our children." David wooed Jo Sullivan Loesser, widow of Broadway legend Frank Loesser, to secure the rights to *Guys and Dolls*. Theater people congratulated him, saying, "It's my favorite show." David knew that was code for, "Don't fuck it up."

17

Jerry Zaks with his parents, Sy and Lily, flanking Zero Mostel. Zaks played Motel the tailor in a touring production of *Fiddler on the Roof* starring Mostel as Tevye. Sy and Lily, Holocaust survivors, were appalled that their son, a Dartmouth graduate, wanted to be an actor instead of a doctor. "Is my boy going to be all right in this fakakta business?" Sy asked Mostel in Yiddish. "Listen to me," Mostel replied in Yiddish. "He's going to be more than all right."

18

George C. Wolfe. Tony Kushner's close friend Oskar Eustis codirected Parts I and II of *Angels in America* at the Mark Taper Forum in Los Angeles. *New York Times* critic Frank Rich praised the play but called the production "stodgy." *Angels* needed a new director for Broadway. Jujamcyn, the the show's producer, picked Wolfe, who had won acclaim for his musical *Jelly's Last Jam*. "We had a lot of faith in George," said Jujamcyn creative director Jack Viertel. "Tony and George got along like a house afire, though they both are very mercurial, difficult personalities." Wolfe won the Tony for his direction of *Angels in America: Millennium Approaches.*

19

Terrence McNally (left) with Edward Albee. McNally and Albee were lovers in the early 1960s. McNally met Albee's mother, Frances. "She wore gloves, hat with a veil—formidable and very unfriendly," he said. Albee and his mother hated each other. He left home at twenty after she discovered he was gay. At one point she disinherited him. But as she began to fade in the late 1980s, they reconciled. A year after she died, he started to write a play about her. The "anger was still there," he said, "but I added something—a little pity." He called the play *Three Tall Women*.

20

Edward Albee at a rally on December 31, 2009, calling on China to release imprisoned activist and writer Liu Xiaobo. The success of *Three Tall Women* restored Albee to the front pew of American playwrights. Lincoln Center Theatre produced an acclaimed revival of *A Delicate Balance*, starring Rosemary Harris, George Grizzard, and Elaine Stritch. And Kathleen Turner and Bill Irwin won raves as George and Martha in a superb Broadway revival of *Who's Afraid of Virginia Woolf?* Albee proved he could still shock audiences with *The Goat, or Who Is Sylvia?*—about an architect who upends his comfortable domestic life by falling in love with a goat. Previews were wild, with people laughing, booing, or walking out. The laughing annoyed Albee, but he loved the walkouts. "It meant he'd gotten under their skin," said his press agent, Sam Rudy.

never heard of the Weisslers. He seated them in the next to last row of the Imperial Theatre. Presenter Hal Linden called them "Fran and Barry Weesler" on national television. When they won for *Othello*, they ran down the aisle—it was a long run—and Barry said to Fran, "Don't trip, don't trip!" She didn't trip. "And that was the start of our life," she said.

Few Broadway shows were as sexually charged as the Encores! production of *Chicago*. The dancers were sexy, the choreography was sexy, the costumes were sexy, even the orchestra was sexy. Sex was the show's calling card, and Barry Weissler knew it had to be exploited. Impressed with the ad campaign for *Rent*, the Weisslers met with Drew Hodges. Hodges had read that *Chicago* was moving to Broadway in Cindy Adams's column in the *New York Post*. Adams played up what could be the show's fatal flaw. "Who's going to pay seventy-five dollars to see a glorified concert?" she wrote. The ad campaign had to convey sex, and wipe away the perception that the show was a "glorified concert."

Hodges thought the campaign should embrace the minimalism of the production. The best way to do that would be to photograph the cast in black and white. "When Calvin Klein runs a black-and-white ad, nobody says he doesn't have the budget for color," Hodges told the Weisslers. "It's an aesthetic choice. Black-and-white fashion photography says minimalism, and that's got to be our point of view." The Weisslers hired Max Vadukul, a fashion photographer known as the "king of black and white," to do the job.

In the meantime, *Chicago* needed a quick ad for the Broadway announcement in *Variety*. The Weisslers selected a black-and-white photo of a sexy Russian model naked from the waist up, a cigarette dangling from her mouth. Hodges was in Fran's office one day sitting on a low sofa next to Tommy Tune. "We're both tall so we're sitting there with our knees literally around our ears," he recalled.

Fran held up the photo of the topless Russian. "What do you think of this photograph for *Chicago*?" she asked Tune.

"Well, Fran, girls love tits. Boys love tits. Everybody loves tits," Tune said. The photo ran in *Variety*, though the breasts were cropped. It was black and white, but for the tip of the cigarette, which was red.

The first photo shoot would only be for the women of *Chicago*. Hodges laid down a rule: no bars. Nobody was to look as if they were in jail. "The girls could be as sexual as you wanted them to be as long as they were in charge," he said. "If they were empowered, they were provocative. If they were victimized, then the sexuality goes off the road."

Fran Weissler thought the clothes for the photo shoot should be by famous designers. William Ivey Long had spent weeks improving his costumes for Broadway, but Fran dismissed them. "We want fashion, William," she said. She dispatched him to meet Nicole Miller, Donna Karan, and Calvin Klein. He took a few items, but was not happy. He told Bobbie, "They want to put the girls in chic little black dresses." No way, said Bobbie. "This is our *Chicago*—no little black dresses."

Vadukul's photo shoot took place backstage at the Martin Beck Theatre. It was a shrewd choice. No matter how fashion-oriented the photos might look, the theater setting reminded everyone that *Chicago* was, after all, a Broadway musical. Long holed up in a dressing room costuming the women. He didn't want to be onstage when the Weisslers discovered the women weren't wearing designer dresses. The shoot began and nobody said anything. He heard Barry was having a good time. Finally he got the nerve to check things out for himself. Then he saw Fran coming down the aisle with her friend Nicole Miller. He ran back to the dressing room. But still no one complained. Miller told Fran, "You're in good hands with William."

The photos were stunning. Tina Paul, all legs, standing next to a ghost light. Sultry Denise Faye—"the Body," as everyone called her—leaning against a wall. Mamie Duncan-Gibbs, shot from the back, looking over her left shoulder, her hands up against the wall. Ann Reinking, crouched on a chair, her right arm massaging her left leg, a cigarette dangling from her mouth. Caitlin Carter, in her bra, panties, and fishnet body suit, seated with her hands on her knees and her legs spread wide apart—"the Sharon Stone," Hodges called it.*

Hodges lined up the black-and-white photos side by side above the title *Chicago*, which was in red, to create the ad. The day it hit the Arts & Leisure section of the *New York Times*, the verdict on Broadway was swift: this was the sexiest ad campaign the business had ever seen.

Chicago moved into the Richard Rodgers Theatre in the fall of 1996 with minimal changes. Long was still putting the finishing touches on his costumes. At the first preview, Bobbie noticed that when Reinking came onstage in just her tights, the audience "was looking up at her pahoopa doopa," said Long. He added a little trapeze dress, the kind Catherine Deneuve wore in *Belle de Jour*, for cover.

The opening-night party took place in a nightclub fitted out like a jail. Scantily clad women were in cages. "Prison food" was served. Before they went to the party, Fran, Barry, and their press agent, Pete Sanders, drove over to the *New York Times* building on West Forty-Third Street to wait for the review. At 9:45 Sanders went into the lobby and grabbed the top copy from the first bundle of papers. He glanced at the headlines and then headed back

* When *Chicago* went on tour, the "Sharon Stone" photo "freaked people out," Hodges said. Some markets pulled it from the ads. But when ticket sales dropped, it always went back in.

to the car. He flipped the paper over and halted. There, below the fold on the front page, was an enormous photograph of Bebe Neuwirth and the merry murderesses of the Cook County jail singing "Cell Block Tango." The caption read "Murder, Corruption and That Old Razzle-Dazzle, Back on Broadway." *Chicago* was the first musical to make the front page of the *Times* since *Guys and Dolls*. Sanders showed it to the Weisslers. They burst into tears.

Jimmy Nederlander called the next morning and told them *Chicago* could stay at the Richard Rodgers. "What about *Steel Pier*?" they asked. "Fuck *Steel Pier*!" Jimmy said. Rocco Landesman called, too. "You must think I'm the biggest schmuck in the world," he said. (He'd feel even worse a few months later when Andrew Lloyd Webber canceled *Whistle Down the Wind* for Broadway.) The Weisslers called Jerry Schoenfeld and told him they no longer needed to move to the Shubert, where *Big* had just bombed. There was a pause. "Do you know what a deal is?" Schoenfeld said. The Weisslers had no choice but to move the show, covering the $480,000 moving cost themselves.

In the end, it didn't matter. *Chicago* ran for six years at the Shubert and then moved to the Ambassador, where it's still running. It's played in thirty countries in twelve languages. The Broadway gross alone stands at nearly $700 million. And Fran and Barry Weissler, "of New Jersey," have a twenty-two-acre estate (complete with an amphitheater) in Westchester to show for it.

CHAPTER ELEVEN

EVERYTHING'S COMING UP ROSIE

With *Guys and Dolls*, *Angels in America*, *Rent*, and *Chicago* grabbing headlines—and older shows such as *Cats*, *The Phantom of the Opera*, and *Les Misérables* making substantial sums of money all over the world—Broadway by the mid-1990s was becoming a big business. Attendance hit eight million in the 1989–90 season, but then dipped to seven million the next season and stayed there a couple of years before rising again. In the 1996–97 season ten million people saw a Broadway show. Gross receipts hit a record high of $499 million.

But there was a sense among the new breed of producers that Broadway wasn't doing enough to sell itself. It had the Tony Awards, broadcast on CBS, but that was one night a year. Broadway shows took part in the annual Macy's Thanksgiving Day Parade, also good exposure. But for the most part, appearances on national television were limited. Broadway had the shows, but needed to attract a wider—and younger—audience.

Rocco Landesman, Barry Weissler, and Michael David pushed for a higher national profile. The best place to start, they thought, was at the League of American Theatres and Producers, the industry's trade organization. Long dominated by the Shuberts, the

League was something of a clubhouse. Its handful of employees handled labor negotiations and the Tony Awards, but selling Broadway as a brand was not a top priority. Producers promoted their own shows so what was the point of spending money to push a "Broadway brand"?

When Harvey Sabinson, a former theater press agent, retired as the head of the League in 1995, Landesman sought to replace him with someone outside the business, someone with a fresh perspective. Jed Bernstein, an executive at the powerful advertising company Wells Rich Greene, became a leading candidate. Bernstein loved the theater, but had not spent his life in it. Bernstein's first interview for the job took place in Landesman's office. He noticed that Jerry Schoenfeld, from the Shuberts, sat behind Landesman's desk, with Landesman off to the side. It was a sign that even though some new producers were on the rise, the Shuberts still had the best seat in the house. Someone asked Bernstein how many times he went to the theater. "About a hundred and fifty times a year," he said. Michael David, who was also at the meeting, laughed and said, "Well, never mind our hiring you for this job. We're just going to send you into therapy."

Landesman called Bernstein a few days later to suggest he meet privately with Broadway's warhorses—the Shuberts and the Nederlanders. Bernstein had lunch with Schoenfeld at Barbetta on West Forty-Sixth Street. "I think you're terrific, but if I let Jimmy Nederlander know you're terrific, he's going to vote against you," Schoenfeld said. Bernstein then had lunch with Nederlander at the 21 Club. "I think you're great, but I can't let Schoenfeld know that, or he won't vote for you," Nederlander said.

Bernstein had no idea where he stood. Landesman called again. "So here's the deal. We're going to announce this next week at a press conference."

"Announce what?" Bernstein asked. "Rocco, are you offering me the job?"

"Oh, yeah, yeah. We're offering you the job."

Before the press conference at 21, Bernstein met Landesman, Nederlander, and Schoenfeld at Jujamcyn. As the four rode down in a tiny elevator, Nederlander and Schoenfeld started screaming at each other about upcoming stagehand negotiations. Landesman said nothing. Bernstein thought, *What have I got myself into?* As they headed to 21, Landesman told him, "Don't worry. They do this all the time. It's going to be fine."

At the press conference, Bernstein played up his advertising background, saying he hoped to create a unified campaign to sell Broadway to a wider public. Landesman said Bernstein would be "what Joe Papp was to the Public Theater. We want him to be the blood and guts and heart and soul of building the theater nationwide and around the world."[1]

Bernstein shook up the clubby League by firing much of the staff and bringing in people with marketing backgrounds. Despite headlines of BLOODBATH AT THE LEAGUE in *Variety*, the producers backed him. He reached out to them and theater owners across the country, "the road" as they were known. The League, with its focus on Broadway and New York, had neglected them. "If Broadway was to be thought of as a national brand, the road had to be part of the equation," Bernstein said.

Bernstein sought ways to get Broadway national exposure. A sports fan, he was impressed at how the National Football League had made its halftime show into a celebrated event. In 1998, Madison Square Garden hosted the NBA All-Star Game. Bernstein called up David Stern, the commissioner of the National Basketball Association. "You guys should have a halftime show, and since you're in New York what could be more quintessentially New York than Broadway?" he pitched. Stern liked the idea. Bernstein secured a pledge that the Broadway halftime show would be broadcast live on NBC. Ten Broadway shows participated. Bebe Neuwirth kicked it off with "All That Jazz" from *Chicago*. The cast of *Les Misérables* ran onto the court waving a flag and singing "One Day More," while the Phantom of the Opera descended from the scoreboard. "It was hollow, so we stashed him in there," Bernstein said. "Unfortunately, he was claustrophobic, so it was stressful." The halftime show was a ten-minute infomercial for Broadway. Nearly 17 million people watched it.

Bernstein and his team cooked up a logo—"Live Broadway." Cynics laughed at the slogan. "Dead Broadway sounds more appropriate," one joked. But theater owners in New York and around the country displayed it in their lobbies and in ads for their shows. Bernstein sought out corporate sponsorships, landing a big one in Continental Airlines. The company wanted to be associated with New York, and what better way than to become the official airline of Live Broadway? Continental created an in-flight Broadway channel and published stories about Broadway in its magazine.* Bernstein estimated that, in the nine years the partnership lasted, the free publicity from Continental amounted to $130 million. "The League had a budget of three million dollars when I got there, so that was a lot of money," he said.

Broadway's best marketing tool was, and remains, the Tony Awards. Founded in 1947 by the American Theatre Wing, a nonprofit organization that ran the Stage Door Canteen during World War II, the award took its name from Antoinette Perry, an actress, producer, and cofounder of the Wing. The first Antoinette Perry Awards (soon nicknamed the Tonys) took place at a dinner in the Grand Ballroom of the Waldorf-Astoria Hotel. Helen Hayes, Arthur Miller, and Agnes de Mille received a scroll, a money clip (for the men), and compact powder (for the women.) The ceremony was an elegant black-tie affair, a chance for the theater community

* There was talk of painting a Broadway plane, but the cost—$500,000—was prohibitive. And if the plane crashed, well "that would be the worst possible thing that could have happened," Bernstein said.

to celebrate itself. The competition was friendly as the stakes were low. Most theatergoers knew little about the industry award.

In 1956, DuMont's channel 5 telecast the ceremony in New York for the first time. In 1967, Alexander H. Cohen, a flamboyant showman who knew a marketing opportunity when he saw one, convinced ABC to broadcast live from the Shubert Theatre a one-hour Tony Award show hosted by the stars of the musical *I Do! I Do!*—Mary Martin and Robert Preston. Cohen became the impresario of the Tony Awards, producing them on television for the next twenty years. He ran the telecast with an iron fist, overseeing everything from the musical numbers to the seating arrangements to the food served at the after party. His wife, Hildy Parks, wrote the script. They profited from the telecast, a little too much some theater people grumbled, but the exposure to a national audience turned the Tony into a powerful marketing tool. Americans who cared about the theater tuned in to see numbers from Broadway's latest musicals. A slick or compelling three-minute number spiked ticket sales. Winning the top awards—Best Musical and Best Play—added years to a run in New York and guaranteed a national tour. The once-friendly gala at the Waldorf-Astoria Grand Ballroom became cutthroat. Producers threatened, cajoled, and begged to get votes. The Tony mantra became "You vote for your show first, then you vote against your enemies, then you vote for your friends."

Cohen lost his perch in 1987 after the Shuberts discovered just how much money he was taking (some might say *looting*) from the Tonys. The Wing, which owned the copyright on the award, joined the League to create Tony Award Productions to produce the telecast. CBS, which had broadcast the show since 1978, stuck with it even though ratings were declining. It was still the classiest award show on television, and its viewers were an advertiser's dream. They traveled, drove Lincolns, bought Chanel perfume, and wore Rolex watches.

Bernstein thought the Tonys could be exploited more aggressively. The award was due to celebrate its fiftieth anniversary in 1996, but when Bernstein asked what plans were in place to mark the milestone, he discovered nobody had given it a thought. Hosted by Nathan Lane, the fiftieth-annual Tony Awards featured an array of past Tony winners—Carol Channing, Hume Cronyn, James Earl Jones, Nanette Fabray, Robert Goulet, Bea Arthur, and Ray Walston. But the reviews were scathing and the ratings abysmal despite the hype surrounding *Rent*. A rerun of *Matlock* on ABC clobbered the Tony telecast. Saving the Tonys became a top priority for Bernstein and the League. To do so they would have to take on the Wing and its antiquated notions of how to run an awards show.

Isabelle Stevenson, the Park Avenue grande dame who ran the Wing, turned her nose up at corporate sponsorships. They cheapened the award's artistic merit, she thought. Roy Somlyo, who had slipped in as the managing producer of the Tonys after Cohen's ousting, didn't like to use presenters who weren't from the theater. He vetoed stars with "too much TV Q," Bernstein said. Somlyo also refused to advertise the lineup of celebrity presenters because it "ruined the surprise," Bernstein said. He barred shows that were not nominated for Best Musical from the telecast even if they featured major stars and were box office hits. When Bernstein called a CBS executive to find out why more money wasn't coming from international broadcast rights, the executive refused to speak to him unless Somlyo gave him permission.

"Everything was a little out of kilter," Bernstein said. "And the producers were becoming quite resentful. The Tonys were built on the backs of their shows. They had to provide hundreds of free tickets to the voters, and they had to pay the cost of having their show on the telecast, and that cost was starting to climb. But they had no power over the show. It would be as if the television industry didn't control the Emmys or the movie business didn't control the Oscars."

The producers wanted more control of the award. That meant Somlyo had to go. But he was a wily showbiz warrior, and when the League struck he was ready. He persuaded Isabelle Stevenson that only he could protect the integrity of the Tonys from the crass producers. The day Somlyo was fired from the Tonys, Stevenson announced she'd made him president of the Wing, giving him even more power.

Somlyo did an about-face on an idea he once floated that Bernstein thought was terrific: move the ceremony from a Broadway theater to Radio City Music Hall. It had six thousand seats. The League and the Wing could make a pile of money from ticket sales. But when the League pushed for the move in 1997 Somlyo opposed it. It was, though, one battle he could not win. In the actress and talk show host Rosie O'Donnell, Broadway had found its ambassador to Middle America. She agreed to host the 1997 Tony Awards. And the only theater that could contain her personality, and ego, was Radio City Music Hall.[2]

Rosie O'Donnell fell in love with Broadway as a kid growing up in Commack, New York. She saw a production of *George M!* at the Westbury Music Fair when she was six. She ran onstage during the performance and into the arms of the leading man. Her mother listened to cast albums while she cleaned the house. O'Donnell told the *New York Times* she "was the only second grader [in Commack] who knew all the words to 'South Pacific.'" When she was a teenager, she started stealing money from her father's wallet, played hooky from school, and attended Broadway matinees. She wanted to be on Broadway, but at an open call for Stephen Sondheim's *Merrily We Roll Along* in 1981, she realized she had no idea what she was doing. She didn't even have a head shot and résumé to give to the casting director. Always quick with a wisecrack, she tried stand-up comedy, honing her act in Long

Island clubs and winning several rounds on *Star Search*. Her movie career took off when she appeared in *A League of Their Own* in 1992. O'Donnell got to Broadway in 1994 as Rizzo in a revival of *Grease*. Reviews were mixed, but she proved a box office draw.

In 1996, she launched *The Rosie O'Donnell Show*, a syndicated morning talk show that earned her the nickname "the Queen of Nice." From the beginning, Broadway played a big part on the show. O'Donnell attended opening nights and, always holding the *Playbill*, talked up whatever show she'd been to on television the next morning. She interviewed Broadway stars and featured extended musical numbers from shows with the casts in full costume. *The Rosie O'Donnell Show* was a hit, third in the ratings to *The Oprah Winfrey Show* and *The Jerry Springer Show*. O'Donnell reached six million people every weekday morning, mainly women who, it so happened, bought most of the tickets to Broadway. When she talked up a show, producers saw a box office spike.

"Broadway could seem elitist, but Rosie made it accessible," Bernstein said. "She was a pop media sensation, and she would do anything to help theater." Her rise coincided with a shift in Broadway demographics. In the 1980s, less than 50 percent of the Broadway audience came from out of town. By the mid-nineties, two-thirds did. Broadway was becoming mainstream, and millions of people were learning about its shows from the Queen of Nice rather than from those Kings of Mean, the New York theater critics.

In 1997, O'Donnell presided over a Tony Awards that was the fiercest in years. The only sure winner was *Chicago*, for Best Revival of a Musical. Best Musical was up for grabs. The contenders were Kander and Ebb's *Steel Pier*; Cy Coleman's *The Life*, about Times Square prostitutes with hearts of gold; *Titanic*; and *Juan Darién:*

A Carnival Mass, an arty Lincoln Center show directed by Julie Taymor. The three commercial shows received mixed-to-negative reviews and were struggling at the box office. The Tony for Best Musical could save the show that won.

Maury Yeston began working on *Titanic* in 1985, the year Robert Ballard discovered the ship at the bottom of the Atlantic Ocean. "The *Titanic* was emblematic of the Edwardian world," Yeston said. "It had the whole social structure in its classes—first, second, third. The Edwardian social class went down with that ship."

In 1986, the Space Shuttle *Challenger* blew up. "And I thought, we haven't learned," Yeston said. "Faith in the infallibility of technology led to the poor teacher and the astronauts being killed." Yeston worked on *Titanic* on and off for several years. But other projects got in the way. Tommy Tune called in Yeston and bookwriter Peter Stone, whose shows included *1776* and *My One and Only,* to doctor *Grand Hotel* in Boston. They turned it into a hit in New York. On opening night, Stone asked Yeston what he wanted to do next.

"I'm writing *Titanic*," Yeston said.

"But that's my show," Stone said.

"No it's not. I've been writing it for years."

"But I've always wanted to write it," Stone said. "Can I write it with you?"

"Yes," Yeston said.

They met regularly at a Chinese restaurant near Stone's town house on the Upper East Side and "talked the show into existence," Yeston said. They decided that every character in the musical would be someone on the ship.

In their research Yeston and Stone discovered Frederick Barrett, a stoker who later testified that he thought the *Titanic* was going too fast. Barrett was in boiler room six when the ship hit the iceberg. He survived by climbing into lifeboat No. 13. "Barrett's

Song" became an anthem for the laborers below deck. Most of them drowned.

The producer of *Titanic* was Michael Brown, an eccentric friend of Yeston's who'd gone to Dalton and Harvard, traveled with the Beatles, assisted Federico Fellini on *8½*, and seemed to know everybody in show business. He dressed like a bum, but "everybody thought he was a millionaire," said Yeston. Brown had never produced a Broadway show, so Flora Roberts, Yeston's agent, called Michael David and the Dodgers to see if they'd coproduce. David was skeptical—"*Titanic*, really?"—but met with Yeston in his apartment to hear the score. "And Maury makes this miracle," David said. "He's a little guy, sitting at the piano, acting out all the scenes, singing all the songs, and making the whole thing come alive. I get tears in my eyes just thinking about it." The Dodgers agreed to put up 50 percent of the capitalization for *Titanic*.

Yeston and Stone auditioned the show for several top directors—Mike Nichols, Jonathan Miller, Nicholas Hytner, Stephen Daldry, even Franco Zeffirelli. Nobody wanted to do it. "I played the show for Trevor Nunn in my living room and he said, 'Honestly, I would not know how to do it.' He also drank two bottles of wine," Yeston said.

They finally found Richard Jones, an English opera and theater director whose avant-garde productions often divided critics. "Richard has a very unusual way of working," Yeston said. "We did a workshop, which was an opportunity for the Dodgers to have people come in, look at the show, fall in love with it, and give us money. Well, that did not happen because Richard decided to cast actors against type. So he had a very short, young, blond girl play the captain. I guess he didn't want the intrinsic nature of the actor to create the character. He wanted to test the material." The Dodgers didn't find many backers that day, but Michael Brown knew everybody in show business, so there was little doubt the money would be there in the end.

As Jones began conceiving his production, David realized that *Titanic* was going to be a big show—the most ambitious the Dodgers had ever produced. The Dodgers lived by the rule never to open a show cold in New York. Always go out of town first. But as the budget grew from $8 to $10 million, a tryout was out of the question. "So we committed the sin," David said. "We're taking this thing called *Titanic* right to Broadway. We could write the one-liners ourselves."

The press did it for them. When word leaked out that *Titanic* would open at the Lunt-Fontanne in the spring of 1997, the press pounced. WATCH 'EM SING, WATCH 'EM DANCE, WATCH 'EM DROWN exclaimed the *Daily News*.[3] Yeston and Stone were ready for the jokes. "When I wrote *Nine*, people told me not to use that title because the critics will say *Nine* is a three," Yeston told the *Daily News*. "I said if it's good maybe they'll call it a ten. So if the critics don't like *Titanic* they'll say it sinks. But if they do, maybe they'll say *Titanic* floats."

The first rehearsal of *Titanic* was called for 9:00 a.m. Everybody showed up except for Michael Brown. He still wasn't there two hours later. Yeston was worried. He told Michael David, "The only way that Michael could not be here is that he's dead." David sent a stage manager to Brown's apartment. There was no answer so the manager and the building superintendent broke the lock on the door—and found Brown dead on the toilet. Yeston tracked down Brown's sister to tell her the news and check some facts about Brown's life for a *New York Times* obituary. His sister laughed at his "facts." Her brother had never gone to Dalton or Harvard. He dropped out of high school, shipped out on a tramp steamer to Europe, and disappeared for several years. When he came back to New York he was homeless for months at a time. Aside from his associations with famous people, which were genuine, everything else about his life "was a lie," Yeston said.

The Dodgers discovered something else about Brown: he had not raised a penny of the $5 million he was supposed to put into *Titanic*. With just four weeks to go before opening night, the Dodgers were on the line for the entire $10 million capitalization. "We were scurrying around," David recalled. "I remember going to a guy's apartment and sitting in the lobby with his doorman until he came down with a check. That's how desperate we were." The Dodgers' finances got a boost when they formed a partnership with Dutch entertainment mogul Joop van den Ende, whose company Endemol produced reality TV shows such as *Big Brother*. Van den Ende loved Broadway musicals and took a large stake in *Titanic*.

Yeston and Stone were still writing during rehearsals. Yeston felt something was missing, a song perhaps, that summed up what had become the driving theme of their show. As he put it, "We dream, we strive, and sometimes we fail, but that doesn't mean it wasn't a worthy dream." He wrote a song for Thomas Andrews, who designed the *Titanic*, called "In Every Age," about man's desire to create great and lasting works, from the Egyptian pyramids to the Great Wall of China. The builders of *Titanic* created a "floating city." After rehearsal one day—"and with great trepidation"—he played the song for Jones and Stone. "It's the best thing you've written for the show," Stone said. "And we're going to put it at the beginning not the end."

"Why the beginning?" Yeston asked.

"Because it's critic friendly," Stone said. It told the critics that, despite all the one-liners they'd heard about the show, *Titanic* was a dramatic musical with something thoughtful to say about a cataclysmic event in history. It wasn't sensational. And it wasn't a joke.

The first preview of *Titanic* at the Lunt-Fontanne ran four hours. The show came to a halt several times as special effects failed. And at the end, the ship would not sink. The cast sang the last song in front of the curtain. Bruce Vilanch, the comedian and writer, turned to me and said, "A show about the *Titanic*, and the ship doesn't sink? Well, that's novel."

News of one of the most disastrous previews in Broadway history raced through Shubert Alley. That week the papers published more stories, and one-liners, about what was shaping up to be a fiasco. At Joe Allen, the theater restaurant where posters of flop shows line the walls, waiters were making space for *Titanic*. To quell some of the gossip, the Dodgers established a war room at the DoubleTree Hotel in Times Square stocked with beer and sandwiches. There they could hash over their problems without some gossipy waiter in a theater district restaurant overhearing and leaking to columnists. As previews continued, tensions mounted between the director and the writers. Jones worked methodically. Yeston and Stone were Broadway firecrackers, expert at saving out-of-town shows in a couple of weeks. They bridled at Jones's slow, detached approach. They stopped speaking to him. "We were holding two meetings a day in the war room," David said. "One in the morning with Richard, and one at night with Maury and Peter." Jones insisted he'd fix each problem, technical or otherwise, starting at the beginning of the show and working through to the end. If that meant the second act wasn't finished—and the ship didn't sink—so be it. The audience would have to understand *Titanic* was a work in progress. "Richard was numb to the pressure everybody else was feeling," David said.

Titanic slowly began to float. But there was a problem in the second act. And it was Stone's fault. He had written a lifeboat scene that was forty pages "without a note of sung music," Yeston said. Characters climbed into lifeboats suspended on the sides of the proscenium arch. Each lifeboat had its own minidrama. Scenes shifted from lifeboat to lifeboat. "The problem was somebody would start talking on the upper right and then somebody else would start talking on the lower left on the other side of the stage, and you couldn't follow who was talking," said Yeston. "It was a mess."

Every now and then Captain Smith popped out of a porthole and shouted orders through a megaphone. "He looked like Porky Pig," said Yeston.

Stone was wedded to the scene, and insisted he could fix it even though opening night was just two weeks away. Yeston, meanwhile, was beginning to think their situation was hopeless. "I came home one night around midnight and I made peace with myself. I said to myself, 'You've been in this situation before and sometimes it doesn't work out. This is a guaranteed flop.'" Then he got into the shower and thought, *It's a flop, but people like a song here, a ballad there, and the first act plays well. What if* Titanic *were someone else's musical and he and Stone had been called in to fix it?* That's when he realized the lifeboat scene was killing the show.

"It was an impossible scene to stage," Yeston said. "Because you know those who get in the lifeboat live, and those who don't die. It's unspeakable. It's not entertainment. It's hideous."

Yeston got out of the shower, sat down at the piano, and wrote a song for John B. Thayer, an executive of the Pennsylvania Railroad, and his wife. They were traveling with their young son. Yeston imagined how the Thayers might shield their child from the gathering terror. The mother kneels down to put a life jacket on her son. We'll be "getting in a lifeboat, but father will be staying behind," she says. "It will be like rowing in the Serpentine." As he wrote the song, Yeston envisioned the boy running to his father and throwing his arms around his knees. The father gently pushes him away, telling him to "go along with mother to the lifeboat." As his wife begins to speak, Thayer stops her. "Don't even say it. I'll be fine. I'll collect you both tomorrow morning, you and this beloved son of mine." Yeston expanded the song to include other characters separating from loved ones, knowing they will never see them again but unable to admit it. He called it "We'll Meet Tomorrow."

"All of sudden here was fifteen minutes of music and lyrics that replaced forty pages of uninterrupted dialogue," he said.

He finished the song at 5:00 a.m. and called Michael David. The producer raced over to Yeston's apartment, heard the song, and said, "We gotta do it."

Breaking the news to Stone, a forceful pro skilled at fighting for his turf, would require the diplomatic skills of Metternich. David called a meeting in the war room that afternoon. When Yeston arrived he saw Stone sitting by himself at one end of the table. Everybody else was at the other end. David spoke. "Peter, we have been working on a critical section of the second act. And we honestly believe that what you have written, and what you are working to improve, can work. We are all united in knowing it can work. But we fear there's just not enough time. And so Maury has a plan B. Maury, please tell us what plan B is."

Yeston did so and "there was a huge silence in the room," he recalled. Stone, isolated at his end of the table, finally broke it. "Well, I completely agree with you that what I have written can work," he said. "But I also agree with you that there's probably not enough time to make it work. I think we should try plan B."

The song, unorchestrated, went into *Titanic* that night. The cast sang it to a piano accompaniment and stopped the show.

All that was left to fix was the final scene. Jones struggled to create a stage image that would strike the right emotional note for a musical that ended with the deaths of fifteen hundred people. He had the survivors, clad in blankets from the *Carpathia*, reprise "We'll Meet Tomorrow." It was sad and tragic but not poignant. And then he got it. Into the ranks of the living, Jones interspersed the dead—wearing the clothes they had on the morning they boarded the ship that could not sink. They were memories now.

"The first time we performed that ending, the audience just stood up," cast member Allan Corduner said. When the curtain came down "there was an incredible sense of elation backstage. People were sobbing and hugging. We felt vindicated."[4]

* * *

The opening-night audience that arrived at the Lunt-Fontanne on April 23 was skeptical. A disaster, as they'd read in the papers, was about to unfold. But at the end of the show, they stood and cheered and cried their way through several curtain calls. The normally voluble Stone was speechless. He held on to his date, Lauren Bacall, who was wiping away tears.

Yeston bounced off the walls at the opening-night party. And then the reviews came out. The show "doesn't sink," Ben Brantley wrote in the *New York Times*. "Unfortunately, that is also probably the most exciting thing that can be said about it."[5] The *Daily News* declared it A TITANIC LETDOWN, while the *Post* jeered, "*Titanic* takes a dive." Coming on the heels of the triumphant opening-night performance, the reviews "struck us like an earthquake," Stone said.[6] The next day the shocked company gathered in the basement of the Lunt-Fontanne for a pep talk. "The show is not going to close," David said. "We are going to fight. This is when we are at our best."[7]

The press mounted a daily deathwatch for *Titanic*, gleefully reporting the show was losing money. David took the unusual step of letting reporters see internal financial records. The show was losing money, he admitted, but ticket sales were building every day. Word of mouth was strong. Yeston went to work on the cast recording, and a CD containing three songs was FedEx-ed to members of the Tony Award nominating committee. The company got a boost when the *Daily News* quoted an unnamed Tony nominator saying he and other nominators admired the show. A few days later *Titanic* picked up five Tony nominations, including Best Musical, Best Score, and Best Book.

But its real lifesaver was Broadway's number one fan—Rosie O'Donnell. She attended the opening and told her millions of viewers she had been moved to tears. "I love *Titanic*," she announced, and then welcomed the cast, who performed the stirring number "Godspeed *Titanic*." Ticket sales jumped 200 percent the next day.[8]

The weeks leading up to the fifty-first annual Tony Awards were tense. *Titanic* had pulled ahead of *Steel Pier* and *The Life* at the box office, but it was by no means a hit. It needed the all-important award for Best Musical. To sway voters, the Dodgers sent them copies of the *New Yorker*, which had given the show its only out-and-out rave. But in the same article the critic dismissed *Steel Pier* and *The Life*. Producer Roger Berlind, who had given Michael David a check for $1 million for *Guys and Dolls*, was furious. He had money in both *Steel Pier* and *The Life*. The *New Yorker* mailing smacked of dirty tricks. The Dodgers protested innocence. They simply had to get the word out to Tony voters that not every critic had tried to sink *Titanic*.

In the end, *Titanic* won every award for which it was nominated. Stone thanked "the drama critics for their absolutely, unbelievable reviews. Where would we be without them?" When David got up to accept Best Musical he crossed the aisle and shook hands with Roger Berlind. Looking like a man who'd just been granted a stay of execution, David said, "This has been a most prolific and exhausting season not just for *Titanic* but all our sister shows with whom we spent 365 days toiling in the trenches."

It was a bittersweet night for John Kander and Fred Ebb. The revival of *Chicago* won six Tonys, but *Steel Pier* won nothing. (It would close three weeks later.) "I feel like my left hand is really happy and my right hand is miserable," Kander told the *Daily News*. Said Ebb, "I was as prepared for what happened to *Steel Pier* as you can be without slitting your throat."[9] If O'Donnell seemed a little stiff as host, she delivered where it mattered: Tony ratings jumped 50 percent. On Broadway, O'Donnell was now more powerful than the *New York Times*.

Behind the scenes, the Queen of Nice flashed claws. She clashed with the Tony's powerful executive producer Gary Smith, a television veteran who got his start on *The Judy Garland Show.* When O'Donnell asked for a bigger budget for her wardrobe, Smith said no. "What do you want me to wear? The Gap?" she snapped.[10] She was invited to host the Tonys again in 1998. Her price? No Gary Smith. His contract was not renewed.

CHAPTER TWELVE

THE MAKING OF A MOGUL

In 1975, Marty Bell got hold of the galleys of E. L. Doctorow's new novel, *Ragtime.* Set at the turn of the century, it wove together the stories of a rich white family living in New Rochelle, a successful black musician from Harlem, and a Jewish immigrant on the Lower East Side. The novel mixed its fictional characters with historical figures from the era: Evelyn Nesbit, Emma Goldman, J. P. Morgan, Harry Houdini, Henry Ford, and Booker T. Washington. Bell was a sportswriter at the time, but he loved the theater and dreamed of becoming a producer. As soon as he finished the novel, he said to his wife, "This is a great musical. I want to do this as a musical."

Ten years later, having produced one play on Broadway, Bell asked Peter Stone and Jerry Herman to adapt *Ragtime* for the stage. Stone, who knew Doctorow from the Hamptons, where they had weekend houses, leapt at the chance, though there was a problem. Stone believed musicals had to be about one person. *Ragtime* was densely populated. So he focused his treatment on the rich white mother in New Rochelle and cut back or eliminated the other characters. Doctorow turned it down. He wanted all his characters in the show. "I was pretty shattered," Bell said.

Several years later, Bell got a call from Garth Drabinsky, the former head of Cineplex Odeon who was now running a theater production company in Toronto called Livent. Drabinsky was looking for a creative director. Hal Prince had recommended his friend Bell. "Go up there and give Garth a lot of ideas," Prince told Bell. "He doesn't really know who the talent is out there."

Bell arrived in Toronto with ten ideas for shows and suggestions of who should write them. *Ragtime* was on his list. Drabinsky had read the novel and saw how "songs could emanate from the storytelling," he said.

Ragtime also had all the makings of the kind of musical Drabinsky loved and believed audiences did too. It would be a lavish spectacle with social relevance. The cast and the orchestra would be enormous, the special effects dazzling. The production would be expensive, but Drabinsky was not an impresario to be hemmed in by the accounting department. As Len Gill, an advertising executive who worked for him, put it, "Garth was the only guy I knew who could overspend an unlimited budget."

Garth Drabinsky has a memory from childhood of running through sprinklers on a hot summer day in Toronto in 1953. He was only three years old, but he can recall "the water as cold as diamonds . . . the heat of the afternoon, the green of the lawn" and "the freedom to run and run and run," he wrote in his memoir *Closer to the Sun*. And then he fell down. His next memory is of his father rushing him in a cab to a children's hospital, where he was diagnosed with polio. His left leg was paralyzed, and for the next eight years he underwent seven major operations in an attempt to save it. In the end, the leg was a useless stump he would drag behind him for the rest of his life. He was fitted with braces, but his strong-willed mother stamped out any traces of self-pity. She made him walk to school in those braces every day.

The activities of a normal childhood denied him, Drabinsky turned inward, losing himself in books and movies. But he discovered a talent for debate and public speaking. He saw a production of Molière's *The Imaginary Invalid* and fell in love with the theater. He staged a production of Peter Ustinov's *Romanoff and Juliet* and cast himself in the lead.

Drabinsky formed a stock club, collecting money from friends to invest in the market. The returns never materialized. Michael Cohl, a concert promoter and theater producer who knew Drabinsky from a pool hall they used to hang out in as teenagers, had a friend in the stock club. "He told me they had to go after him because he bought a car," Cohl said. "He never bought any stocks."

Drabinsky studied law at the University of Toronto and founded a magazine about the movie business called *Impact*. He wrote *Motion Pictures and the Arts in Canada*, a well-received book about entertainment law. His magazine, though, was hemorrhaging money. To save it, he turned to Nat Taylor, Canada's version of a Hollywood mogul. Taylor owned theaters and a production studio and was a major shareholder in television stations. He also created the first multiplex theater, the Elgin in Ottawa. Taylor liked Drabinsky's ambition and energy, but thought his magazine was doomed. Close it, he told him, and then offered Drabinsky a job editing his magazine, *Canadian Film Digest*. Taylor became Drabinsky's mentor, teaching him the business of movies.

Drabinsky was too ambitious to be an editor of a film magazine for long. He wanted to be in the game. So he turned to producing. One of his first movies was *The Silent Partner*, a heist movie starring Christopher Plummer as a vicious bank robber and Elliott Gould as a meek bank clerk. Budgeted at $2.2 million,* *The Silent Partner* was the most expensive Canadian movie ever made up to that point. It was a nifty thriller, but, unable to find a major

* Unless otherwise specified, figures in this chapter are in Canadian dollars.

distributor in the United States, it only returned 70 percent of its investment. Undeterred, Drabinsky embarked on an even more expensive movie—*The Changeling*, for which he paid its star George C. Scott the princely sum of $1 million. Drabinsky financed the $5.5 million movie by floating shares to the general public. Myron Gottlieb, a financial whiz popular on Bay Street, the Toronto equivalent of Wall Street, helped Drabinsky draw up his prospectus and raise money. Their plan drew the attention of *Maclean's* magazine, which unloaded with a hatchet piece calling Drabinsky "arrogant and unpopular" and "unrepentantly belligerent." The article also questioned the soundness of his financing scheme and pointed out the high fees he awarded himself as producer, lawyer, and distributor. A furious Drabinsky sued, eventually winning a $75,000 settlement. *The Changeling* got made, though it went over budget and was a bust at the box office.

Drabinsky turned his attention to Broadway, raising money from Toronto investors for *A Broadway Musical*, by Charles Strouse and Lee Adams, about a sleazy theater producer. The critics crucified it and the show closed the night it opened at a loss of more than US$1 million. "I learned never to produce from a distance," Drabinsky said. "I saw how a show gets destroyed, and I said I would never do that again."

In 1979, Drabinsky teamed up with his mentor Nat Taylor to open an eighteen-screen movie theater in the underground parking lot of a mall called Eaton Centre in Toronto. They showed art films and foreign movies and served cappuccino. The theater took off, and Taylor and Drabinsky formed Cineplex to build multiplexes throughout Canada. Gottlieb joined the company as vice president, charged with raising money. And Drabinsky always needed money. Cineplex expanded quickly, taking on debt before it nearly toppled in 1982. Its competitors in Canada—Famous Players and Canadian Odeon Theatres Ltd.—had exclusive access to movies made by the major Hollywood studios. Cineplex could not survive on art films alone, no matter how many cappuccinos it sold. Drabinsky, in a brilliant legal move, convinced Canadian authorities to allow competitive bidding for Hollywood movies. A bank held off on calling in a loan, and Drabinsky and Gottlieb threw $3 million of their own money into the company to keep it afloat. A year later Drabinsky enticed the Bronfmans, one of Canada's richest families (they owned Seagrams), to take a 10 percent stake in the company.

There are two stories as to why the Bronfmans decided to go into business with Drabinsky. One, which Drabinsky tells, was that they wanted to be in show business and liked his vision for Cineplex. The other was that Cineplex could not pay its rent for its multiplex in Eaton Centre, which the Bronfmans owned. The space was useless for retail, so the Bronfmans made the investment to keep Cineplex afloat. Whatever the truth, their stake enabled Drabinsky to gobble up a competitor, Odeon, for the bargain price of $20 million.

The new company—Cineplex Odeon, now publicly traded—expanded at a dizzying clip, snapping up old theaters or opening new ones all over North America. These weren't shabby theaters with horsehair seats and sticky floors. Drabinsky built movie palaces that featured Italian marble, carpeting imported from England, Parisian-style cafés, state-of-the-art sound and projection, scientifically countered seats, and plenty of neon.[1] Drabinsky decreed that real butter rather than the cheaper flavored oil be used on Cineplex Odeon popcorn.

Drabinsky lived a mogul's life, marshaling helicopters and private jets to take him around the country to check up on his growing empire. Cineplex Odeon hosted lavish parties for movie stars in Los Angeles, Cannes, New York, and Toronto. Drabinsky impressed the movie business. His posh theaters brought in audiences that the industry feared were being lost to HBO, Showtime, and videocassette players. But his sharp elbows, brashness, arrogance, and litigiousness did not make him popular in Toronto or Hollywood. When the *Toronto Star* questioned the cleanliness of one of his theaters, Drabinsky sued the paper for $2 million.

By 1985, Cineplex Odeon was booming, its theaters filled with such hits as *Ghostbusters* and *Back to the Future.* The company made $13 million in its first year. "Garth looked like a genius," said board member David Fingold. A year later Drabinsky convinced Lew Wasserman, head of the Music Corporation of America (MCA) and the most powerful man in Hollywood, to go into business with him. MCA acquired one-third of Cineplex for US$75 million. Drabinsky's stake in his company dwindled to just 7 percent, but MCA's money helped him retire debt and keep expanding. A friend warned him that MCA would not be a silent partner. He might wake up to find that he was no longer the Caesar of the empire he created. But Drabinsky brushed aside the warnings.

Drabinsky was competitive, and he had a vindictive streak. He eliminated Odeon by buying it, but his other rival, Famous Players, hung on. Drabinsky never forgot—and never forgave—the company for blocking him from getting mainstream Hollywood movies when he started Cineplex. Across the street from his office in Toronto was Famous Players' flagship theater, the Imperial Six. He discovered that a ninety-year-old widow in Michigan owned half the theater. "Famous Players was trying to destroy this little woman," Drabinsky said. He convinced her to sell him her half of the lease. Two days later, Drabinsky descended on the building with a security detail, guard dogs, and carpenters. Drywall and chain-link fences went up to divide the building in half. Famous Players could only access its theaters through a fire exit. The theater had to close.

With MCA's backing, Drabinsky returned to producing films, including *Madame Sousatzka* and *Talk Radio*. They were hardly blockbusters. He spent US$7 million on Martin Scorsese's *The Last Temptation of Christ*. Christian groups hated the movie and picketed MCA. Wasserman was furious. Drabinsky operated as if Cineplex were his fiefdom, and that, too, irritated Wasserman.

Friction erupted over MCA's ambitious plan to build a Universal studio tour in Orlando, Florida, in partnership with Cineplex. Costs escalated out of control, placing an undue burden on Cineplex's balance sheets.

Drabinsky's aggressive, snarling personality grated on Wasserman and Sidney Sheinberg, his second in command at MCA. They were as ruthless as Drabinsky was. They were "considered to be the most challenging guys to deal with in the film business," Drabinsky said. But their ruthlessness was cloaked in silk. Drabinsky's came in burlap. "Garth would take people to task—scream and holler and carry on at meetings," David Fingold said. "After one meeting I took him aside and said, 'Garth, I don't understand why you are like this. You've arrived. You're not fighting to stay alive now like you were years ago.'"

Another aspect of Drabinsky's nature was a drive to expand. Cineplex continued to grow at an astounding rate, and pile up debt along the way, much to the chagrin of MCA and the Bronfmans. Drabinsky always maintained that Wasserman urged him to use leverage rather than equity to build the company. But others believed Drabinsky did deals behind MCA's back. In 1987, Cineplex Odeon was valued at US$1 billion but lost US$78 million and was beginning to stagger under crippling debt. When the market crashed, the company entered an even more fragile position. Analysts began to question "liberal" and "unorthodox" accounting practices. As Sheinberg put it, "My God, we're in business with a madman."[2]

Drabinsky, meanwhile, chafed under MCA's and the Bronfmans' increasing oversight. Whenever he and his partner, Myron Gottlieb, met privately with Fingold, they called Cineplex "our company." Whenever Fingold met with MCA and the Bronfmans, they called it their company. In 1989, Fingold "began to smell it"—an irreparable rift between Drabinsky and MCA. He cashed out. He and his brother had bought shares of Cineplex Odeon at its start for between $2 and $3 million. They sold them for $36 million. "The only person who ever made big money with Drabinsky was a Fingold," Fingold said.*

Drabinsky had to regain control of Cineplex soon because MCA was plotting to push him out. He and Gottlieb put together a group of investors to buy out the Bronfmans, who were only too happy to exit a nightmare. The price: $17.50 a share for a total of $125 million. Drabinsky, in an interview in 2020, objected to the characterization that MCA wanted to oust him. He went after the Bronfmans' stake because he wanted to own more equity in "my company."

When Wasserman learned of Drabinsky's overture to the Bronfmans, he set out to destroy him. Court battles ensued. Things became so petty that MCA pulled ads in *Variety* celebrating Cineplex Odeon's tenth anniversary and canceled tables it had booked for the celebration. In the end, MCA decided it wanted out, too. MCA offered to sell Drabinsky the company, but at the same share price he was offering the Bronfmans—$17.50. Battered Cineplex Odeon shares were now trading at $14. The price for Drabinsky to regain his company shot from $125 million to $1.3 billion. And he had just five months to raise the money. Wasserman put the knife in further. An audit of Cineplex given to the press revealed loans to Drabinsky and Gottlieb had been misrepresented in an annual report. Drabinsky claimed they were for advances against bonuses, but the stench of shifty accounting grew worse.

* Fingold's departure shifted more control to MCA. Furious, Drabinsky urged the Ontario Securities Commission to investigate Fingold for insider trading. It did, but Fingold was cleared.

Drabinsky and Gottlieb scrambled to raise $1.3 billion. And they came close, but not in time. Lew Wasserman had what must have been to him the delicious pleasure of stripping Drabinsky of Cineplex Odeon on November 27, 1989. Drabinsky was shaken, almost defeated. He began planning his comeback. And he had a good building block: *The Phantom of the Opera.*

CHAPTER THIRTEEN

BE AT THE FUCKING MATINEE

Garth Drabinsky acquired the Canadian rights to *Phantom* while he was still running Cineplex. Sid Sheinberg saw an early performance in London and told Drabinsky it was going to be a massive hit. "The jungle drums are beating across the Atlantic," Sheinberg said. Drabinsky, while in London inspecting new movie theaters, snagged a seat under the balcony from which he could barely see the falling chandelier. But he knew one thing: *Phantom* "would be the biggest piece of entertainment I would ever see in my lifetime."

And he had just the place in Toronto to put it: the Imperial Six, which he had wrestled away from his rival Famous Players and was now calling by its original name, the Pantages. Getting the rights to *Phantom* would not be easy. Lloyd Webber and Cameron Mackintosh generally controlled their shows wherever they played. Drabinsky made headway with Lloyd Webber by showing him plans for the restoration of the Pantages.

He met Mackintosh at the opening of *Phantom* in Hamburg. "I saw this man striding, or rather limping, across the foyer, and as I did not know anything about his polio I rather unfortunately said, 'Has your leg fallen asleep?'" Mackintosh said. After he recovered from his embarrassment, and over the course of a few months, Mackintosh discussed terms with Drabinsky. He didn't like him. "I thought he bulldozed through the creative process and really didn't understand it," he said. "And that's just not the way I work." But Mackintosh had a problem. He was opening productions of his other smash hit, *Les Misérables*, all over the world, including Toronto. "I just couldn't do two shows back to back," he said. Lloyd Webber, meanwhile, wanted to roll out *Phantom*, an even bigger hit than *Les Misérables*, as fast as possible. So Mackintosh relented and gave Drabinsky the rights.

As part of their exit package from Cineplex Odeon, MCA allowed Drabinsky and Myron Gottlieb to buy the Pantages and *The Phantom of the Opera*. MCA executives weren't interested in live theater and scoffed at Drabinsky's assertion that the show would run in Toronto for at least four years. It had an astonishing advance sale of $24 million,* but the executives thought there weren't enough people in all of Canada to keep it going for four years.

Drabinsky and Gottlieb paid US$65 million for the theater and the show, using their severance packages, selling their shares in Cineplex Odeon, and securing loans from friends and banks. They called their company the Live Entertainment Corporation of Canada, or Livent, for short. It was a scrappy start-up, but Drabinsky had absolute control. "I will never go public," he told his lawyer Dan Brambilla. "I will never be a public company again."[1]

The day he left Cineplex, Drabinsky ordered the cast of *Phantom* to meet him backstage at the Pantages. Champagne flowed. A giant cake came out bearing the name Livent and its logo, a phoenix. "Out of the ashes of one empire, we are going to build Livent," he announced. "And *Phantom* is the rock on which we will build it."

Drabinsky wanted his Canadian *Phantom* to be as good—better, if possible—than the Broadway production. He hired Colm Wilkinson, the star of *Les Misérables*, to play the lead, signing

* Unless otherwise specified, all figures in this chapter are in Canadian dollars.

him up for several years and paying him an enormous amount of money. Drabinsky's production would not be a rollout from New York, directed by some stage manager. He wanted the real director—Hal Prince—to stage it. Prince moved to Toronto for two months to oversee the production. To Drabinsky, Prince was the greatest director alive. He treated him with deference and respect.

Toronto was a sleepy theater town in 1989. Ed Mirvish, founder of Honest Ed's famous discount store, owned most of Toronto's theaters. He loved the theater but wasn't a producer, opting instead to fill his houses with road companies of Broadway hits. Drabinsky was a far more aggressive producer. He launched an ad and marketing blitz for *Phantom* the likes of which Toronto had never seen. There were billboards everywhere, full-page ads in all the papers, huge radio and television buys. Drabinsky's *Phantom* didn't just open in Toronto, it invaded Toronto.

The city's theater audience largely came from the suburbs and Buffalo, on the other side of Lake Ontario. Drabinsky realized he could extend his reach deeper into America. The Canadian dollar was cheap—his *Phantom* was a US$65 ticket—and audiences could get into it a lot sooner than they could the Broadway production. He advertised *Phantom* in Rochester, Syracuse, Cleveland, Akron, Detroit, and Pittsburgh. He created the *Phantom* Express, a bus that would bring up Americans from those cities for the day. If the trip was too long, he threw in a discounted hotel for the night. "A massive chunk of the Midwest suddenly was going to see shows in Canada," said Chris Jones, the theater critic for the *Chicago Tribune*. Cameron Mackintosh seethed. Drabinsky was cutting into his audience and there was nothing he could do about it.*

* When Drabinsky opened a *Phantom* in Vancouver, he advertised in Seattle, which was where Mackintosh had a *Phantom* tour playing. "I was running effectively open ended and he was running for three to five weeks," Drabinsky said. "I certainly didn't [advertise] to hurt Cameron Mackintosh."

Drabinsky threw a lavish *Phantom* opening, inviting just about every Canadian celebrity alive. He got Lloyd Webber to come as well, but couldn't get Mackintosh. When Mackintosh caught up with the production a few months later, he was given a tour of the Pantages. Surveying the gilt paint, the velvet wallpaper, the plush carpeting, he said, "Ah, yes. Garth always did have taste. Acres of taste."

Working for Drabinsky could be a nightmare. He treated Prince and other artists with "gossamer and charm," said Richard Ouzounian, Prince's assistant director on the Toronto *Phantom*. But he could be brutal to underlings. "You're a fucking useless piece of shit" was a phrase he hurled at assistants. Drabinsky checked up on the *Phantom* regularly—and expected Ouzounian to do so as well. Ouzounian got a call late one night. "Why weren't you at the theater tonight?" Drabinsky demanded. Ouzounian said he'd been there the night before and would be there the next day. "I don't think I have to be there every night," he said.

"Well, Colm was overacting terribly so you'd better check up on him."

"I'll come tomorrow night," Ouzounian said.

"No not good enough. Come tomorrow afternoon."

"Garth, it's my daughter's fourth birthday, and we have twenty kids coming over."

"Who pays you the money to let you have twenty fucking kids come over? Be at the fucking matinee."

Ouzounian went. He sat in the last row taking notes. Fifteen seconds before the show ended, Drabinsky opened the back door, looked at Ouzounian, nodded, and left.

Drabinsky's *Phantom* was the smash he knew it would be, returning its investment within a couple of years and grossing $1 million a week, unheard of for a show in Canada. Drabinsky got the rights from Lloyd Webber to *Joseph and the Amazing Technicolor Dreamcoat*. He produced a revival starring Donny Osmond that was a hit in Toronto and on the road (it would run sixteen months in Chicago).

But Drabinsky wanted to do new shows. He found his first in John Kander and Fred Ebb's *Kiss of the Spider Woman*. Based on Manuel Puig's novel, it told the story of a gay window dresser in prison in Argentina for corrupting a minor. He endures torture and humiliation by fantasizing about a movie diva. Hal Prince directed an early version that Marty Bell produced at SUNY Purchase in Westchester. Frank Rich panned it. Drabinsky, who had invested in the movie, saw the production and told Prince it was too tame. "You're trying to let the audience off too easily," he said. "It's a complex piece of work. Consider reworking the show and bring it to me." Kander, Ebb, and writer Terrence McNally rewrote the show. Prince gave Drabinsky the new script. He read it and told Prince, "Let's do the show." He produced it in Toronto and in London, splashing star Chita Rivera's face from one end of the Shaftesbury Theatre to the other. The show lost money in both cities, but Drabinsky didn't care. He had bigger plans.

Jon Wilner, co-owner of a prominent New York theatrical ad agency, got a call one day from Mary Bryant, Prince's longtime press agent. "I'm in London with Garth Drabinsky," she told Wilner. "He's producing *Kiss of the Spider Woman* and he's bringing it to New York. Chita's in it. You have to come to see it." Wilner had driven to Westchester in the rain to see the first version. "I didn't know what was worse, the weather or the show," he said. But he went to London and thought the show was much better. A few days later Bryant called and told him he had to go to Toronto to meet Drabinsky. "Mary, who's paying for this?" Wilner asked. "I went to London and he didn't pay for anything." Bryant replied, "He'll pay. You send him a bill. He'll send you a check."

Livent's offices in Toronto impressed Wilner. The décor was expensive Sante Fe—all beige and other desert colors. An art gallery featured paintings and sculpture by Canada's top contemporary artists. The men wore suits, the women business jackets and skirts. Everybody seemed to have an assistant. "It was all very strange to me," Wilner said. "I was used to producers who were sort of a one-man band smoking a cigar. This felt very corporate, and all of a sudden this larger than life character with hair everywhere came in and started charming me. He knew everything about me. He knew every show I had ever worked on."

In the large, sleek conference room, Drabinsky introduced Wilner to his two Canadian ad agencies. Wilner sensed what was up. Drabinsky was the kind of boss who pitted people against one another to see who came up with the best idea. Wilner listened to the Canadians' ideas for *Spider Woman* and then chimed in. Their biggest problem, he said, was that they were up against *The Who's Tommy*, which was coming into New York on the strength of rave reviews from the La Jolla Playhouse. As far as New York was concerned, *Spider Woman* was damaged goods. The advertising and marketing would have to overcome that perception. The Canadians, Wilner recalled, didn't seem to know what *Tommy* was. Wilner thought, *I'm dealing with a bunch of Toronto local yokles.* For their part, the Canadians thought Wilner was "this crazy guy from New York," said Barry Avrich, creative director at one of the Canadian agencies. Wilner wore skintight red pants, no socks in the winter, talked fast, and could be flamboyant in his contempt for their ideas. The Canadians and Wilner did not mix. But Drabinsky loved the give-and-take and appreciated Wilner's grasp of the politics of Broadway. Drabinsky asked him to be his advertising agent in New York.

Drabinsky, in an interview in 2020, disputed Wilner's belief that he pitted advertising agencies against one another. "If you're going to run a show for years and years and years, in the case of *Phantom*, for example, there is not one single advertising agency that is going to come up with a novel idea year after year," he said. "I had to have ideas all the time, and that's why we had three agencies."

Drabinsky drew attention to *Spider Woman* in New York by outspending rival shows, including *Tommy*, on marketing and advertising. The morning of the Tony nominations announcement at Sardi's, directly across the street from the Broadhurst Theatre where *Spider Woman* was playing, Wilner arranged for a man with a crane to be under the marquee. He put up the phrase "Nominated for"—blank—"Tony Awards, including Best Musical." As soon as *Spider Woman* snagged its last nomination, Wilner ran out of Sardi's and told the man, "Eleven! Put up eleven!" When all the Broadway power brokers left Sardi's they looked up and saw the marquee trumpeting the show's eleven nominations. The producers of *Tommy* were stunned. Drabinsky loved it.

Before the Tony telecast, Drabinsky extracted a promise from CBS not to show him walking to the stage if he won. He did not want the world to see his limp. *Spider Woman* collected seven awards, beating out *Tommy* for Best Musical. Four years after his humiliation at the hands of Lew Wasserman, Drabinsky was on his way to conquering Broadway.

Money was now coming in from *Phantom*, *Joseph*, and *Spider Woman*. But it was not enough. So Drabinsky violated his declaration never to be a public company again and floated shares in Livent on the Canadian stock exchange and, eventually, NASDAQ. Some who worked for Drabinsky thought he went public because of an overweening ambition to build another empire. Humiliated in Hollywood, he wanted to be a mogul again, this time in live theater. But Drabinsky claimed he went public because he was under pressure from his backers to "monetize" or "liquidate" their investments. The cash flow from his shows paid down lines of credit from banks or went into producing new shows, he said.

A company that produced live theater—with all of its risks and, unless the shows are smashes, no reward—had never before gone public.

The money that flowed in from the public offering allowed Drabinsky to expand his empire. He acquired theaters in Vancouver and Chicago. He was creating a "vertically integrated" company that would control everything—the shows, the theaters, the merchandising, the cast albums, the marketing and advertising, even the means of production. (Livent would have its own costume shop in Toronto.) It was the old Hollywood studio system applied to the theater. Livent impressed investors. Its shares climbed.

Drabinsky was always on the hunt for hits. He wanted Cameron Mackintosh's *Miss Saigon*, but Mackintosh preferred working with the Mirvishes. They were building a new $20 million theater especially for the show. Drabinsky gummed up the works by insisting the Mirvishes abide by a city law requiring a parking garage near the theater. The Mirvishes had to spend another $5 million on a parking garage, delaying the opening of *Miss Saigon* by nine months. But *Saigon* was a winner. Drabinsky wound up with Andrew Lloyd Webber's *Aspects of Love*, which had flopped on Broadway. He put together his own production, and opened it in Edmonton. The morning after opening night, Barry Avrich told him, "It's a loser."

"What the fuck do you know?" Drabinsky snarled. "Your taste is up your ass."

The show was a loser, but Drabinsky refused to close it, sending it to Toronto and on tour—and spending enormous amounts of money to advertise it. Avrich began to realize something: as long as *Aspects* was running somewhere it could be listed as an asset on Livent's books. It was, after all, an Andrew Lloyd Webber show. What the books would never show was just how much money it was losing, and just how much money Drabinsky was spending to make it appear to be a hit.[2] The creative accounting

Drabinsky had been accused of using at Cineplex Odeon was taking root at Livent.

In 1990, Drabinsky caught a revival of *Show Boat* in London. He didn't care for the cheap production but the story and Jerome Kern and Oscar Hammerstein II's score moved him. Florenz Ziegfeld produced the original in 1927. Drabinsky envisioned a Toronto production that would be even grander than Ziegfeld's. Hal Prince agreed to direct a cast of seventy-one actors, including Robert Morse as Cap'n Andy and Elaine Stritch as Parthy. *Show Boat* opened in Toronto in October 1993 at Drabinsky's new theater, the North York Performing Arts Centre. Jeremy Gerard from *Variety* raved, as did the Toronto critics. But the show was so expensive—$8 million—Gerard urged his readers to journey to Toronto to see it because "only an act of charity will bring this production to Broadway." Gerard was shocked a few months later when Drabinsky announced he would open another production of *Show Boat* on Broadway at the Gershwin Theatre in October 1994. This production would cost US$10 million, making it the most expensive revival in theater history. The weekly overhead would be more than US$600,000.

On opening night he and Prince took center stage at the curtain call. They beckoned the backstage crew to join them and their seventy-one actors. Arthur Cantor, a wily old producer, began counting the number of people onstage. "Jesus Christ," he said. "This show can never pay back." He was onto something.*

Drabinsky's next production was a play, *Barrymore*, about the actor John Barrymore, starring Drabinsky's old friend Christopher

* Cantor was my date for the opening.

Plummer. He paid the actor a small fortune—between US$15,000 and $20,000 a week—for a tour and then a Broadway run. Plummer could be a diva at times, but his wife, Elaine, always calmed him down. Drabinsky wanted her to tour with him. He offered her US$5,000 a week. When she turned him down, he called Plummer's agent and said, "Ask her what she likes in jewelry. I'll buy her a diamond necklace."[3]

Drabinsky paid Elaine Stritch US$15,000 a week to do *Show Boat* in Toronto, bumping it up to US$20,000 in New York. She sang one song—"Why Do I Love You?"—to a baby in such a way that Stephen Sondheim said, "I don't know if she's going to sing to that baby or eat it."

When Drabinsky needed to replace John McMartin as Cap'n Andy (an exhausted Robert Morse chose not to reprise the role in New York), he offered the part to John Cullum, a Tony Award–winning musical theater leading man. But Cap'n Andy doesn't have a song and Cullum's wife feared Broadway would think he couldn't sing anymore. He passed. Jeff Berger represented Cullum. Drabinsky called him one day and said, "What the fuck do I have to do to get John Cullum in my show?" Berger drew a number out of the air. "Pay him twenty-five thousand dollars a week." "You got it," Drabinsky said and then hung up. He also threw in a chocolate-brown Rolls-Royce to drive him home from the theater every night.

Drabinsky's free spending irritated rival Broadway producers. He dropped hundreds of thousands of dollars a week to advertise *Show Boat* and *Spider Woman*. Everybody knew *Spider Woman* wasn't the hit Drabinsky made it out to be. (Its grosses did improve for a time when he cast Vanessa Williams in the lead.) But they'd open the *New York Times* and see pages and pages of ads. They could not match it, but they had to try or risk being overwhelmed. They also couldn't match what he was paying actors. Actors' quotes were going up all over Broadway. "Garth Drabinsky money," as it was called, was increasing costs for everybody.

Up in Toronto, Livent was churning on all fronts. *Phantoms* were going to Hawaii, Vancouver, and Singapore. *Spider Woman* was launching an American tour, and productions of *Show Boat* were being planned in Chicago, London, and Vancouver. Livent was preparing *Sunset Boulevard* starring Diahann Carroll for Toronto. Future projects included *Ragtime* and a musical version of the movie *Sweet Smell of Success*. Drabinsky had his fingers in everything. He called box offices around the world to find out what the grosses were that day, sometimes what they were that hour. If he didn't like the numbers, he'd slam down the phone. He read scripts, listened to new songs, checked out carpet patterns for theaters he was restoring. And he was all over the marketing and advertising, two areas he had mastered at Cineplex Odeon.

Every Tuesday morning he presided over a marketing and advertising meeting. People entered the conference room in fear. "It was a gladiatorial forum. Who's going to get thrown to the lions today?" said Norman Zaiger, the head of Livent's publicity office. Avrich and the Canadians presented their ads. Then Jon Wilner, in from New York wearing his skintight red pants ("sometimes they were green," Avrich recalled) and dripping with contempt for the "yokels," presented his. If Drabinsky liked something, he'd say, "That's it!" If he didn't, he'd bellow, "This is shit!" At some point during the meeting, he would target someone, usually a low-level employee, for humiliation. One day he lit into an underling in the marketing department—a "lovely, talented young woman," a person who was there said—because she didn't have the answer to one of his questions. She broke down in tears. "If that's the way you're going to react, get up and get out," Drabinsky said. The meetings could run as long as three hours, at which point Drabinsky would have his driver bring in a plate of sandwiches and soup from a nearby deli. But he was the only one who could eat. "We're all salivating, and he'd be slurping his soup," Zaiger said.

Underneath the bravado, arrogance, and sharp temper was—people close to Drabinsky sensed—deep insecurity. When he was in doubt about something, he'd asked anybody in sight for an opinion, even the security guard at the front desk. He was most sensitive about his limp. A former employee recalled making a minor mistake and receiving a call at night from an irate Drabinsky. The employee was battling diabetes and was in danger of losing his leg. "I'm on painkillers because of my leg," the employee said. Drabinsky replied, "I'll trade my leg for your leg any fucking day."

Bill Taylor, the head of Andrew Lloyd Webber's company, ran into Drabinsky at a fundraiser in New York one night. They had business to discuss so Drabinsky had his assistant book a room in the hotel for an hour after the dinner. "Unfortunately, the room was a long way from the elevator and Garth had to struggle to walk down the hallway," Taylor said. "He was so annoyed with his assistant he turned around and slapped him in the face."

In January 1996, Drabinsky staked a claim in New York, unveiling ambitious plans to combine the Lyric and the Apollo, two derelict theaters on Forty-Second Street, to create a state-of-the-art 1,825-seat theater to house Livent musicals. The cost was estimated at US$22.5 million, which Drabinsky said he would raise from private institutional funders. City officials and the media greeted the plan enthusiastically. The Walt Disney Company was restoring the New Amsterdam Theatre across the street for nearly US$40 million. The two theaters would become anchors for the resurgence of Forty-Second Street and Times Square after decades of squalor and decay. Drabinsky said his new theater would be part of a "strategic circuit" that would enable him to move Livent's shows from his theaters in Toronto to New York and then to Chicago and Vancouver.[4]

This plan sounded attractive to Wall Street. But old Broadway hands remained skeptical. Jeremy Gerard, the theater editor for *Variety*, regularly prowled Times Square to get a feel for the business on the street. He'd slip into theaters and count the house. He stopped by the Gershwin, where *Show Boat* was running, one weeknight and noticed it was half-empty. Outside on the street he scooped up discarded ticket stubs and was shocked to see the price—ten dollars or sometimes nothing. The show was being papered and heavily discounted, and yet Drabinsky was reporting weekly grosses of US$900,000 to $1 million. When Drabinsky released a statement announcing *Show Boat* had recouped its US$11 million cost, Gerard refused to print the news. "Garth was furious," Gerard recalled. "He called me into his office and dressed me down. 'I've got the books. The books are right here. I can show you!' he said. And I said, 'I'm sorry Garth. I don't believe you.'"

Up in Toronto, some of the financial people at Livent were becoming alarmed at just how much money Drabinsky was spending. *Phantom* was throwing off a ton of cash, but *Kiss of the Spider Woman* was "eating a ton of cash," said Robert Topol, Livent's chief operating officer. But Drabinsky wouldn't close it. As long as it ran on Broadway or on tour, he could list it as an asset. Drabinsky's plans for *Show Boat* appalled Topol. He wanted to roll out productions in Vancouver and Chicago and on tour that would be as big and as expensive as the Broadway production. "It was insane," Topol said. "You don't send out road shows with a hundred people." When the productions opened, they weren't hits despite the lavish spending on advertising and marketing.

Drabinsky's foray into Vancouver was also on shaky ground. As it turned out, Vancouver was not the theater town he had envisioned. "In Toronto there was a sense that you didn't want to miss out on the latest show," said Jordan Fiksenbaum, who worked in ticketing at Livent. "But nobody wants to be inside in Vancouver during the summer. They love outdoor activities. It's a different mind-set. They're West Coast laid-back. There's no urgency to see the latest show." Many of the shows Drabinsky produced in Vancouver lost money. "If you know *Sunset Boulevard* is bombing with Diahann Carroll in Toronto, why take it to Vancouver?" said Fiksenbaum. There was an answer. As long as it was running it was another asset on the books.

Whenever he needed money, Drabinsky would send his quiet and unassuming partner, Myron Gottlieb, to Bay Street to raise it. "Somebody was always doing due diligence on us for the next round of money," said Livent lawyer Dan Brambilla. "It was like a book-of-the-month club, but we always called it the offering-of-the-month club."

It was becoming increasingly clear around the Livent offices that what the company needed was another *Phantom of the Opera*. And in *Ragtime* Drabinsky thought he had one. He called up Sam Cohn, E. L. Doctorow's agent, to get the rights. Cohn set up a lunch meeting for the three of them in his booth at the Russian Tea Room. Drabinsky was nervous. "I hadn't done something like this with this level of a writer before," he said. Doctorow, looking professorial in a bow tie and tweed coat, arrived. First he wanted to know what Drabinsky thought of Milos Forman's *Ragtime* movie. "Truthfully, I thought the film was a complete disaster," Drabinsky said. "Forman didn't understand your structure. You wrote a book that is essentially an equilateral triangle. If you take any one of the sides out everything collapses. Forman skewed his film to Coalhouse, ignoring the Jewish immigrant and the WASP family. There is only one way to do the musical and that is to maintain the triangle you created." Doctorow turned to Cohn and said, "Make a deal with him."

Terrence McNally turned in a treatment in 1994 that incorporated all of the characters from the novel. Drabinsky and his creative director, Marty Bell, gave the treatment to ten different composers and lyricists, paid them each US$2,000 and asked them to come up with three or four songs as an audition for writing the full score. One of the teams they approached was Lynn Ahrens and Stephen Flaherty, who had a Broadway hit with the charming *Once on This Island*.

Ahrens and Flaherty submitted four songs, including the opening number "Ragtime" and "Gliding," a tender waltz for the Jewish immigrant to sing to his daughter. Drabinsky brought Doctorow to his office one day to listen to all the submissions, which included songs from Jason Robert Brown and Canadian composer Leslie Arden. "I could see Doctorow was getting impatient," Bell said. "Everybody had one or two good songs, but then one or two that weren't good. Then we played him Ahrens and Flaherty and he loved the opening number and the anthem 'Till We Reach That Day,' and we were off."

The phone rang in Ahrens's apartment: "Hey, it's Garth Drabinsky. This is only the beginning. You've got the job. And if you don't do an amazing job, I'm going to fire you." Ahrens, Flaherty, and McNally headed to Toronto to start workshops for *Ragtime*. Their cast, mainly American and some of the brightest talents on Broadway, included Brian Stokes Mitchell as Coalhouse Walker, the Harlem musician; Audra McDonald as Sarah, the servant girl he impregnates; Marin Mazzie as the rich woman from New Rochelle; and Peter Friedman as the Jewish immigrant. At one point in the workshop, Ahrens and Flaherty realized McDonald, possessed of one of the great Broadway voices ever, was sitting around. So they wrote a song for her—"Your Daddy's Son," one of the most haunting in the show. "I want to hear it, I want to hear it!" Drabinsky said. Ahrens and Flaherty said they needed time to teach it to McDonald. Drabinsky was throwing a barbecue that night for the company. Unless he heard the new song by the end of the day, Ahrens and Flaherty would not be invited.

The first cast read through of *Ragtime* lasted three hours, "and it was as rough as could be," said Ahrens. Drabinsky invited Ahrens, Flaherty, and Bell to dinner. He came into the restaurant and put a document with a blue cover in front of everyone. "Flap, flap, flap," Ahrens said. It was fifteen pages of notes, all typed. He had comments on everything. "I have to have this," the notes read. "And I want that." One note read: "On page seventeen of the novel the characters say this, and I want it in the show." Ahrens was furious, but held her tongue. Later she let Bell know how upset she was. At six the next morning, Drabinsky called her. "I understand you're angry with me." Before she could reply, he started shouting: "You will do what I tell you! This is my project, and you're going to make it what I want!"

The outburst lasted five minutes. When it was over Ahrens asked, "Are you through?"

"Yeah," Drabinsky grunted.

"All right, now let me tell you a thing or two. From this moment on you will never do this again to me or any other writer. You can express your concerns and your confusions and your worries. But you will never again tell me what to write. You don't give me solutions. I give you solutions. And not only that, you can never give us your notes until you hear our impression of our work first. We're probably sensing the same problems you are, but it would be nice to let us say it first."

"All right," Drabinsky said, "I hear you."

"And from then on he never did it again," Ahrens said. "And he was fabulous. He would give us notes saying, 'I want more Klezmer music,' but it was all very respectful."

Ahrens, Flaherty, and McNally were doing some of the best work of their careers on *Ragtime*. They struggled with Coalhouse Walker. He dreams of owning a Ford Model T, and the writers feared he was coming off as materialistic. "And somehow it became apparent that his dream wasn't about the car at all," said Ahrens. "It was about his young son and the tangible future Coalhouse wanted to provide for him and Sarah. The Ford became a physical representation of the American dream as well as access to it." The song originally was called "America's Child," but Ahrens found a better title—"Wheels of a Dream." The first time Brian Stokes Mitchell sang it in rehearsal everyone was in tears.

What Drabinsky pushed for most was spectacle. His unshakable belief was that audiences still wanted lavish musicals, even though *Rent*, without any special effects, was becoming a sensation. "Garth didn't like *Rent*," Bell said. "We saw it together. I was dazzled by it. He was cursing it out."

Drabinsky demanded special effects and big sets—an enormous clock at the top of the show, a gigantic diorama, and a huge stereopticon that nobody but Drabinsky liked. "It was ugly, and it turned out it cost seventy-five hundred dollars a week in overtime for somebody to come in at six o'clock every night and preset it," McNally said. Drabinsky spent US$65,000 for a trick for Houdini that opened the second act. And he ended the show with an onstage fireworks display. *Ragtime* had a cast of fifty-five. It was playing in a suburb, but most of the actors had apartments downtown. "There were car services galore," said McNally. "Even Emma Goldman had a limo."

Ragtime opened in Toronto on December 8, 1996. Local critics raved. "There are few works in contemporary music theater to rival *Ragtime*." "A consistently marvelous work." "Audacious." The *Los Angeles Times* called it "a defining musical for the end of the American Century." Ben Brantley, in the *New York Times*, praised the show's "visual grandeur," Ahrens and Flaherty's score, and the "excellent" cast. But he thought it was heavy-handed on social issues and had one too many anthems. "By the end, you may feel you've been sitting through a multi-million dollar reunion of a folk protest group like the Weavers," he wrote. His reservations had no impact. *Ragtime* was the biggest hit Toronto had seen since *Phantom*.

The day after the opening, Bell went to his office and found a large envelope on his desk. It contained stock certificates in Livent and a handwritten note from Drabinsky: "Thank you for the work you've done. You own 500 additional shares of stock."

Ragtime still needed some fine-tuning, but it had energy and buzz. Everyone in New York was talking about it. Jon Wilner and Mary Bryant urged Drabinsky to move it to Broadway right away. *Show Boat* was set to close in January 1997 at the Gershwin so he could open *Ragtime* there in the spring. Best of all, the field of new musicals that season was weak. *Steel Pier*, *The Life*, and *Titanic* could not compete with *Ragtime*. "You're going to win every Tony in sight," Bryant said. But Drabinsky had other plans. Hal Prince wanted to direct a revival of *Candide*, and Drabinsky was going to produce that at the Gershwin. *Ragtime*, he said, was not yet ready for New York. He would fine-tune it in Los Angeles and then bring it to Broadway to open his new Forty-Second Street theater—The Ford Center for the Performing Arts—in January 1998. It was, he said, the perfect musical for his perfect theater.

"Stop," Bryant said. "Put your ego away. You will have a hit if you listen to us."

"We begged him," Wilner recalled. "We begged him like teenagers wanting to take out the car. But he wouldn't do it. He would not do it. And it was the beginning of the end."

CHAPTER FOURTEEN

THE LION QUEEN

Michael Eisner, the chairman of the Walt Disney Company, had no interest in bringing the Magic Kingdom to Broadway. He loved the theater. Growing up in New York City, he'd seen just about every Broadway musical from the time he was six until he went off to college. But when he was running Paramount Pictures in the early 1980s, the company produced Tommy Tune's *My One and Only* and it was "the biggest nightmare of my life," he said. The show was in trouble in Boston and while Tune, with the help of Mike Nichols, Peter Stone, and Maury Yeston, turned it into a hit in New York, "it took more time than anything I was doing at Paramount," Eisner said. "I decided never again. This is a hobby we can do without."

And then Frank Rich raved about Disney's animated movie *Beauty and the Beast*—"the best Broadway musical score of 1991"—and Eisner reconsidered. He ran into Andrew Lloyd Webber at an event in North Carolina and "began probing," Lloyd Webber recalled, about the theater. The hundreds of millions of dollars *Cats* had made around the world impressed Eisner. Broadway, like the movies, had become a global business. But when Eisner proposed a stage version of *Beauty and the Beast*, nobody at

Disney wanted to do it. "Fine," Eisner said. "I'm the CEO of the company, so I'll do it. And we'll do it only with people who work at Disney."

Eisner hired Robert Jess Roth, who staged a show Eisner had seen on the *Queen Mary*, to direct *Beauty and the Beast*. The musical—at $20 million the most expensive in Broadway history—opened at the Palace Theatre. The critics dismissed it as a theme park show, but the family audience flocked to it. It became a blockbuster. The Broadway crowd snubbed it by giving the 1994 Tony for Best Musical to Stephen Sondheim's short-lived *Passion*. "But we won the Bank of America award, so it was okay," said Eisner.

With Disney now committed to Broadway, architect Robert Stern, who designed the company's Features Animation Building in Burbank, suggested the company also get involved in Times Square. Mayor Rudy Giuliani was trying to clean up the Crossroads of the World, and Disney's support would give the plan a lift. Eisner "ignored" his friend Stern. Then he found himself seated next to Marian Sulzberger Heiskell, of the *New York Times* family, at a charity event. As chairwoman of the New 42nd Street, Inc., she was involved in saving Times Square. She told Eisner about the New Amsterdam Theatre, a once-grand but now decrepit theater on Forty-Second Street. Disney, she suggested, should acquire it. "I ignored her, too," Eisner said.

On his way to see his son play hockey in New Jersey one spring morning in 1993, Eisner decided to take a look at the theater. Cora Cahan, of the 42nd Street Development Project, gave him a tour. "It was dark, it was raining inside," Eisner said. "Birds were flying around. But it was amazing." Eisner looked past the decay and saw the remnants of the theater's former glory: the art nouveau details, the faded friezes depicting scenes from Shakespeare, the remains of an Irish-marble fireplace in the lounge. A few months later, he brought Frank Wells, the president of Disney, to look at the theater. Two hookers propositioned Wells on the sidewalk.

Eisner met with Giuliani and told him Disney couldn't be on a street full of prostitutes, peep shows, and porn houses. "They'll be gone," Giuliani said.

"Mr. Mayor, in all deference, I come from New York, and I know you just can't move somebody out," Eisner said. "They've got rights, there's the ACLU—it's very difficult."

"Look me in the eyes," Giuliani said.

"What do you mean?"

"Just look me in the eyes."

Eisner did.

"They will be gone," the mayor said.

"OK, so I guess they'll be gone," Eisner said.

Disney began negotiations with the city to take over and renovate the New Amsterdam Theatre. By the time negotiations finished, Eisner had a show in mind for the space—a stage version of the highest-grossing animated film of all time, *The Lion King*.

Jeffrey Katzenberg, the chairman of Walt Disney Studios, came up with the idea for *The Lion King* movie. He was flying on a private plane with Peter Schneider, the head of Disney Animation, to Europe to promote *The Little Mermaid*. They were talking about what movies to do next and Katzenberg suggested a story about the moment a boy becomes a man. He'd had such a moment himself as a teenager working on New York mayor John V. Lindsay's campaign for president in 1972. Katzenberg collected cash contributions, including a fat envelope from a businessman who later profited from dealings with the city. An investigation ensued, and Katzenberg was subpoenaed before a grand jury. The case went nowhere, but as James B. Stewart writes in his book *DisneyWar*, "it was a searing education in money and politics for Katzenberg."[1]

Fascinated by Africa, where he'd once worked on a film set, Katzenberg thought that would be a good setting. Schneider wasn't convinced—*What the fuck is the story?* he thought—but Katzenberg was his boss so he had to come up with something. A story emerged about a lion cub having to take his father's place as king. The working title was *King of the Jungle*. "The B team was working on it," said Schneider, "because it didn't have princesses, and everybody wanted princesses. The A team was working on *Aladdin*."

Tim Rice, the lyricist of *Evita* and *Jesus Christ Superstar*, was at the Disney Studios doing "song placement—whatever that means," he said, for a Dolly Parton movie called *Straight Talk*. He'd hit a rough patch in his theater career after the failure of his Broadway musical *Chess*. A memo he wrote about where to put certain songs in *Straight Talk* impressed Katzenberg, so "I was just hanging around Disney Studios and saying, 'Got another job for me? I really like to write songs. I'm quite good at that.'"

Rice met with Schneider and his number two at Animation, Tom Schumacher. They told him about *King of the Jungle* and asked him if there was a composer he'd like to work with. Elton John, he said. "I thought he had the great combination of great melodies with a rock feel, like *Superstar* and *Evita*. Of course I was thinking only of me at that point, trying to salvage my career. I knew working with Elton couldn't hurt."

The plot of *King of the Jungle* was still vague, though it was beginning to resemble *Hamlet*. "*Hamlet* with fur," as Rice called it. He and John wrote two songs—"Can You Feel the Love Tonight" and "Be Prepared," for Scar, the evil lion who plots against his brother to take over the kingdom. Rice and John didn't work in the same room, as John was always on tour. John liked to have the lyrics first. So Rice would write some verses, peck out his own little tune on the piano to make sure they "sang," and then faxed them to John. "I got quite attached to my little tunes," Rice said. "My 'Can You Feel the Love Tonight' was like Tammy Wynette. And then a cassette would arrive and there was Elton singing my words with a completely different tune. And I thought, 'That's not as good as mine!' And then after about half a verse I thought, 'Actually, that is as good as mine.' And after two verses I thought, 'It's a lot better than mine.'"

When Katzenberg heard a tape of John singing "Can You Feel the Love Tonight" and "Be Prepared" he was not impressed. *The Little Mermaid* and *Beauty and the Beast* had Broadway-style scores by Alan Menken and Howard Ashman. "Can You Feel the Love Tonight" was a pop ballad; "Be Prepared" had a tinge of rock. "We were not writing in the tradition of Alan and Howard," Rice said. So he got Lea Solonga, a Broadway star from *Miss Saigon*, to record a demo of "Can You Feel the Love Tonight." He also performed "Be Prepared" for Katzenberg, Schneider, and other executives himself, putting it over as a theatrical song for the villain. "I was quite good," Rice said. "I kind of felt I should have the part, frankly."

This time the songs worked. Rice and John wrote an opening number. It was a bouncy ditty that listed all the animals in the jungle. Don Hahn, one of the producers of the movie, rejected it. "We've got to have something to really open the film but big," he said. Rice found a line in the script: "It's the circle of life." *Good title,* he thought. He began crafting a lyric "that was more serious, a little philosophical." He and John happened to be in London at the same time so they met to work on the song. John was at the piano playing around with rhythms. Rice fed him lines—"From the day we arrive on the planet," "band of hope," "wheel of fortune"—while John developed a melody. He hit a crescendo and said, "Can I have one more line?"

"On the path unwinding!" Rice called out.

"Don't know where that came from," Rice said years later, "but it's nice."

They finished "Circle of Life" in about an hour and a half.

Disney executives liked the song, but it sounded like a pop tune. What was missing, Schneider and others realized, was an authentic African sound. Somebody—nobody's sure who anymore—thought of film composer Hans Zimmer, who had used African choirs and instruments in his score for a movie set in South Africa called *The Power of One*. Zimmer listened to "Circle of Life" and said he'd "play around with it" for a couple of days. On *The Power of One* Zimmer teamed up with Lebo M., a singer and songwriter from South Africa who once worked as a parking attendant in Los Angeles. He dropped by Zimmer's studio one afternoon while Zimmer was fiddling with "Circle of Life." Lebo listened to the song and added some Zulu vocals, including the phrase *Nants ingonyama bagithi baba*. Zimmer recorded his version of the song and sent it off to Disney.

"The minute we heard it we all knew it was perfect," said Schneider. "It was the eureka moment."

The Disney marketing machine wasn't so sure about the movie, now called *The Lion King*. It was about animals. There were no people in it. And the lead character, Simba, was male. The lead characters in a Disney movie were usually girls, preferably princesses. "It was still the B-team movie," said Schneider.

The Disney equivalent of a Broadway out-of-town tryout is a screening, usually in a suburb of Los Angeles, several weeks before a movie's release. Disney screened *The Lion King* for a family audience in Woodland Hills one afternoon and then added a second screening for the date-night crowd. "All these eighteen-year-olds came in hanging all over their girlfriends," Schneider recalled. "And we thought, 'What the fuck are we doing?'" At the end of "Circle of Life," the eighteen-year-olds stood up and cheered. "And that was the first moment we knew we had a huge hit on our hands," Schneider said.

Peter Schneider joined Disney Animation in 1985 "because it fundamentally meant no difference who they hired," he said.

"Animation? Who cares? It wasn't making any money. As a matter of fact, it was losing money. I got hired because they were not picky and I was at the right place at the right time."[2]

Schneider came to Burbank by way of the theater. Raised in Wisconsin, he graduated from Purdue University with ambitions to be a director. He made his way to New York and landed a job as the company manager of *Little Shop of Horrors*, where he met Alan Menken and Howard Ashman. He had a good mind for business and marketing. His artistic tastes ran toward the avant-garde. Fast-talking, informal, and wiry, he preferred jeans, T-shirts, and sneakers (usually red) to business suits. While running the theater division of the 1984 Olympic Arts Festival in Los Angeles, he shared a small office with Thomas Schumacher, a junior member of the Mark Taper Forum staff. Schumacher had worked in puppet and children's theater in San Francisco and Los Angeles. The two became friends. When Schneider took over the entire Olympic Arts Festival, he hired Schumacher as his line producer. Schumacher went on to become associate director of the experimental Los Angeles Festival of the Arts.

The celebrated Disney Animation department—birthplace of *Snow White and the Seven Dwarfs*, *Dumbo*, *Pinocchio*, and *Fantasia*—was a shadow of itself by the 1980s. *The Rescuers* and *The Fox and the Hound* were box office hits, but hardly in league with *Sleeping Beauty* or *The Jungle Book*. *The Black Cauldron*, released in 1985, was the low point. It cost $44 million and was a critical and box office dud. The entire Walt Disney Company was in trouble in 1984, fending off takeover bids. When Roy E. Disney, Walt's nephew, gained control in 1984, he brought in Michael Eisner to salvage the company. Eisner wasn't much interested in animation—the money was in live action movies and theme parks—but Roy Disney was. He took over Animation and, at the suggestion of some friends, brought in Schneider. A few years later Schneider hired Schumacher. They made a good team. The high-strung

Schneider had a temper, especially if he hadn't eaten. Underlings called his eruptions "three-veiners" because of the veins that stood out on his forehead when he yelled. Schumacher, always dapperly dressed with a neatly trimmed mustache and designer glasses, smoothed things over with wit and charm. He could sense a three-veiner coming on and, one person said, headed it off with food.

Schneider and Schumacher brought their theater training to bear at Animation. They hired Howard Ashman and Alan Menken to write *The Little Mermaid*, approaching it as if it were a Broadway musical. Previous animated movies "had been a series of scenes, excellent scenes, but not necessarily tied together in an effective story arc, all the things we learned in our college English and theater courses," Eisner said. "Walt did that, but it was all in his head. It was never put on paper. Before we went to a storyboard, we had a script. We thought about the evolution of the characters and the plot. That was the key change. And it worked." *The Little Mermaid* was a critical and box office smash as were *Beauty and the Beast*, *Aladdin*, and *The Lion King*.

Disney was thrown into turmoil on Easter 1994 when Frank Wells died in a helicopter crash in the mountains of Nevada. Jeffrey Katzenberg assumed he'd take over Wells's job as president of the company, but Eisner took on the responsibilities instead. Furious, Katzenberg left the company a few months later to form DreamWorks with Steven Spielberg and David Geffen.

As the corporate intrigue swirled, Eisner asked Schneider and Schumacher to take over Disney's theater division, which was booming thanks to the success of *Beauty and the Beast*.

"I always thought that Michael did that to keep Peter and me excited," said Schumacher. "I think he wanted to keep us in the boat, at a time when the boat might be coming apart because Jeffrey was leaving to start his own animation company."

Fearing Katzenberg might poach two of his most valuable employees, Eisner put them in charge of what they loved most—theater. Their first project was a stage version of *Aida*, with a score by Elton John and Tim Rice. But Joe Roth, who had replaced Katzenberg as the head of the movie studio, had another idea. Walking across the Disney lot one afternoon with Eisner, he said, "Why aren't you doing *The Lion King*? How can it miss?" When Eisner proposed a *Lion King* stage musical Schumacher said, "Michael, that's a terrible idea." *Beauty and the Beast* was conceived as a musical, but *The Lion King*, Schumacher thought, was more of a film with a few songs amid Hans Zimmer's haunting score. But Eisner kept pushing. One thing he was adamant about: *The Lion King* had to be different from *Beauty and the Beast.* He knew if Disney produced another theme park show "we'd be killed." He wanted to do something "a little more adventurous." Schneider and Schumacher agreed. For two theater people who had worked with artists such as Peter Brook and Pina Bausch, *Beauty and the Beast* was too literal a rendering of the movie. It was tame and predictable. They went back to their offices to come up with a plan. Schumacher thought of someone whose work had impressed him when he was running the Los Angeles Festival of the Arts. "Peter," he said, "I'm just going to call Julie Taymor."*

Born and raised in West Newton, a tony suburb of Boston, Taymor joined the Boston Children's Theatre when she was ten. She staged plays with neighborhood kids at her large house on Fairfax Street. One neighbor said Taymor was "very determined, very disciplined, and very intense" as a teenager. She was drawn to experimental theater and, after traveling through Sri Lanka and India one summer, Asian theater. She studied mime in Paris and,

* While at the Los Angeles Festival of the Arts, Schumacher had tried to book Taymor's *Liberties Taken*, a bawdy romp through the American Revolution. It didn't work out, but he kept in touch with her.

at Oberlin College, joined an experimental theater troupe led by Herbert Blau. Taymor embraced Blau's belief in ideographs—pared down, abstract forms of expression. An example: if Blau or Taymor were to stage *Sweeney Todd*, a victim sitting in the barber chair might pull a red handkerchief from his neck to indicate his throat had been cut.[3]

After college, Taymor, thin, beautiful, and brainy, traveled through Indonesia, Japan, and Eastern Europe, learning mask work, puppetry, shadow puppetry, and Bunraku, Japanese puppetry in which the puppeteer is in full view of the audience. She lived in Indonesia for four years and established her own company called Teatr Loh. Back in America, her career took off in experimental theater with works such as *The Haggadah*, *The Transposed Heads*, and *Juan Darién, A Carnival Mass*, which featured animal puppets. Schumacher was especially impressed with her production of Stravinsky's *Oedipus Rex* starring Jessye Norman. The singers wore sculpted masks on top of their heads. "You're not going to put a mask over Jessye Norman's face," Taymor said. The audience saw the performer's face and the mask at the same time—"duality," as Taymor called it.

She demanded a lot from her actors and her audiences. When Lincoln Center Theater produced *Juan Darién*, Taymor wanted to stage the nearly three-hour work without an intermission. "Julie, the audience needs a break," the director Gregory Mosher told her. "I'm not doing it for the audience," she said. But her work was daring, gorgeous, and unexpected. The MacArthur Foundation gave her a "genius" grant in 1991.

Taymor was directing Wagner's *The Flying Dutchman* in Los Angeles when Schumacher called about *The Lion King*. She had to admit she had "not seen the animated film—or cartoon, as I would have called it," she said. "I think Tom was a little surprised." He sent her a video. "It was beautiful," she said, "and I was taken with the challenge of how to put it onstage. How was I going to stage the stampede [of the wildebeests]?" Schumacher also sent her *Rhythm of the Pride Lands*, a CD inspired by *The Lion King* with songs by Hans Zimmer, Lebo M., and Mark Mancina—including "He Lives in You"—that were not in the movie. Taymor loved it.

Eisner had never heard of Julie Taymor. "Peter and Tom told me she does this stuff in Indonesia," he said. "She does puppetry and masks and blah, blah, blah. So I studied her stuff a little bit and it sounded like a pretty good idea. Putting an artist on a very commercial idea is something I've believed in my whole life." Eisner checked out *Juan Darién* at Lincoln Center with Schneider and Schumacher. Ten minutes into it, he turned to them and whispered, "I think we have the right person."

Taymor made maquettes of the animals to give Disney an idea of what she planned to do with *The Lion King*. She took her maquettes to Orlando to show Eisner. She put them on his desk and began playing around with them. One of them was a gazelle wheel, a three-wheeled contraption that, as the wheels turned, made five gazelles leap and fall as though running across the plain. Taymor explained to Eisner that the audience would see the puppeteer pushing the gazelle wheel across the stage. "If you understand this idea, you want me," she said. "This is what I do. If you don't want to see the puppeteers, you don't want me."

"Fine," Eisner said. "We'll do it." Disney was taking a risk with Taymor. She had never worked in the commercial theater. But the company protected itself. Taymor would have to do periodic presentations to Eisner and other executives. If they did not like the direction she was going in, they could sever the relationship at any time. Taymor had a few demands of her own. She liked John and Rice's songs, but she insisted that Lebo M. join the team to fill out the score with new songs and songs from *Rhythm of the Pride Lands*.

Another demand: "I thought women were missing gravely from the story. The lionesses are really the ones who go out and get the food and run the show. The big lions are sleeping all the time.

I knew it still had to be *The Lion King*, but I wanted to develop Nala." Taymor called her friend Thuli Dumakude, a South African singer who was in *Juan Darién*, to get some names of other South African singers to be in the chorus. "There's really no role for you because there's not really any adult women in it," Taymor told her. Dumakude laughed. "There are never any parts for women," she said. A thought struck Taymor: Why not make Rafiki, the baboon medicine man, female? Disney agreed to the change.* As Eisner put it, "Eh, fine. You can do that. That's not really changing the story. It's a monkey, okay?"

As Taymor studied the animated movie, she discovered a hole in the plot. After Simba thinks he caused his father's death, he runs away from Pride Land. Scar takes over and destroys the kingdom. Nala coaxes Simba to come back, fight Scar, and take his rightful place as king. "But he doesn't go through enough of a trial to earn the mantle of king," Taymor said. So she came up with a new second act. Simba runs off into the desert and sees a city of lights, a Las Vegas–Disneyland of the Sahara. The inhabitants are half human, half animal. "Humanimals," Taymor called them. Simba falls in with some bad characters and descends into decadence. Nala, along with Simba's friends Timon, a meerkat, and Pumbaa, a warthog, save him. They convince him to return to Pride Land and confront Scar.

Taymor explained her new second act to Schumacher and "his mouth hit the floor," she recalled. "Julie, here's the thing," he said. "That's a really interesting idea. But I want to expand the material that we have. I don't want to do your version. But if your version is really important to you, then I guess we're at the place where we don't do this together." Taymor thought for a moment and said, "No, no. It was just an idea."

* Dumakude did not play the part. It went to Tsidii Le Loka, who received a Tony Award nomination.

She went back to the original script, but began to play around with the notion of the "humanimal." She wanted the audience to see the puppeteers as they manipulated the puppets. But what if she put the puppeteer, still visible, *inside* the puppet? A cheetah, for instance, with the front and back parts of the animal attached to the puppeteer who manipulates the paws with rods. Or a life-size Timon puppet attached to the actor at the feet, the actor shadowing the puppet. Or an actor on four stilts with a neck and head sprouting from the top of his head: a giraffe.

"People always think Julie's designs came first," Schumacher said. "But she focused on the plot and the character and that really liberated the big design idea."

Taymor assembled her team, few of whom came from Broadway: Michael Curry, designer and builder of puppets; Richard Hudson, from Zimbabwe and a set designer from the opera; Garth Fagan, a Jamaican choreographer from the world of modern dance; and lighting designer Donald Holder, who lit *Juan Darién*. Lebo M. continued to write new songs, with Taymor pitching in to write the lyric to "Endless Night." Taymor put together a multiethnic cast, with a chorus of singers from South Africa whom she planned to fold into the show as the landscape. At one point they would wear boards of grass on their heads to symbolize the grasslands. At her studio in the Flatiron District of New York City, Taymor, Curry, and an army of designers sculpted mask headdresses out of clay, silicone rubber, and carbon graphite—the regal Mufasa, the demented Scar, the serene Sarabi. They were working around the clock to prepare for the first reading and presentation of their designs to Disney executives in the summer of 1996.

The presentation took place at 890 Broadway (once the headquarters of *A Chorus Line*'s creator Michael Bennett) for Eisner and the "California crowd," as one person called them. Taymor displayed her designs. The actors read through the script and demonstrated puppet techniques. Mario Cantone, a comedian, played Timon. He hadn't had time to work out the puppetry so he wound up overdoing the comedy. "He was very funny, but he upstaged the puppet," Taymor said. As the day wore on, the "California crowd" became more and more skeptical. One of the executives could not grasp the idea of a mask on top of an actor's head. Is the audience going to look at the actor or are they going to look at "that African thing on their head?" the executive wanted to know.

"Do you know Bunraku?" Taymor asked the executive. He had no idea what she was talking about. Schumacher shot her a look that said, "They're film people." "Have you seen my work?" Taymor persisted. "Of course he had not," she said, "so I just shut up at that point."

Taymor had made some mistakes. The masks for Mufasa and Scar were too big, and they were white because she hadn't painted them. She knew that when completed and properly lit the audience would have no problem taking in the mask and the actor's face at the same time. But in a brightly lit rehearsal in the middle of the day, with Disney executives sitting just a few feet away from the performers, her designs were a bust.

Eisner and the other executives got into their SUVs, leaving Taymor, Schneider, and Schumacher "sick to our stomachs" at the curb, Schumacher recalled. Then Schneider turned to Taymor and said, "We failed you, Julie, because we put your stuff in a room where it couldn't be properly evaluated. We need to get this back in front of Michael."

Taymor had a thought. "I'm not pushing the puppetry," she said. "There are different ways we could do this." She asked if she could present three versions of Timon, Scar, and Zazu. Disney could then decide which version it liked best. "Just give me a couple of weeks," she said. Her "puppet workshop," as it was being called,

21

Fran and Barry Weissler, circa 1970 (I date the picture from Barry's shirt). Barry, a struggling actor, formed a theatrical company that did Shakespeare plays in small theaters in New Jersey. Fran, in the process of getting a divorce, volunteered to work in the box office at a theater in West Orange the day Barry's production of *The Taming of the Shrew* came to town. Barry noticed her, and struck up a conversation. She was not impressed. "He was short compared to my husband. And he had no money. All he had was a dream of going to Broadway one day."

22

William Ivey Long's costume sketch for Denise Faye, one of the merry murderesses in *Chicago*. Long had a costume budget of just $2,000 for the four-performance concert at City Center. He told the actors to wear their own clothes, which he supplemented with pieces of clothing he found in second-hand stores. For a photo shoot before *Chicago* moved to Broadway, Fran Weissler told Long she wanted the actors to wear clothes by famous designers. "No way," said director Walter Bobbie. "This is our show." Long pretended to look at designer clothing but used none of it. During the photo shoot, he hid in a dressing room.

23

The author with James M. Nederlander, on his ninety-second birthday. Nederlander gave Fran and Barry Weissler the Richard Rodgers Theatre for *Chicago*, but only for nine weeks. "I've got *Steel Pier* coming in next season," he told them. "That's the new Kander and Ebb show. You've got the old chestnut." The morning after *Chicago* opened to raves, Nederlander called the Weisslers and said, "Fuck *Steel Pier*!"

24

The author with Fran Weissler (center) and Betty Jacobs at a dinner party at the Weisslers' estate in Westchester. The success of *Chicago* enabled the Weisslers to buy the twenty-two-acre estate, which boasts an amphitheater designed by artist Beverly Pepper. Posters of the Weisslers' many shows line the wall of a long hallway in the main house. Giving a tour to a visitor, Fran said of the *Chicago* poster, "This is the show that built this house." When she came to *Seussical, the Musical*, which lost $10 million, she said, "And this is the show that almost made us sell this house."

25

Isabelle Stevenson, a Park Avenue grand dame, and her husband, John Stevenson, ran the American Theatre Wing, which owns the copyright on the Tony Award. Stevenson fiercely protected the integrity of the award, fending off the League of American Theatres and Producers, which wanted to exploit the Tony's marketing potential. But Stevenson could be a little old-fashioned when it came new musicals such as *Rent*. She once asked Angela Wendt, the show's costume designer, where Wendt had found the costumes. When Wendt said Daffy's and the Salvation Army, Stevenson "almost fainted," Wendt recalled.

26

Garth Drabinsky surrounded by the cast, creative team, and crew of *Ragtime* on the first day of rehearsal in Toronto. The show was a smash in Toronto, winning raves and breaking box office records. Jon Wilner, one of Drabinsky's advertising executives, pleaded with him to move it to Broadway immediately. But Drabinsky wanted to wait until The Ford Center for the Performing Arts was finished. *Ragtime*, he said, was the perfect musical to christen his perfect theater. He took the show to Los Angeles first, where it lost millions of dollars. When *Ragtime* opened in New York, it was up against Disney's *The Lion King*. "And that was the beginning of the end," said Wilner.

27

Lyricist Tim Rice with his EGOTs—Emmy, Grammy, Oscar, and Tony. Still smarting from the bruising failure of his Broadway musical *Chess*, Rice was hanging around the Disney studios in Los Angeles doing "song placement—whatever that means," he said, for a Dolly Parton movie called *Straight Talk*. One day Rice met with Peter Schneider and Thomas Schumacher, who were running Disney's animation department. They told him about a movie they were working on called *King of the Jungle*, about a lion cub named Simba, who must earn the right to take over his murdered father's kingdom. Schneider and Schumacher asked Rice if there was a composer he'd like to work with. "Elton John," Rice said. "I was trying to salvage my career at that point. I knew working with Elton couldn't hurt."

28

Julie Taymor working on the mask of Scar. The mask of Mufasa is to the right. Taymor worked in experimental theater, winning acclaim for her productions of *Juan Darién, A Carnival Mass* and Stravinsky's *Oedipus Rex*, starring Jessye Norman (who wore a Taymor-sculpted mask on top of her head). Thomas Schumacher was a fan of her work and called her about directing a stage version of *The Lion King* for Disney. "I had not seen the animated film—or cartoon, as I would have called it," she said. Schumacher sent her a video. "It was beautiful," she said.

29

Julie Taymor selecting patterns for the lionesses' costumes. Not a single detail of *The Lion King* escaped Taymor. But when she presented her first workshop of the show to Disney executives, they were not impressed. As Michael Eisner and his retinue climbed into their black SUVs after the workshop, Taymor, Peter Schneider, and Thomas Schumacher were left standing on the curb "sick to our stomachs," Schumacher recalled. Schneider said, "We failed you, Julie, because we put your stuff in a room where it couldn't be properly evaluated. We need to get this back in front of Michael."

30

Julie Taymor rehearsing John Vickery as Scar. A classically trained actor, Vickery admired Taymor but sometimes thought she paid more attention to the puppet than him. Previews in Minneapolis were stressful, grueling, and sometimes dangerous. The actor operating the four stilts on the giraffe puppet "went splat," Vickery recalled. "For a few seconds we thought he was dead." Vickery went to an army surplus store and bought the stage managers medic helmets. "That's the kind of humor we had about it," he said.

31

Julie Taymor with Disney's Thomas Schumacher during rehearsals at the Orpheum Theatre in Minneapolis for *The Lion King*. Taymor is seated on a Barcalounger to ease the discomfort from having had her gall bladder removed. The crew dubbed her throne the "Bark-a-lounge" because she barked instructions from it over a microphone. Taymor, Schumacher, and Peter Schneider nervously huddled at the back of the theater for the first public performance. They had no idea how it would go down. "If I were an older man, I would have pooped my pants," Schumacher said.

32

Julie Taymor takes a rare break from directing *The Lion King* in Minneapolis. Seated next to her is Tsidii Le Loka, who would be nominated for her unforgettable performance as Rafiki. Le Loka opened "The Circle of Life" with a Zulu chant. As the giant, shimmering sun rose above the stage, giraffe puppets loped out, and the parade of animals came down the aisles, theatergoers at the first preview in Minneapolis gasped in astonishment. Then they stood on their seats and cheered and cheered and cheered. John Vickery, as Scar, had to go on next. *How the fuck am I going to follow this?* he thought. "It was like going on after the Beatles," he recalled.

33

Julie Taymor with the creative team on the opening night of *The Lion King* at the New Amsterdam Theatre. Roger Allers (far left), bookwriter; Garth Fagan, choreographer; Michael Curry, puppet designer; Lebo M., composer; Elton John; Mark Mancina, composer; Thomas Schumacher (wearing glasses) and Peter Schneider, the Disney executives who produced *The Lion King*. Towering above them all is lyricist Tim Rice. The opening-night audience was packed with celebrities, including Rosie O'Donnell. Director Francis Ford Coppola, standing on his seat, led the ovation for Taymor when she took her bow.

34

Costume designer William Ivey Long with Victor Garber and producer Elizabeth Williams at the opening night party for *Crazy for You* in 1992. Susan Stroman, who choreographed the show, got to know Long and set designer Robin Wagner on *Crazy for You*. During the Washington, D.C., tryout, she came to the theater early one morning to work out some choreography and found Wagner with a can of paint touching up his set and Long, down on all fours, painting the showgirls' shoes. "I knew then these were the two men I always want to work with," she said.

35

William Ivey Long's sketch for Roger de Bris' costume for "Keep It Gay" in *The Producers*. "I'm supposed to be the Duchess of Anastasia," De Bris (played by Gary Beach) says. "But I think I look more like the Chrysler Building." De Bris introduces his creative team, all flamboyant gay men but for his lighting designer, a lesbian. "Well, if we're going to go there, we might as well go all the way," Long said. He designed a BDSM leather outfit; a lavender suit with lavender shoes and glasses; and a crop top and bell-bottomed pants. He put the lighting designer in a baggy flannel shirt and work boots. For kicks, he threw in the sailor and the Indian chief from the Village People.

36

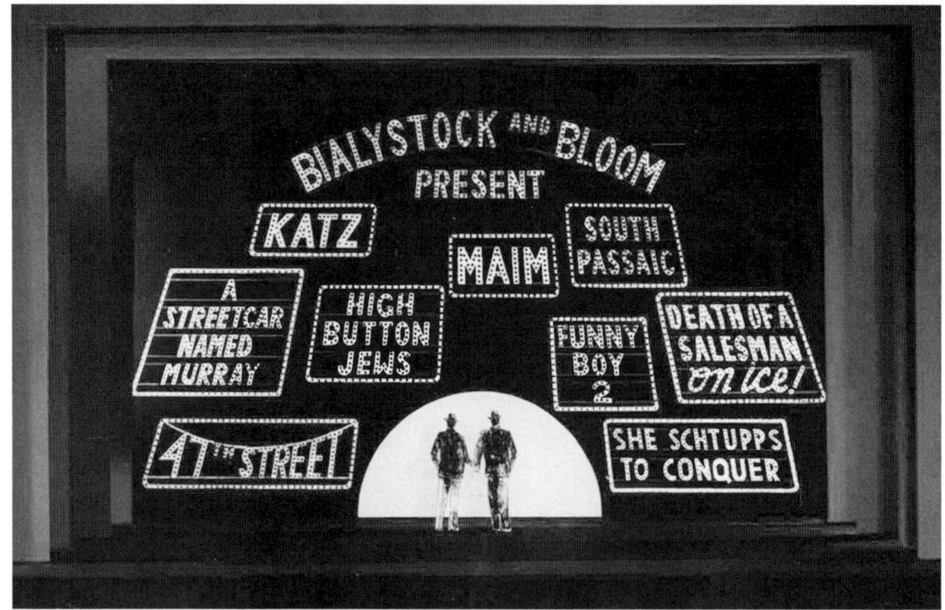

Robin Wagner's set design for the final scene of *The Producers*, as Max and Leo walk off arm-in-arm and point to all the shows they're going to produce. Wagner, Mel Brooks, and Tom Meehan came up with the funny titles. *The Producers* tipped its hat to many great shows of the past, and so did Wagner's sets, which evoked *Follies; Kiss Me, Kate; Gypsy*; *Cabaret*; and *A Chorus Line*. Brooks loved all of Wagner's designs until he saw this one. "Are you crazy?" he said. "That's not how you spell *shtups*!"

37

Matthew Broderick and Nathan Lane rehearsing *The Producers*. Lane joined the production as Max Bialystock early on. Broderick kept reading in theater columns that Brooks wanted him to play Leo Bloom, "but nobody called me," he said. Then he met Brooks and some Hollywood producers about doing a movie. After the meeting, Brooks took him aside and invited him to hear some songs he'd written for *The Producers*. Broderick then did a reading of the show with Lane. It went well, but both actors thought some of the jokes were from another era and might land with a thud in 1999. "This is either going to be the biggest hit or the biggest flop ever," Lane told Broderick.

was done at the Palace Theatre for an audience of one—Michael Eisner, seated in the tenth row so he was not on top of the actors John Vickery (Scar), Geoff Hoyle (Zazu), and Max Casella, now playing Timon.

First up was a traditional rendering of the animals. Vickery was in a lion costume "that was sort of like *Cats*," he said. Casella was in a meerkat outfit. Hoyle wore a beak and did not have the hornbill bird puppet on his head. Next came a hybrid of the animal costume and the puppetry, with Vickery wearing a half mask on his face. Finally, Taymor presented her original designs—the Scar headdress on top of Vickery's head; the Timon puppet attached to Casella, shadowed by him; Hoyle with Zazu on his head. The masks, now in proper proportion, were painted, the actors were in costume and makeup, and Donald Holder did the lighting.

"I'm going with your original idea, Julie," Eisner said. "The bigger the risk, the bigger the payoff."

At which point Vickery decided to quit. The forty-pound headdress was giving him headaches. The electronics used to operate it "worked less than fifty percent of the time." And as the headdress extended out over his head and neck, "I was doing things the human body isn't supposed to do." He told Disney, "This is going to injure me." Disney threw enough money at him that he stayed, but his fear of injury was not unfounded. Taymor's puppets made extraordinary demands on the actors.

Rehearsals for *The Lion King* began in May 1997. Everything was compartmentalized. The dancers worked with Fagan in one studio. The actors worked with their puppets in another. They had to learn in a few months what puppeteers in Indonesia and Japan spent lifetimes mastering. The cast rehearsed musical numbers in one room, dramatic scenes in another. New lyrics by Tim Rice were coming over the fax machine. It was as though armies were marching on several fronts, with Taymor—"General Patton," as some called her—in command of it all. She had the whole show mapped out in her mind, and always seemed to know what she wanted. A cardinal rule: never upstage the puppet. "Sometimes you got the feeling she was directing the puppet and not you," Vickery said. But she was open to good ideas no matter whose they were. Kevin Cahoon, playing one of the hyenas, told her he thought his character was the runt of the litter. "He always gets the scraps," he said. "I wish we could see his ribs." Great idea, Taymor said, and then redesigned the costume.

The actors were never quite sure what was going on, but there were moments when they realized *The Lion King* was reaching for, and achieving, artistry. When Fagan, who kept his dancers sequestered, first presented the lionesses' dance to the whole company, Hoyle was knocked out. "It was so beautiful and very touching," he said. But the dance was so demanding he wondered how the women would be able to do it eight times a week. "If you're in a modern dance company, maybe you do it three nights, and then you take a break," he said. There were no breaks on *The Lion King*. "We were being pushed beyond the limits of the human body," Vickery said.

Taymor spent a lot of time putting together "Circle of Life." It was the opening, and the staging had to capture the spirituality of the song. It begins with the sun rising over the Serengeti. "I could do a sunrise with a projection," Taymor said, "but I made a commitment to doing theater at its most poetic. And that is often minimalist." She made her sunrise out of bamboo rods and pieces of silk. "It was a pile on the ground and then as that incredible song happens the audience sees the strings that make it rise, and I knew because of Don Holder's lighting and the natural air, it would do the shimmer," she said.

It was impossible to see in the rehearsal studio what Taymor saw in her head. There was no Don Holder lighting, no animal procession coming down the aisles of the theater. The actors playing the giraffes couldn't wear their long neck headdresses because the ceiling was too low. And Pride Rock, designed by Richard Hudson to spiral up from below the stage, elevating Mufasa, Sarabi, and baby Simba, was still being built in the scene shop. Kevin Cahoon was assigned to be the right leg of a life-size elephant puppet, which was still being developed. He and the three other legs "just walked side by side in rehearsals."

As Taymor was rehearsing *The Lion King*, Michael Eisner was getting ready to unveil the refurbished New Amsterdam Theatre. At one point the man who did not want to be on Broadway got a little carried away with some plans for Forty-Second Street. He wanted to close it and build a deck above it featuring a New York–themed entertainment park. "And then somebody pointed out to me that the exit out of the Lincoln Tunnel depends on Forty-Second Street," Eisner said. "So that didn't happen."

Disney cut a good deal with the city to redo the New Amsterdam. With tax breaks and subsidies, "basically the New Amsterdam was given to us," said Eisner. But now that Disney was coming to Times Square, other companies were as well, including AMC, the movie chain; Condé Nast, publisher of *Vanity Fair* and *Vogue*; and Madame Tussauds. And directly across the street from the New Amsterdam, Garth Drabinsky was building his theater for *Ragtime*.

Mayor Giuliani deployed zoning laws and policing to get rid of the peep shows, porn houses, drug dealers, hookers, hustlers, and muggers. Some of his solutions were, and remain, controversial, but they got results. As Darrell Deckard, a black hustler, said at the time: "*More* police; and *less* money. People be scared now, you know what I'm sayin'? They stay home. Makes you wanna get a regular job."[4]

Disney opened the New Amsterdam Theatre on May 18, 1997, with a concert version of *King David*, a new musical by Alan

Menken and Tim Rice. Disney put a tent over West Forty-First Street from Seventh to Eighth Avenues and threw a lavish party. *King David* had some good songs, but even Rice thought the concert was "boring." The critics were tepid, but they raved about the refurbished New Amsterdam Theatre. And that was the point.

The Lion King decamped to Minneapolis in May to prepare for its first public performance on July 8 at the Orpheum Theatre. So began perhaps the most grueling technical rehearsal in the history of the American theater. Taymor was a perfectionist, spending an entire day teching a scene that lasted two minutes. It took five days to tech "Circle of Life."

A week or so into rehearsals Taymor fell ill. She thought it was food poisoning. It turned out to be her gallbladder. It was removed, but she was back at the Orpheum the next day. She directed prostrate on a Barcalounger. The crew dubbed it the "Bark-a-lounge" because she'd "bark" instructions from it over a microphone.

Much of Taymor's work was simple and poetic. A large piece of blue silk pulled through a hole in the stage symbolized a drought. Mourning the death of Mufasa, the lionesses pulled long pieces of white crepe paper from the eyes of their masks to symbolize tears. But the production had some enormous sets, including Pride Rock and an elephant graveyard, both of which spiraled up from beneath the stage. Taymor had solved the problem of putting a wildebeest stampede onstage by creating a series of giant rollers with wildebeests attached to them. The contraption weighed more than a ton. And sometimes the wildebeests would fly off. The backstage choreography was as intricate as it was onstage. If you were in the wrong place at the wrong time "you might get killed," one actor said. Stage managers told Taymor there were so many costume changes in the first act that it was "chaos" backstage. They urged her to come back and take a look. "I don't think I should," she said, "because then I'll feel bad. You guys work it out."*

Performers did get injured. The dancers called the show's love duet "Can You Feel the Pain Tonight?" Disney employed physical therapists to massage sore backs and muscles. The four stilts in one of the giraffe puppets gave out one day and the actor "went splat," said Vickery. "For a few seconds we thought he was dead." Vickery went to an army surplus store and bought the stage managers medic helmets. "If that happens again, just kill him and drag him off the stage," he told them. "That's the kind of humor we had about it," he said later.

Tempers flared. One day, Vickery got stranded in an elevator on one side of the stage for two hours. When he got out, he exploded at Taymor. "It really wasn't her fault," he said, "but I'd just had enough. I said, 'Fuck you. I'm going to have a cigarette. I'll be back when I feel like it.'" Taymor, working on little sleep, remained focused and determined. But even she had a meltdown one day. Nobody remembers the cause, but she locked herself in the ladies' room. Her assistant—patient, calm—coaxed her back to work.

Hovering over it all were Schneider and Schumacher. Schneider sometimes lost his temper if he didn't eat ("Eat meat, Pete," people would tell him). Schumacher, the "master schmoozer," as Eisner called him, made jokes to diffuse tense situations. They had worries of their own, though. *The Lion King* wasn't selling as well as they'd hoped. It went on sale in New York that spring and promptly took in $5 million. But in the summer, sales tapered off. And they were not great in Minneapolis. The July 8 preview was only half sold. They thought about canceling it. They still had not run the show from start to finish. A few days before the first preview they realized to their horror that there would be a long

* They did, and when Taymor eventually watched the show from backstage she wept. "They had done such a beautiful job," she said.

delay in the first act. Two scenes featuring gigantic sets—the elephant graveyard and the stampede—were back to back. It would take several minutes to change the scene.

As the audience settled into its seats at the Orpheum Theatre on July 8, 1997, Schneider and Schumacher walked onstage. They introduced themselves and explained that what was about to unfold was a work in progress. "Tonight, not only do you get an intermission, you get a pause during the first act," they said. "Now, intermission is very different from a pause. Intermission is you get up from your seat and go to the bathroom. A pause, which is a few minutes, is when you turn to your neighbor and say, 'It's going well, isn't it?'" The audience howled. Watching from the back of the theater, Chris Boneau, the show's press agent, thought Schneider and Schumacher were like "Hope and Crosby."

Their curtain speech over, the two bolted to the back of the theater to sit with Taymor and watch the first public performance of *The Lion King*. "We were terrified," said Schumacher. "If I were an older man I would have pooped in my pants."

The house went dark and then Tsidii Le Loka, as Rafiki, pierced the silence with a Zulu chant. She called out to South African singers scattered in the boxes of the theater. They called back. The orchestra began playing, slowly at first, Elton John's theme as the giant sun, nothing but bamboo and silk, rose from the back of the stage. Two life-size giraffe puppets loped in from stage left. A cheetah puppet appeared from stage right, licking its paw. A bird woman fluttered across the stage, followed by three zebras, their heads attached to the puppeteers' chests, their hindquarters attached the puppeteers' backs. Three dancers holding gazelle puppets in both hands with a third gazelle attached to their heads leapt across the stage. The audience, stunned at the beauty of what they were seeing, began to cheer. Children stood on their parents' lap to take it all in. Then they whipped around to see a procession of animals—a rhinoceros, more bird ladies, a giant elephant followed by its baby—make its way down the aisles of the theater. Kevin Cahoon, peering out from a slit in the elephant's leg, saw astounded looks on both children and adults. People were clutching each other and pointing everywhere. Many people, he noticed, were wiping away tears. Pride Rock spiraled up from below the stage. Mufasa and Sarabi, holding baby Simba, climbed to the top. Rafiki joined them to bless the lion cub. As she hit the last note of the song she held Simba high above her head for everyone to see. Blackout.

And then came a roar from the audience unlike anything the performers had ever heard in a theater before. People were standing on their seats cheering and applauding. At the back of the theater, Taymor, Schumacher, and Schneider looked at one another and burst into tears.

John Vickery was not in the opening number. He was in the next scene. When "Circle of Life" ended he thought, *How the fuck am I going to follow this?* "It was like going on after the Beatles," he said.

The rest of the show couldn't top the opening number, but there were many wonders along the way—the grass heads, the gazelle wheel, the lionesses' dance, the Timon and Pumbaa puppets, Mufasa's giant face materializing from out of nowhere during "He Lives in You." The show may have been a bit long. But the audience didn't care. They would have stayed all night. Houses for the first week of previews were three-quarters full. By the second week there wasn't a seat to be had. *The Lion King* was the biggest hit Minneapolis had ever seen.

It took a few days for reports to filter back to New York. Nancy Coyne, a partner in the advertising firm Serino, Coyne & Nappi, was one of the first to hear something special was happening in Minneapolis. She wasn't doing the ad campaign. Disney had hired the powerful Grey Advertising. But a friend said to Coyne, "There's a show in Minneapolis. I don't know what they're doing with the advertising, but they're not doing it right. You should go out there and see it." She did, buying her own tickets and not letting anyone from the show know she was there. "I swear it was not a scouting expedition," she said. "I just wanted to see it." She expected another *Beauty and the Beast.* "Ten minutes into it I knew I had to be on the show," she said. She heard the show wasn't selling well in New York. She analyzed the ad and marketing campaigns. Disney was targeting the traditional family audience by offering "a gazillion little plastic *Lion King* watches" with the purchase of a ticket. But the show she had seen was not just for kids. Disney had it backward. They were going after the family audience first. The family audience "would always be there," Coyne said. "My goal was that people who've already bought four tickets to *The Lion King* will not take their children first. They will take the husband's client and take their children later."

Coyne arranged a meeting with Schumacher and Schneider, whom she'd never met. Rick Elice, her creative director, went with her. "Our pitch was rather brilliant and very, very simple," he said. "Well, we didn't know that it was brilliant, but we knew it was simple. The ads say 'Disney presents *The Lion King.*' Our premise was: What if it says 'The Royal Shakespeare Company presents *The Lion King*'? What would the media buy be then? Who would we target? The cognoscenti, the tastemakers, the opinion makers, the people who wouldn't go to see *Beauty and the Beast*, but who will go to see Julie Taymor's brilliant artwork."

Schneider and Schumacher listened to the pitch. "That's a brilliant strategy, brilliantly articulated," Schumacher said. Grey was out. Serino, Coyne was in.

Press agent Chris Boneau was already working the cognoscenti. He gave *Time* exclusive access to the creative team during the Minneapolis tryout. The favorable article alerted *Time*'s millions of readers that *The Lion King* was no *Beauty and the Beast*, and that Julie Taymor was a genius. Boneau had to deal with the most powerful tastemaker of all—the *New York Times*. The paper, somewhat hostile to Disney and the "Disneyfication of Broadway," assigned one of its star reporters, the much-feared and powerful Alex Witchel (Frank Rich's wife), to profile Taymor. Witchel wanted to shadow her on the day of the Minneapolis opening. She wanted to be with Taymor when she picked up her boyfriend, composer Elliot Goldenthal, at the airport. She wanted to write about the designer dress Taymor had selected for the big event and where she was having her hair done.

"That's insulting," Taymor said. "If they want to do a story about me as an artist, fine. But I'm not doing a story about what I'm going to wear."

Boneau had to tell Witchel the story was off. She was furious. A few days later, while taking a break on Fire Island, Boneau got a phone call. "Hi, it's Virginia for Michael Eisner. Please hold for Michael." Boneau's legs buckled. "I just got a call from Frank Rich," Eisner said. "He's not happy that you told Alex we're not doing that story for the *Times*. What's going on?" Boneau, fearing he was about to be fired, told Eisner what Taymor had said.

"Well, Frank's pissed, but Julie's right and you're right," Eisner said. "You did the right thing. It's okay. Good-bye." Boneau let out a deep breath. But now he had another problem: the *New York Times* had one more reason not to like Disney or *The Lion King*.

Another crisis erupted when Ward Morehouse III, the widely read but unreliable theater columnist for the *New York Post*, reported that the show was scaring children. It wasn't remotely true—and it was never clear if Morehouse had even seen the show in Minneapolis—but it wasn't helpful. The *New York Daily News* sent me to check out the show. With some time to kill the night I arrived in Minneapolis, I wandered over to the Orpheum to eavesdrop on audience members. I walked around to the back of the theater a few minutes after the show had started and heard a strange sound. It was a roar coming through the concrete wall. Whatever was going on inside sure wasn't scaring kids. The next day I took my seat in the orchestra. I'd heard the show was good, but I was skeptical. I didn't care for *Beauty and the Beast*, and while I admired Taymor, I couldn't see how she fit into the Magic Kingdom. I was, frankly, hoping "disaster's in the air," as Tim Rice wrote. At the end of "Circle of Life," I was on my feet with fifteen hundred other audience members cheering and applauding. After the show I met for the first time Schneider, Schumacher, and Taymor. They asked what I thought. "I think you have the biggest hit on your hands since *The Phantom of the Opera*," I said.

Garth Drabinsky hadn't been paying much attention to *The Lion King*. It was a kids' show, he thought. But now he, too, was hearing the buzz from Minneapolis. He dispatched Hailey Lustig, a production assistant at Livent, to check it out. She was to tell no one she was going. Drabinsky didn't want anyone to think he was worried. "I lied and called in sick," she said. Nobody from Disney knew she was there. "I remember being stunned at the opening and then the stampede," she said. "There was something magical about the production." Lustig had to write up a report for Drabinsky. She was "terrified" to tell him the truth. Her report stressed that *The Lion King* was a family show and would "court a much different audience from *Ragtime*." She concluded with a brilliant thread of the needle: "Having both shows run across the street from each other will only serve to make Forty-Second Street the most important destination for theater this year."*

* "She wasn't sent by me," Drabinsky said of Lustig's trip to Minneapolis. "She worked underneath Marty Bell."

* * *

The Lion King played its first preview at the New Amsterdam Theatre on October 15, 1997. Disney invited Rosie O'Donnell to an early preview. She went back the next day with her two-year-old son. On her television show, she called it "the best show I have seen in my thirty-five years," and told her millions of viewers to get tickets before the reviews came out. That endorsement, along with the tremendous word of mouth racing around the city, drove the advance to nearly $20 million by November 13, opening night.

The cognoscenti and the opinion makers turned out for the opening. O'Donnell was there for the third time. Elton John, seeing the show for the first time, broke down at intermission and told friends that Princess Diana, killed that summer in a car crash in Paris, "would have loved it."[5] Director Francis Ford Coppola, standing on his seat, led the ovation for Taymor at the curtain call.

Garth Drabinsky sat across the aisle from me that night. He joined the standing ovation, but I noticed the color had drained from his face.

CHAPTER FIFTEEN

THE UNMAKING OF A MOGUL

With *Ragtime* selling out in Toronto, Drabinsky turned his attention to the $4.5 million revival of *Candide*, directed by Hal Prince. The musical, with a celebrated score by Leonard Bernstein, Richard Wilbur, and Stephen Sondheim, had been done on Broadway twice, but in recent years had migrated to opera houses. At a meeting in Toronto, Marty Bell told staffers Livent's *Candide* "is going to be the greatest revival of all time."

"Has anybody in this room heard of *Chicago*?" Jon Wilner asked.

"That's just a concert," Drabinsky said.

"Yeah, a concert that's selling out eight performances a week on Broadway," Wilner said.

Candide opened to tepid reviews at the Gershwin in April 1997. Philip J. Smith, the president of the Shubert Organization, was at the opening-night party. "This is a tough one," he told Drabinsky.

"Don't worry," Drabinsky replied. "All I have to do is spend a few more dollars." And he did. He ordered Wilner to run ads in the *New York Times* promoting free parking with the purchase of full-price orchestra seats. Wilner exploded. "No one is buying a full-price seat! It's not happening. They don't want to see the show. You think they're going to come for fucking free parking? You should say they only have three weeks left to see the show. At least you're being honest." Mary Bryant, Hal Prince's press agent, was furious, too. "You think you did Hal a favor by bringing this show in? Well, you didn't do Hal a favor." In the end, even Drabinsky couldn't pretend the show was hit. He closed it after just 104 performances.

Drabinsky prepared a second company of *Ragtime* to open at the Shubert Theatre in Los Angeles in the summer of 1997. He wanted to return in triumph to the town that had humiliated him. He bore down on *Ragtime*, refining and tinkering with it. He conducted audience focus groups. "He made us sit in a room with a two-way mirror and people would be asked 'Who is your least favorite character?' or 'What song do you like the least?'" Terrence McNally said. "Nobody ever asked, 'Who's your favorite character? What's your favorite song.' I remember one woman saying, 'I thought there'd be more Charlestons in it.'"

Ragtime opened to a star-studded first night crowd in Los Angeles—Morgan Freeman, Ian McKellen, Quincy Jones, Bob Mackie—and strong reviews. But Los Angeles is a notoriously tough town for theater, and *Ragtime* couldn't conquer it. Drabinsky threw money at the $10 million production, but it staggered to a close. "It was a disaster," said Robert Topol, Livent's chief operating officer. "*Candide* was a disaster. We were bleeding cash."

In New York, Drabinsky was rushing to finish his theater on Forty-Second Street for the opening of *Ragtime* in January 1998. He claimed the theater was coming in on budget, but people around him had doubts. Wilner could see the construction site from his office window. Drabinsky came to the office one hot summer day and surveyed the scene. "There was a big hole in the street and tons of construction workers and they're not doing anything," Wilner said. "There's not a bulldozer, there's not a wrench, there's nothing. Just two hundred people sitting around eating lunch."

Drabinsky and Wilner rushed to the site. "I'm Garth Drabinsky. Where's the foreman?" Drabinsky bellowed. The construction workers weren't impressed. "We're waiting for the steel," someone said. "Can't do anything until the steel comes."

Every day, no matter where he was in the world, Drabinsky would call Wilner and ask, "Is the steel there?"

"No steel yet," Wilner would say. A month later, Wilner was able to report, "Garth, I see steel. The steel is here." Drabinsky was overjoyed. Wilner heard him over the phone tell his staff, "The steel is there! The steel is there!" The staff applauded.

As *Ragtime* was faltering in Los Angeles, *The Lion King* was exploding in New York. The advance climbed to $30 million with no end in sight. Even the *New York Times*, whose critic Ben Brantley praised Taymor but turned up his nose at the "heartwarming storytelling," had to get into the act. The paper published a pretentious editorial praising Disney for allowing Taymor to "unmask" and "de-cloy" the "anthropomorphism of [the company's] animated animal films."

The elite tastemakers Coyne had urged Disney to pursue flocked to the show. Every night Kevin Cahoon looked out from his slit in the elephant leg and saw, "Warren Beatty's astounded face and Aretha Franklin's astounded face and Gerald and Betty Ford's astounded faces."

Rosie O'Donnell, the musical's biggest champion, talked about it on her show many times. She wanted the cast to perform "Circle of Life." Disney was reluctant. Much of the number's power came from the element of surprise. Audiences had never seen anything like it. But the Queen of Nice knew when to be tough. "Do you want my support?" she said. The cast performed the opening number for the first time outside the theater on her show.

Drabinsky countered *Lion King* hype by spending obscene amounts of money promoting *Ragtime* in the papers and on television and radio. "I think Garth was starting to get desperate," said Wilner. "We had to have a different ad, a different logo every week." Drabinsky wanted ads that said, "This is the musical everyone should see." An exasperated Wilner snapped, "No, it should be the musical everyone *wants* to see."

An odd incident occurred one day that rattled Wilner. One of Drabinsky's accountants showed up at his office and asked if he could have some of Wilner's billing stationery. Wilner said no. Then he told his business partner, "Lock up the stationery. Something's funny. Lock it up."

Drabinsky was promoting *Ragtime* on all fronts. On the Forty-Third Street side of the Ford Center, he placed a replica Ford Model T and, in enormous letters, the phrase "Wheels of a Dream." The creators were horrified. The *New York Times* building was across the street. The *Times* might think the show was pandering to the Ford Motor Company. "Are you crazy?" said Ahrens. "Take that down now."

Ragtime played its first preview on December 26, 1997. Drabinsky was in a good mood. He'd given his girlfriend, Karen, a pair of diamond earrings for Christmas. Drabinsky was still married to his first wife, Pearl, whom he met at university, but had walked out on the marriage years earlier. (Pearl kept his office in their home exactly the way it was the day he left.) Now he was talking about getting a divorce and marrying Karen. "Look at the earrings Garth gave me," Karen said at intermission. Norman Zaiger, Livent's press agent, said, "Yeah, I picked them out."

"Karen's head did a Linda Blair," Wilner recalled. "There was a big fight at intermission. She made mincemeat of Garth right there."

Watching the first preview, Terrence McNally had a sinking feeling. "It felt a little tired," he said. "What was raw in Toronto was over-rehearsed. We picked at it too much. It was noble and high-minded and felt self-important. And with all the publicity, and putting that car out in front of the theater, there was maybe a certain smugness." Wilner had the same feeling. "It was like they were doing the Ten Commandments. It felt heavy."

Drabinsky couldn't, or wouldn't, acknowledge that. *Ragtime*, he said, "is the great American musical." He was so confident in the show he created the VIP suite. For the price of $126, the highest ever on Broadway, VIPs got prime orchestra seats, free coat checking, a souvenir program, and free food and drinks in a private room at intermission. Drabinsky claimed the seats were sold out for a year.[1]

As befitting "the great American musical," he threw a lavish opening-night party at the Waldorf-Astoria. While Drabinsky held court, accepting congratulations from Broadway's power brokers, Wilner and Bryant slipped away to pick up the early edition of the *New York Times*. They read Ben Brantley's review in Wilner's office.

"Blessed with beauty, ambition, a smashing wardrobe, and a social conscience, 'Ragtime' would seem to be the kind of musical that brings Broadway audiences to their knees in adoration," he wrote. "Then why does this ten million dollar show . . . feel so utterly resistible?" It went downhill from there. *Ragtime* lacked "a distinctive human personality." It was "static" with the "earnestness of a civics lesson." Then he slit its throat. *The Lion King* . . . "is stamped with the idiosyncratic vision of one person, Julie Taymor, its director and designer. 'Ragtime,' on the other hand, has the aura of something assembled by corporate committee."[2]

Wilner, his business partner Peter LeDonne, and Bryant sat in silence. Drabinsky arrived with Karen and a pizza. Wilner read the review from start to finish betraying no emotion. When he was done Drabinsky got up and went to the men's room. LeDonne followed him. Drabinsky stood over a sink and spit up blood. LeDonne tried to give him water, but Drabinsky brushed him aside. "I'm fine," he said. Then he and Karen left the office.

Wilner and Bryant collected the other reviews, most of which were favorable. Wilner weaved the money quotes into a bright, splashy ad featuring colored lights and fireworks. Drabinsky arrived the next morning and approved the ad. It ran once, but then "the committee in Toronto" nixed it, Wilner said. *Ragtime* was an important new American musical. Wilner's ad "made it look like Radio City Music Hall," the Toronto people said. They designed a more dignified ad to convey the show's significance. Wilner threw up his hands in disgust.

A few weeks after the opening of *Ragtime*, I interviewed Drabinsky for the *Daily News* in his lavish new offices above the Ford Center. His window looked down on *The Lion King* marquee on the other side of Forty-Second Street. Drabinsky was affable until I brought up rumors that Livent was in financial trouble because of lavish spending. "I hope you put this cost thing to bed," Drabinsky said, pounding his desk so hard that my tape recorder fell off it. "There is no organization that can produce shows with more discipline and frugality than we do." When I brought up Drabinsky's tenure at Cineplex Odeon and wondered if perhaps Livent was overexpanding, Drabinsky erupted. "Stop! Don't write that. We set in motion a game plan in 1993 to build new theaters. We need those theaters to fulfill the commercial and artistic aspirations of our company. That game plan is nearly complete, and we are not doing anything else. So it isn't a question of overexpansion." The eruption passed. Drabinsky leaned back in his chair. Speaking quietly he said, "I hope people understand that my motivations are purely one of love for this industry. I work hard to achieve my objectives, artistic and commercial. And I am dedicated to spending the rest of my life in this business."[3]

Ragtime's many good reviews, and Drabinsky's spending to advertise them, drove ticket sales. The musical had an advance of several million dollars. But as winter gave way to spring, Robert Topol, monitoring ticket sales hourly from Toronto, could see softness. The advance wasn't climbing. And for a show with a weekly overhead of more than $500,000 that would soon become a problem. Topol looked at his spreadsheets and thought, *Unless* Ragtime *wins the Tony, it's history.*

Ragtime picked up thirteen Tony nominations in May, edging out *The Lion King* by two. Both were nominated for the top prize—Best Musical. Drabinsky's Tony strategy was simple: drive home the point that *Ragtime* was an important new American musical. Tony voters might be impressed with Taymor's puppets, but surely they were not going to give Best Musical to a kiddie show. "We're going to win," he told anxious Livent employees. Norman Zaiger thought Alan Cumming, starring in the acclaimed revival of *Cabaret*, would beat Brian Stokes Mitchell. "Bullshit!" Drabinsky yelled, then chewed out Zaiger for "mentioning the unthinkable," Zaiger said.

Peter Schneider and Tom Schumacher were not optimistic about winning Best Musical. They wanted the Tony. It would validate Disney as an artistic force on Broadway. But they figured they'd have to settle for Best Director for Taymor and a slew of design awards. Nancy Coyne disagreed. *The Lion King* could win the top prize. The problem wasn't that it was a "kiddie show." The problem was that Disney was an impersonal company in Burbank that had invaded Broadway. The company needed a face, and in Schneider and Schumacher, it had two bright ones. They weren't corporate people. They were theater people who happened to work for a corporation. Coyne, Rick Elice, and press agent Chris Boneau mapped out a strategy. "If we can demonstrate that it's not Disney, but two guys—a guy who worked as the company manager on *Little Shop of Horrors* years ago, and a guy who did puppet shows in high school and college—we can humanize you," Elice said. "And at the same time we can position *The Lion King* as a work of art."

To begin, there would be no bragging about the show's success. The assumption was that nobody could get a ticket for years. Coyne created ads that read, "Three easy ways to get a ticket." Disney was a master at customer service, something that had never been Broadway's strength. A trailer with extra box offices went up outside the New Amsterdam so people didn't have to wait in long lines.

Serino, Coyne's twentieth anniversary coincided with the run-up to the Tonys. Coyne threw a big bash to mark the milestone. She invited more than two hundred people, many of them Tony voters. "It was something she would never do because it would seem self-aggrandizing," said Elice. "But it wasn't really an anniversary party. It was a get-to-know-Tom-and-Peter party." Coyne told them, "Don't leave until you've met twenty-five people you've never met before. And remember their names."

The month before the Tony Awards, Broadway's calendar is packed with lesser awards and benefits—an unending succession of cocktail parties, lunches, and black-tie dinners. Though Schneider and Schumacher were still living in Los Angeles and running Disney Animation, they didn't miss a single pre-Tony event. "We lived on the corporate jet," Schumacher said. "We had our pajamas on the plane. We would leave an event, take off our tuxedos, put on our pajamas, sleep on the way to Los Angeles and go to the studio that morning. Then we'd get back on the plane for the next event in New York."

They honed the Crosby-and-Hope act they developed in Minneapolis to cover the six-minute "pause." When they spoke in public, they were charming, self-deprecating, appreciative, and humble. "Two theater geeks who will be around long after Garth Drabinsky is gone," Coyne said.

She relished going up against Drabinsky. She met him just once, in the lobby of the St. Regis Hotel in 1993. He wanted her to work on *Kiss of the Spider Woman*. Before the meeting, she called her friend Philip J. Smith, executive vice president of the Shubert Organization and one of the shrewdest men in the business. "Phil," she said, "it all smells to me, everything about Garth Drabinsky." He replied, "That's right. It's just a Ponzi scheme." How long before it falls apart? she asked. "It'll take about twelve years," he said.

During the meeting, Drabinsky asked her about billing practices. "We bill weekly," she said. "Do you collect from the Shuberts every week?" he wanted to know. Yes, she said. "Well, I don't believe you, and that's not how I do business," he snapped. Then he started to yell at and "humiliate me," she said. When he left, a bellhop came over to see if she was all right. "Just a lover's quarrel," she said.

Boneau made Schneider and Schumacher available to all media outlets, no matter how small. The *New York Times*, though, resisted their charms. A dinner was arranged at Gabriel's in New York so they could meet Frank Rich. He'd migrated to the Op-Ed page as a political columnist, but he still held sway over the paper's culture section. "We talked about who we were, where we came from, and it didn't go well," Schumacher recalled. "Frank called Michael Eisner the next day and said, 'Those boobs are going to lose the Tony for you because they're so incompetent.'" Alex Witchel dubbed them "the Disney clowns."*[4]

If Drabinsky picked up on Disney's strategy to put its two "Disney clowns" out and about, he did little to undercut it. "I never lobbied for the award," he said. "I always believed there would be a backlash if we lobbied. The show spoke for itself. I relied on the goodwill of the show and the integrity of the Tony voters." His only concession to the politics of the Tonys was to join the

* Schneider and Schumacher got their due from the *New York Times* in October 1998 with a positive profile by Barry Singer. He later told Schumacher his editors wanted the story to be tougher, but he resisted. Like most of the theater community, he thought Schneider and Schumacher were smart and fun.

Broadway League, which negotiated theater contracts. Livent did its own negotiating, but the League was loaded with Tony voters, and they might take offense if Livent continued to stand aloof.

Before the Tony Awards on June 7, Disney threw a cocktail party at the Rainbow Room in Rockefeller Center. Schneider and Schumacher came up to me and *Newsday* theater columnist Patrick Pacheco, another champion of *The Lion King.* "We're going to lose tonight, aren't we?" Schneider asked us through clenched teeth. Yes, we said. *The Lion King* is an artful spectacle, and voters will give it plenty of awards. But the top prize will go to *Ragtime* because it's a great American musical.

Michael Eisner didn't bother to attend the Tonys. "I went to the *Beauty and the Beast* one and it was such a horrible experience, I didn't want to go through it again," he said. Schneider and Schumacher gave Eisner's tickets to Coyne and Elice in appreciation for all they had done.

Rosie O'Donnell kicked off the fifty-second annual Tony Awards with a salute to Broadway divas—Patti LuPone, Jennifer Holliday, and Betty Buckley singing their signature songs from *Evita*, *Dreamgirls*, and *Cats*. Then O'Donnell introduced the opening number from *Ragtime*, calling the show "the star-spangled blockbuster." The audience responded enthusiastically. Here and there some people stood up. As expected, *The Lion King* swept the design awards, and Taymor became the first woman to win Best Director of a Musical. *Ragtime* won for its book and score, and Audra McDonald won Best Featured Actress in a Musical. To the theater press huddled in a bunker deep in Radio City, the Tonys were unfolding as they'd predicted. And then the cast of *The Lion King* performed "Circle of Life," and five thousand people stood on their feet and cheered and cheered. "*The Lion King*," O'Donnell said when the number ended, "the most astounding show I've ever seen in my life." The mood was shifting. But Schneider and

Schumacher still had doubts. They had a car waiting at the curb to whisk them away as soon as the telecast finished. During the final commercial break, O'Donnell told the audience, "Okay, guys, we're up against it. We only have a minute left. Nathan Lane [the presenter] is going to be in position. We're cutting his pre-thing. He's just going to say the nominees, and then say who won. Whoever you are say 'thank you.' There's no time for a speech. Get off."

The telecast resumed. Lane ran onstage, looked at his watch and rattled off the nominees. "And the best new musical of 1998 is . . . *The Lion King*." His eyebrows shot up so high they almost hit the roof of Radio City. Schneider and Schumacher raced down the aisle, Schumacher tripping on a cable. They squeezed in a speech, ping-ponging back and forth as they'd been doing since "the pause" in Minneapolis. Then they ran offstage and right into Isabelle Stevenson, the head of the American Theatre Wing. She took them in her arms and said, "I voted for you boys."

Though the mood was bleak at Livent after the Tony loss, Drabinsky plowed ahead with his next show, *Fosse*, a revue of songs and dances from Bob Fosse musicals. Chet Walker, a Fosse veteran, was putting it together, with Fosse's widow, Gwen Verdon, keeping watch. The developmental costs were high. Drabinsky produced an elaborate workshop with twenty dancers. It didn't work. Marty Bell thought Richard Maltby Jr. should take a look. Maltby had done three acclaimed revues: *Ain't Misbehavin'*; *Starting Here, Starting Now*; and *Closer Than Ever*. He watched a video of the workshop and thought, *Fosse's just repeating himself. I thought he was better than this.* Then he realized the numbers were never meant to be seen side by side. That's when he had "an epiphany." Everybody knew the trademark Fosse moves, and they were all over the revue. Maltby wanted to "keep the cat in the bag for as long as we can." He wrote a treatment explaining his idea of holding back the familiar moves for as long as possible, tantalizing the audience with a finger snap here, a shoulder roll there, but not doing the obvious numbers—"Big Spender," "Steam Heat," "Nowadays"—until later in the revue. His version would open with "Life Is Just a Bowl of Cherries," from the musical *Big Deal*, "float around for as long as possible," and then move into "Bye, Bye Blackbird" from *Liza With a Z*. "It's one of his tiniest numbers," Maltby said. "It's almost whispered, and then it explodes and disappears."

He got the job. Drabinsky turned on the charm. "The thing about Garth is, if he hires you, then you are, by definition, the absolute best person on the face of the earth to do that job because he wouldn't deal with anybody who wasn't the best," Maltby said. "You know it's a con, but you want to believe." Drabinsky also paid him well—3.5 percent of the gross—"the biggest deal I'd ever had."

Maltby and Walker began assembling the revue, using obscure numbers and delaying the big Fosse moments for as long as possible. Verdon attended a presentation. She left the room without a word, and then disappeared for several days. Worried, Walker went to her house to see if she was all right. She opened the door and lashed into him for the way he and Maltby had arranged Fosse's work. "How dare you?" she said. "You are a traitor. I don't ever want to see you anywhere near this work again. You are dead to me. You're dead to Bob."

She did return to rehearsals, "but she was a sullen force," Maltby said. "I finally said to Garth, 'We have to make this woman go away.'" Drabinsky finessed the dicey situation. He brought in Verdon's daughter, Nicole, to act as a buffer between her and the show. But he "stayed completely true to the idea I sold him right at the beginning," Maltby said. "He never veered from it." At Verdon's urging, Drabinsky brought in another Fosse veteran, Ann Reinking. He then eased out Walker "gracefully," said Maltby.

Drabinsky spared no expense on the show. Maltby was on a week's vacation in Aspen when Drabinsky summoned him to a meeting with Reinking in New York. A private plane picked him up at the Aspen airport and flew him to Denver where he caught a flight (first class) to New York. A limousine took him to Drabinsky's office. He met with Reinking for about an hour. Then the limo took him back to the airport to catch a flight to Dallas, where another private plane was waiting to return him to Aspen. "All in one day," he said. "You wonder why Livent went bankrupt?"

Broadway veterans were becoming increasingly skeptical of Livent's viability. Rumors swirled that Livent was buying its own tickets to inflate grosses of shows in New York, Toronto, and on tour. Gerald Schoenfeld told Maltby that the Ford Center could never make enough money to cover the debt service on the cost of the renovation. He also scoffed at Drabinsky's favorite phrase—"vertical integration." Sure, it sounds good to have your own costume shop, Schoenfeld said. But a production only needs a costume shop for about two months. Then it sits empty, though fully staffed, until another show comes along. Livent had a lot going on, but not enough to support its infrastructure.

Livent started making odd deals for touring shows. Pace Theatrical, which began as a producer and promoter of monster truck shows and tractor pulls, had branched out in the theater business in the early 1980s by acquiring theaters across America. The company flourished with hugely profitable tours of the British megamusicals—*Cats*, *Les Misérables*, *Phantom*, and *Miss Saigon*. But that pipeline had run dry. And so Pace was eager to do business with Drabinsky. "Garth exuded confidence," said Scott Zeiger, a Pace executive. "Here was a new impresario bringing big talent and big ideas and big shows to the boards. We got swept up in it." Miles Wilkin, another Pace executive, thought Drabinsky was "a jerk and a know-it-all," but there was no doubt he was a prolific producer.

Pace had secured the British shows by offering Cameron Mackintosh and Andrew Lloyd Webber attractive touring deals. The company would advance them several million dollars in each market, minimizing their risk. Pace recovered the money from ticket sales when the shows played the markets. Livent made the same deal for a tour of *Kiss of the Spider Woman*, though the tour ultimately went bust. But for tours of *Show Boat* and *Ragtime* Livent wanted to change the wording in the contracts. It wanted Pace's money to be seen as an investment rather than an advance. That way it could report it on its books as revenue.

"Garth had crazy, squirrely language that was making our accountants and lawyers tear their hair out," said Wilkin. Pace protected itself legally, but Drabinsky's unorthodox demands made everyone uneasy. That unease turned to anxiety when Pace realized the *Show Boat* tour was sinking. "We find ourselves biting our fingernails every Monday morning when we look at the grosses of where the tour is because we're now sweating whether the tour is actually going to get to us so we can take our money back from the box office," Wilkin said. "If it doesn't get to us, our four or five million dollars has, poof, gone."

Around the offices of Livent, people began to hear rumors of financial trouble, of bills not being paid on time or at all. A woman who made a specialized item for *Show Boat* that was sold in the gift shop in Chicago told Eleanor Goldhar, now running the press office, that Livent owed her $15,000. "I'm a little independent person," she said. "This is going to bankrupt me." The ad agency in Toronto was supposed to be paid every Friday. But the check always came so late in the day it couldn't be cashed until the following week. Len Gill, one of the ad people, started getting nervous. He told his friend Michael Cohl, "Garth owes me so much money. I could have a problem here." Employees who happened to go to the offices on Saturday noticed Drabinsky, Gottlieb, and people from the accounting department huddled in closed-door meetings. One Saturday an employee had some business to discuss with Drabinsky. But when the employee tried to go into Drabinsky's office, Drabinsky said, "Get out. We're busy."

Dan Brambilla, the Livent lawyer, couldn't make sense of what was happening. Drabinsky announced the company had a positive cash flow of $100 million. But Brambilla knew the shows were losing money. *We probably have a $100 million* negative *cash flow*, he thought.

A few financial journalists started to take a close look at Livent. Analyzing the company's financial reports from 1996, one columnist wrote, "Costs are growing faster than revenues," adding that much of the wording in the reports "fogs up the picture." The columnist concluded, "So beware, as one superpalpitating bit of hype about Garth and his grand vision could send Livent on a seeming rocket ride to the moon. Don't chase it, because this is one ride that might wind up right back where it started."[5]

In the spring of 1998, Livent reported a net loss of nearly $31 million in 1997. The stock price had long since fallen from $25 to $8. Rumors of the company's collapse gripped Broadway. And then Drabinsky startled everyone by announcing he'd found two angels—Michael Ovitz, cofounder of Creative Artists Agency, and Roy Furman, a billionaire investment banker who had become a producer. Ovitz invested $20 million in Livent and put in place a new management team led by Furman. Drabinsky remained with the company as vice president in charge of creative affairs. "I am exhausted," he told the *Daily News*. "I am tired, frankly, of having to raise money and run every aspect of a company that is growing. My true passion is really on the creative side of this business."[6] Livent's stock rose on the news of the management shakeup. Drabinsky told Marty Bell, who always received stock after opening nights, "You've got twenty-five thousand shares, and now with Ovitz coming in the stock is going to go much higher. You're probably worth four million dollars, Marty."

There was much speculation around Broadway as to why Ovitz and Furman would invest in a company clearly in trouble.* For Ovitz it represented a return to show business after his humiliating dismissal by his ex-friend Michael Eisner as president of the Walt Disney Company. Now he'd be competing against Disney on Broadway. Furman loved the theater—the *thee-ate-or,* as he called it. And though Livent had financial challenges, Ovitz and Furman were picking it up at a bargain. For a mere $20 million—"a rounding error for Ovitz," said Barry Avrich—they were getting theaters, *Ragtime*, which appeared to be a hit, and promising shows in the works—*Fosse, Seussical, Sweet Smell of Success.* Livent employees were thrilled about the change in management. "I thought we finally had some adults in the room," Brambilla said.

The honeymoon lasted barely a month. Ovitz installed an associate, David Maisel, as president. The morning after the first preview of *Fosse*, Drabinsky asked Maisel what he thought. "There's a lot of good stuff, but it's too long, and it's not that well organized," he said. Drabinsky exploded. "What the hell do you know about creating shows or storytelling? Don't tell us what to do. We know what to do. We've been doing this our whole lives."

Brambilla recalled a meeting with Robert Webster, the new head of finance in the Ovitz regime. In the middle of the meeting Webster took a call from the accounting department. He turned pale. "Dan, we have to continue this meeting some other time," he said, and then bolted downstairs to see the accountants.

After the opening-night party for *Fosse*, Drabinsky headed to an editing room with Avrich and Marty Bell to start cutting commercials advertising the show's good reviews. Drabinsky was munching on candy when his phone rang. It was Furman ordering him and Myron Gottlieb to be at a meeting first thing in the

* Furman turned down a request to be interviewed for this book. Ovitz never responded to an email request made through his secretary.

morning. "Now Garth is bothered," said Avrich. "And very distracted." They finished editing around three in the morning. The review from Canada's *Globe and Mail* was not yet out. Drabinsky told Bell he'd call him as soon as he got it. At 6:30 a.m., Bell's phone rang. But it wasn't Drabinsky. It was Furman. "Meet me at the Four Seasons in an hour," he said.

"And that's when he told me there were two sets of books and they were firing Garth and Myron," Bell said.

The accounting department had come clean with Ovitz and Furman. For several years, under intense pressure from Drabinsky—"bullying," as one of the accountants later testified—the department had cooked the books. It hid losses or turned them into revenues. It shifted the costs of a show about to close to another that was running so they would not have to be reported. Advances and loans became investments and revenues. The set of books shown to investors and regulators made the company look profitable. The set of books known only to Drabinsky, Gottlieb, and a few others cataloged an ever-widening sea of red ink. Ovitz and Furman had been duped. Livent was a fraud.

Employees showed up to work that morning to find the offices crawling with Royal Canadian Mounties. Yellow tape outside the building turned Livent into a crime scene. Eleanor Goldhar, from the publicity office, saw police with bulletproof vests and guns. "It was a SWAT team, which you never see in Canada," she said. Computers, files, phone records, every scrap of paper was impounded. Bell got on the phone to all the creative people to tell them what was happening, but not to worry. The shows, he said, would go on.

Drabinsky and Gottlieb publicly protested their innocence. Privately, Drabinsky told friends and associates he'd be back at Livent within a few days. A week after Drabinsky was fired, Bell was driving out of the parking garage of his apartment. He stopped at a red light and saw Drabinsky, in his car, coming in the other direction. Drabinsky waved at Bell to follow him. They stopped in a parking lot behind a supermarket. Bell got into Drabinsky's car.

"You have to quit," Drabinsky said.

"Garth, you made me move up here," Bell said. "My wife gave up her job. I got a young kid. We don't have a New York apartment anymore. How can I possibly quit?"

"If you don't quit, people are going to think I'm guilty. If you quit, it will show everybody that I'm telling the truth and they're lying."

"I can't do it," Bell said.

"Oh, you want the job then?" Drabinsky snarled. "You want to be the big shot. You want to run the show."

Bell got out of the car.

"Fuck you," Drabinsky said.*

Drabinsky and Gottlieb never returned to Livent. They were indicted in Canada and the United States on several counts of fraud and conspiracy. Ovitz and Furman bailed out the only way they could: Livent declared bankruptcy, taking down with it many smaller companies that were owed millions of dollars, including Jon Wilner's ad agency. SFX Entertainment, which had acquired Pace Theatrical, eventually bought what was left of Livent's assets for $100 million. SFX looked at *Phantom* in Toronto, discovered it had been losing money for years, and closed it. The lavish headquarters in Toronto were also closed. SFX cut costs on *Ragtime*, but the show only lasted until January 2000, closing at a loss. *Fosse* turned out to be a gold mine. It won the Tony for Best Musical in 1999 and cleaned up on Broadway and on tour.

Marty Bell lost his job on November 30, 1998, shortly after Livent declared bankruptcy. He framed his shares of Livent stock and hung them on a wall in his apartment.

* Drabinsky said he does not recall the conversation.

CHAPTER SIXTEEN

THE PLAYMAKERS

During the Christmas week of 1996, Broadway sold nearly $14 million worth of tickets, the highest weekly gross in its history. In May 1997, the Broadway League reported that the industry had its best season ever, with gross receipts hitting $500 million. Producers and creators of musicals had much to celebrate. Eighty percent of that $500 million came from their shows. Playwrights, though, began to fret. The commercial play, once a staple of the Great White Way, seemed endangered. Changing demographics had a lot to do with its plight. Tourists flocked to Broadway in the mid-1990s, with more than 60 percent of the theater audience coming from outside the New York City region. And they wanted to see shows they'd heard of—*Cats, Phantom, Les Misérables, Rent, Chicago, Sunset Boulevard.*

As Rocco Landesman put it, "The upper-middle-class, upper-age, Jewish West Sider is moving to Florida or dying out. That educated theater audience is getting harder to find."[1] Playwright Arthur Laurents complained to the *New York Times* that "entertainment is killing theater," adding that Times Square was in danger of becoming an arcade. Producer Alexander H. Cohen said, "Tourists want falling chandeliers and swimming pools."[2]

Nonprofit theaters such as the Public, the Roundabout, and Lincoln Center produced plays, and some moved to Broadway. But it was not a robust pipeline. Hollywood stars could sell a play, but most were reluctant to commit to a run of more than a few months since they'd lose out on far more lucrative film roles. The Broadway Initiative, a coalition of theatrical producers, theater owners, and theater unions, lobbied for a fund to be created from the sale of air rights in Times Square to subsidize new plays. What nobody could foresee was that plays were about to make a comeback, though not American plays. The British (and the Irish) would soon launch another invasion of Broadway. This time they would come not with chandeliers and helicopters, but with intimate, gripping dramas starring some of the finest actors in the world.

David Hare needed a break from epic plays. *The Absence of War*, about the defeat of the Labour Party in the 1992 general election, premiered at the National Theatre in London in 1993. It was the last installment of his state-of-the-nation trilogy. The first, *Racing Demon*, tackled the Church of England. The second, *Murmuring Judges*, examined the judicial system. All three plays featured casts of nearly thirty actors. "I was tired of throwing lots of characters onstage," Hare said. "I felt I wasn't going deep enough. So I decided I'd write what I called 'a play in a room.'"

The "room" turned out to be a modest apartment belonging to Kyra Hollis, a teacher at a public school in the East End of London. Hollis had an affair years ago with Tom Sargeant, a successful restaurant owner. The affair ended after his wife found out about it. His wife now dead, Tom turns up at Kyra's apartment one night. He makes fun of her shabby surroundings. Her idealism, he thinks, has prevented her from making money. Though Kyra and Tom clash ideologically, they're still attracted to each other and end up sleeping together. Hare called the play *Skylight*. Richard

Eyre, then running the National Theatre, agreed to direct. Lia Williams played Kyra. For the part of Tom, Eyre cast Michael Gambon. He was not a star, but had won rave reviews for his stage performances. Hare caught him in a revival of Arthur Miller's *A View from the Bridge* at the National in 1987. He played Eddie Carbone, a longshoreman sexually obsessed with his niece. His performance impressed Hare. He told Gambon, "You came on as this big longshoreman, but by the time you left the stage you were tiny. You had shrunk." Gambon was pleased. "That's all I was trying to do. Come on big. Leave small."

The barrel-chested Gambon was imposing, but he could, without warning, become delicate and tender. One day in rehearsal, after Tom has made love to Kyra, Gambon started doing ballet pliés. Hare was amazed. "It was just a little bit of business, his going up and down, but it was there to say, 'I've made love to her. I feel absolutely great. I feel fantastic.' I could never have written anything like that."

Gambon had trouble with the second act, when his character reveals a painful vulnerability to Kyra. "This is not what blokes do," he told Hare. "He's abasing himself in front of her. He's allowing her to have power."

Hare replied, "You know, Michael, he's in love with her."

"Yeah, but you never show it, do you?"

"Well, you may never show it, Michael," Hare said, "but there are some men who do."

Gambon struggled, but Hare knew he would get there. He did, turning in the play's most touching scene.

Gambon sometimes had trouble remembering lines. When he went dry he'd throw in a few *fucks* until he got his bearings. Princess Margaret came to the show one night in 1996 and "it was a particularly fuck-heavy night," said Hare. The princess met Hare after the play. "You're a very good writer," she said, "but rather too fond of the f-word, if I may say so."

The critics adored *Skylight*, and after a sold-out run at the National, producer Robert Fox moved it to the West End. Fox got the play because he made a stink about the way the National was doing business. Michael Codron, a prominent West End producer, was on the theater's board and always seemed "to get first dibs" on its plays, Fox said. Fox thought that was the theatrical equivalent of insider trading and said so publicly. Eyre defused the embarrassing situation by offering Fox *Skylight*. Codron was furious, but there was nothing he could do.

Fox was close to some powerful New York producers—the Shubert Organization, Scott Rudin, and Roger Berlind, a gentle, elegant investment banker who'd made a fortune on Wall Street in the 1970s. They wanted to bring the show to Broadway, but a play, especially one without a big star, was risky.* So they came up with a formula that made economic sense. Hare and Eyre did not take much money up front and kept their weekly royalties at a minimum. The actors worked for a relatively small weekly salary. But everybody would share in the profits at the end of the limited three-month run. *Skylight* came in for $750,000, received glowing reviews, and recouped in just seven weeks. The remainder of the run was "pure profit for everyone," said Fox. Gambon was nominated for a Tony and emerged well on his way to becoming a star. He sent Hare a note saying, "Thank you. You changed my life."

In 1998, more imports from Great Britain captivated New Yorkers. *Art*, by French writer Yasmina Reza and translated into English by Christopher Hampton, had been a blockbuster in London. In

* Ralph Richardson had dubbed Gambon "the Great Gambon," so press agent Adrian Bryan-Brown insisted everyone call him that so New Yorkers would think he was a big star.

New York, with Alan Alda, Alfred Molina, and Victor Garber playing three men whose friendship is tested over a work of modern art, it was an immediate sellout. Scott Rudin brought over a revival of Ionesco's *The Chairs* with, as *Variety* put it, "the glorious double-act" of stars Richard Briers and Geraldine McEwan. And from the Druid Theatre Company in Galway, Ireland, came *The Beauty Queen of Leenane*, about a vicious struggle between a mother and her daughter by new writer Martin McDonagh. The Tony nominators showered nominations on all three plays, prompting the *New York Times* to note that the rivalry between *The Lion King* and *Ragtime* "was all but upstaged by the surprisingly strong showing of straight plays after a long Broadway eclipse."[3]

Hare, Eyre, and the team that produced *Skylight* then came through with *The Judas Kiss*, starring Liam Neeson, now a household name from Steven Spielberg's *Schindler's List*, as Oscar Wilde. It was not ideal casting. "We wanted to reconceive Oscar Wilde, but to cast Ireland's most famous heterosexual was perhaps pushing the envelope too far," Hare said. Playing Wilde's lover, Lord Alfred "Bosie" Douglas, was another straight actor, Tom Hollander. "Richard wasn't gay, I wasn't gay, Liam wasn't gay, and Tom wasn't gay," said Hare. "It was a gay-free play about Oscar Wilde. That was hopeless arrogance." Broadway wags dubbed *The Judas Kiss* "Schindler's Lisp."

With the *Skylight* formula in place—Neeson's share of the profits would be between 12 and 15 percent—the plan was to debut *The Judas Kiss* in London and transfer it to Broadway. But the London critics pummeled the play. Hare and Eyre wanted to close it and cancel the Broadway transfer. Fox and Rudin asked a simple question: What are we going to do with the $3 million advance sale in New York? Hare and Eyre agreed to work on the play. It got better, but not good.

"We're going to get murdered," Eyre said.

"Yeah, we're going to get murdered," Hare replied. "It's not going to be the most pleasant experience because we've made some mistakes, but we're just going to have to march to the goal."

Neeson took Hare aside one day and said, "David, I'm going to get killed in New York for this, aren't I?"

"It's not going to be fair, but you're going to get killed," Hare said.

The night *New York Times* critic Ben Brantley came to see the play, Hare went to Café Un Deux Trois, a popular theater restaurant, during the show and knocked back several drinks. After the performance he went backstage to see Neeson. "Was the *New York Times* in tonight?" Neeson asked. "Yes," Hare said. "Oh, Christ. Let's go have a drink," Neeson said.

"I've never, ever, ever been so drunk as the night the *New York Times* went to see *The Judas Kiss*," said Hare. "As I walked home, the pavement had waves."

Brantley didn't "murder" everybody, but he dismissed the play as a "dense marble monument" and Hare's rendering of Wilde as "a bit of a snooze." The Tony nominators snubbed *The Judas Kiss*. But it didn't matter. Neeson was such a big star that there were plenty of profits to go around.

Sam Mendes, a young director out of Cambridge who was running the Donmar Warehouse, a pocket-size theater in Covent Garden, asked Hare to write a modern adaptation of *La Ronde*, Arthur Schnitzler's play about sex and class in Vienna in 1897. Hare was reluctant—"I rather disapproved of adaptations that update," he said—but agreed to write a few scenes. To his surprise he enjoyed the exercise. "This is fantastic," Mendes said. "Nicole Kidman's going to do it."

Hare was shocked. "When has she ever acted in the theater?" he asked.

"Now," Mendes said, "because she's very open to learning."

Kidman had done theater in Sydney, Australia, as a teenager, but moved into television and movies. She was best known, however, as the wife of Tom Cruise, whom she'd met while filming *Days of Thunder* in 1989.

Hare reduced the cast of *La Ronde* from nine to two—a man and woman, who would play all the parts—and set it in contemporary London. He renamed it *The Blue Room*. Iain Glen, an up-and-coming Scottish actor, was cast opposite Kidman. From the first reading, Hare was struck by Kidman's understanding of the play's sexual politics. "There wasn't a situation between a man and a woman Nicole didn't know about," he said. She was, though, "a little bit short of technique. She really didn't know how to act onstage at all."

In one scene Glen appeared naked. Kidman wore clothes. "Would the scene be better if I were naked, too?" she asked Mendes during the dress rehearsal.

"If you're okay with that, yeah, I think it would be," Mendes said.

"I'm fine with it," she said and disrobed. The scene was better, but it was just fifteen seconds so nobody thought much of it.

Hare, who was performing his one-man show *Via Dolorosa*, couldn't get to a preview, but his wife, fashion designer Nicole Farhi, attended an early one. "Nicole Kidman is an absolute knockout," she told her husband. Hare said, "I'm sure she's quite good, but I don't think she's a knockout." Go see her, his wife said. He attended a matinee and left stunned. "The rather hesitant, uncertain person in rehearsal had totally disappeared. She was brilliant."

Previews were sold out, largely because audiences had heard that Cruise was there most nights. "They found a place to put him behind glass because if he was in the audience, the event became completely distorted," said Hare. After the opening-night performance, Charles Spencer, the theater critic for the *Daily*

Telegraph, headed to the Garrick Club in Covent Garden to bang out his review. He thought the play was a little thin, but praised Kidman as "a terrific actress who brings all five of her roles to instantly distinctive life." He sent off the review and was about to head home when his editor called. The review came in a little short for the space. Could he add another paragraph? Spencer opened his laptop and wrote: "The play still strikes me as a cleverly executed, glibly cynical jeu d'esprit rather than a profound meditation on human relationships. In this production, however, you might as well lie back and enjoy the sheer style and sexuality on display: It's pure theatrical Viagra."

The phrase—"pure theatrical Viagra"—ricocheted around the world, ending up in newspapers from New York to New Delhi, Berlin to Buenos Aires.

Hare didn't think the play should go to New York. It was too intimate for Broadway. But Gerald Schoenfeld knew "pure theatrical Viagra" would be pure theatrical gold at the box office. Mendes also objected to Broadway, thinking the play better suited to a smaller theater. But Schoenfeld brushed him aside. "We have an understanding that all plays by David come to our theaters and we'll coproduce," Schoenfeld said. Fox was amused. There was no formal agreement to that effect. "But okay—if you say so Jerry," Fox said years later with a laugh.

Using the profit-sharing model that had worked so well for *Skylight* and *The Judas Kiss*, *The Blue Room* arrived in New York at the Cort Theatre on December 13, 1998. Night after night a thousand people stood in the freezing cold to catch a glimpse of Kidman and Cruise as they left the theater. Sometimes the block had to be cordoned off. The critics were indifferent to the play, but it didn't matter. Scalpers were getting nearly $1,000 for seats with a prime view of Kidman's buttocks. She made the cover of *Newsweek*. "Nicole Kidman bares all—about her daring Broadway debut, her marriage to Tom Cruise, and their fight for privacy." Not since Henry Fonda starred in *Mister Roberts* on Broadway in 1948 had *Newsweek* put a nonmusical play on its cover.

In the midst of it all was "my poor little play," said Hare. One night as he and Mendes surveyed the throngs waiting outside the theater, he was reminded of what the critic F. R. Leavis had said of the Sitwells. They "belong to the history of publicity rather than poetry."

The four-act plays of Eugene O'Neill inspired Hare's next play. Nobody was writing four-act plays anymore, so Hare thought he'd try. His play, which unfolds over sixteen years, centers on Esme, a famous stage actress; Amy, her daughter; and Amy's husband, Dominic, a movie buff who hates the theater and with whom Esme has a contentious relationship. Hare called it *Amy's View*. When Richard Eyre read it, he said of Esme, "This is Judi Dench." Dench, however, disagreed. "I have no idea why you think this is me at all," she said after reading the play. "I don't connect with this at all." Eyre urged her to think it over. Finally, she said, "Looking back, I can see the plays that I didn't understand at all were always the ones that I had the greatest success in. When somebody gave me something I went, 'Oh, yes I can do this,' it was kind of boring."

Dench signed up for the play, and had what Hare called one of "the most hideous rehearsal periods" of her career. Esme shuns modernity and lives in the past. Dench could not understand her. She also found Esme's long speeches frustrating. "The sentences are so long," she said. "I am a Shakespearean actor, but I can't manage a sentence with 146 words in it!"

And then late in the rehearsal period her daughter gave birth, and she was running off to the hospital to be the doting grandmother. Her mind off the play, something clicked and at a run-through she turned in a performance that was no longer labored but spontaneous.

"You're brilliant," Hare told her.

"Am I?" she asked. "I really don't know what I'm doing."

She settled into the role and opened to a cheering first-night audience at the National Theatre in the late spring of 1997. As an opening-night gift, she gave Hare a piece of paper on which she'd written out, in medieval handwriting, his 146-word sentence that drove her mad. At the bottom she added, "Fuck you, David." The critics raved. Some called it the best performance she'd ever given. Not that she paid any attention to reviews, however. Her method of dealing with them was to sweep into the theater the day after they came out and announce, "I haven't read them, but I hear they're very good."

In between the London run of *Amy's View* and the Broadway opening in the spring of 1999, Dench became an international movie star. She appeared as Elizabeth I in *Shakespeare in Love* for about eight minutes and made off with the Oscar for Best Supporting Actress. New Yorkers clamored to get tickets to *Amy's View*, pushing its advance sale to $5 million, then a record for a nonmusical play.

Hare was performing *Via Dolorosa* at the Booth Theatre while Dench was a few blocks north at the Ethel Barrymore. She'd call him every night to boast about all the celebrities who'd been to her dressing room. Hare had a few, too, including Kurt Vonnegut and Paul Newman. "Well, I've had *both* Clintons," Dench said. Hare said he'd had all the Hitchcock heroines—Teresa Wright, Eva Marie Saint, Janet Leigh, and Kim Novak. "Judi was white with jealousy," Hare said. It was all good, theatrical fun. And then, three or four weeks before the end of her run, Dench learned that Michael Williams, her husband of nearly thirty years, had lung cancer. On her days off she flew to London to be by his side, returning to New York Tuesday mornings to give eight performances a week. "She's more than a pro," Hare said. "She is a very, very good person who would never let the company down. But Michael's illness blighted the end of the run." He died in 2001 at the age of sixty-five.

The formula for attracting big stars to Broadway by offering them limited runs and a share of the profits reinvigorated the market for plays. Kevin Spacey, working for a weekly salary of $1,325, turned in a brilliant performance as Hickey in *The Iceman Cometh* in 1999. The show made a profit of nearly $2 million, 15 percent of which went to Spacey. Movie stars now saw Broadway as a place to burnish their careers—and make some money without having to commit to a run of more than three or four months. Denzel Washington returned to Broadway in 2005 in *Julius Caesar*, following it up a few years later with a Tony Award–winning performance in a revival of August Wilson's *Fences*, which grossed more than $1 million a week.

One of the biggest movie stars of the decade—Julia Roberts—made her Broadway debut in 2006 in Richard Greenberg's *Three Days of Rain*. Her costars were a relatively unknown Paul Rudd and an unknown Bradley Cooper. Her reviews were not great, but that didn't matter. The show, which ran just twelve weeks, opened with an advance of $10 million, and made such an enormous profit that one of its producers, feeling guilty about the "easy money," donated a substantial portion of his share to three nonprofit theaters—the Public, the Vineyard, and Second Stage.

Two other nonprofit theaters—Lincoln Center and the Roundabout—operated on Broadway in the 1990s. In the 2000s, Manhattan Theatre Club and Second Stage joined them. Commercial producers grumbled about competing with the nonprofits, which had tax advantages and lower salary scales. "There's no profit like nonprofit," Jerry Schoenfeld said so often that an exasperated Todd Haimes, the head of the Roundabout, once responded, "If I hear him say that again, I'm either going to shoot myself or him."

But there was no denying the nonprofits contributed significant straight plays to the terrain, including *Proof, Doubt, The Tale of the Allergist's Wife, War Horse*, and *The Humans*.

In the fall of 2019, plays accounted for nearly a third of the productions on Broadway, led by *Harry Potter and the Cursed Child*; *The Sound Inside* with Mary-Louise Parker; *The Height of the Storm* with Eileen Atkins and Jonathan Pryce; and *The Inheritance*, Matthew Lopez's two-part, seven-hour post-AIDS epic. Musicals are still the engine of Broadway—always have been, likely always will be—but it's been a long time since anybody complained that all the tourists want are "falling chandeliers and swimming pools."

CHAPTER SEVENTEEN

IT'S GOOD TO BE THE KING

Cats played its final performance September 10, 2000, at the Winter Garden Theatre. It ran eighteen years and grossed more than $400 million. Andrew Lloyd Webber told the closing-night crowd, which included more than a hundred performers who had been in the show, "This is only the last night of *Cats*'s first run on Broadway, so don't get too excited." After the performance, there was a laser show outside the theater and then Lloyd Webber, Cameron Mackintosh, Trevor Nunn, the Shuberts, and many others who'd made fortunes from *Cats* made their way to Chelsea Piers for a farewell bash.

Cast member Jeffry Denman spotted me at the party. He introduced himself, saying he was still a little annoyed with me for attacking a short-lived show he was in called *Dream* in 1997. But the affable Denman was pleased to learn that I'd enjoyed the final performance of *Cats*. I asked what he planned to do next. He told me he'd recently been cast in the ensemble of Mel Brooks's *The Producers*.

"Oh, I can't *wait* to see that," I sneered. "It has all the makings of a floperoo."

Denman said, "Yeah, I guess we'll see," took a swig of his Jack and Coke, and made a getaway.[1]

Of course I was right. Well, at the time. Mel Brooks writing a musical? The last musical he wrote was *All American*, which ran just two months back in 1962. I loved his movies—*Young Frankenstein, Blazing Saddles, High Anxiety*—but they were from the 1970s. The more recent *Robin Hood: Men in Tights* was not in their league. As for *The Producers*, if you were in show business, you loved the movie. If not, you probably never saw it. It was a cult film. Brooks seemed like someone whose time had come and gone. And he was from Hollywood, and what do Hollywood types know about the theater? Blake Edwards, another movie director whose career was on the wane, had flopped on Broadway in 1997 with *Victor/Victoria* even though his wife, Julie Andrews, played the lead.

That fall on Broadway the buzz was not about *The Producers*. It was about *The Full Monty*, a musical adapted from the 1997 British film about unemployed steel workers who form a male striptease act to pay the bills. Terrence McNally shifted the action to Buffalo, New York, and wrote a funny, moving script. The score, by newcomer David Yazbek, was contemporary, witty, and tuneful. Directed by Jack O'Brien, the musical also featured show-stopping performances from Patrick Wilson, André De Shields, and Kathleen Freeman. I'd seen *The Full Monty* at the Old Globe in San Diego that summer and praised it in a column. At the opening-night party in October, I told Yazbek that at the next year's Tonys "you're going to win everything in sight."

Four months later, McNally got a call from his friend Nathan Lane, who was in Chicago for the out-of-town tryout of *The Producers*. He was playing Max Bialystock. The musical was in the middle of its first preview. Act I had just ended. Lane was calling from his dressing room.

"It's intermission," he told McNally, "and they're still laughing."

* * *

In 1960, Brooks intended to write a novel about "a guy who was a caterpillar who wanted to become a butterfly." His caterpillar was an accountant who falls in with Bialystock, a down-and-out Broadway producer. When the accountant, Leo Bloom (a name Brooks took from *Ulysses* and apt because the character does "bloom"), notes that under the right circumstances a producer can make more money with a flop than a hit, Bialystock has an idea. Find the worst show imaginable, raise far more money than the actual production costs, close the show after one performance, and pocket the difference.

A small-time producer Brooks worked for when he got out of the army inspired Bialystock. Brooks always claimed that the real-life producer raised money by sleeping with little old ladies. The plot of taking the world's worst show and turning it into a hit was not original. George S. Kaufman came up with it for his 1925 comedy *The Butter and Egg Man*, the only play he wrote without a collaborator. Brooks, of course, never saw the play (he was born in 1926) and added his own characters and sense of humor to the premise.

At the time he was writing his novel, he lunched every Tuesday with friends in Chinatown. Among them were the novelists Joseph Heller and Mario Puzo. Heller had challenged Brooks to write a book. "You wrote sketches all your life for *Your Show of Shows* and they were brilliant, but you're fucking second rate until you write a novel," he said. Brooks showed his friends what he'd written. Too much dialogue, they told him. "You know what this is?" Puzo said. "It's an incredibly good play." So Brooks reworked it, dropping in a Busby Berkley–style number featuring singing and dancing Nazis. He called the play *Springtime for Hitler* and gave it to his friend Kermit Bloomgarden, the producer of *Death of a Salesman* and *The Music Man*.

"It's funny, it's daring, it's brave," Bloomgarden said. "Too many scenes. Listen, we producers have a secret code, and that code is: one set, five characters. We can't make money unless it's one set, five characters. You've got thirty scenes. It's not a play. It's a movie."

So Brooks turned *Springtime for Hitler* into a screenplay. Sidney Glazier, who started out as an usher at a burlesque theater and had gone on to produce an Academy Award–winning documentary about Eleanor Roosevelt, thought it was hilarious. He vowed to make the movie, but could not find a distributor. Finally Joseph E. Levine, the owner of Embassy Pictures, agreed to become Glazier's partner. Levine had produced a string of low-budget adventure movies. As Brooks put it, "He did *Hercules*, then *Hercules Unchained*, then *Hercules Chained Again*, then *Hercules Nearly Chained But Gets Away*." Levine made one demand: change the title. Most exhibitors were Jewish and when Levine told them about *Springtime for Hitler*, they said, "No Hitler on our marquee." Brooks changed the title to *The Producers*.

As Brooks worked on his screenplay in 1963, his wife, Anne Bancroft, was playing the title character in a Broadway production of Bertolt Brecht's *Mother Courage*. A young actor named Gene Wilder played the chaplain. He and Brooks started hanging out backstage. "Why is the audience always laughing at me?" Wilder asked Brooks. "Sometimes I'm amusing, but most of the time I'm trying to be sincere."

"Why do they laugh at you?" Brooks said. "Go to the mirror and take a look. They have every right to laugh. God made you funny." He paused and then added, "You know I'm writing a movie about an accountant who becomes a producer, and you're him. You're Leo Bloom. You look like Leo Bloom. You talk like Leo Bloom. You're Leo Bloom."

"Okay," said Wilder. "Whenever you get the money let me know."

A few years later, Levine's check in hand, Brooks went to visit Wilder backstage at another play. "I've got the money," he said.

Wilder burst into tears and exclaimed, "I don't believe it, I don't believe it!"

Brooks wanted Zero Mostel to play Bialystock. "And Zero said no right away," Brooks said. "He said, 'He's a bad guy. He's a shithead. I don't want to play him.' So I got to his wife, Kate, and said, 'Read this.' And she banged him over the head with it and said, 'If you don't do this, I'm leaving.'"

Brooks shot the film in eight weeks at a studio on West Twenty-Sixth Street in New York. Money was tight. During a break from shooting the "Springtime for Hitler" number, Brooks went out and bought the company sandwiches and coffee. He came back carrying a heavy cardboard box. But when he tried to get back in the studio, a woman at the door said, "Where the hell do you think you're going? They're making a movie in there."

"I know," said Brooks. "I'm the guy making it. I'm directing it!"

"You're directing it?" the woman said, and burst out laughing.

The Producers opened in the spring of 1967 to mixed reviews. "Some of it is shoddy and gross and cruel; the rest is funny in an entirely unexpected way," Renata Adler wrote in the *New York Times.* She thought Brooks made a "terrible . . . mistake" by having the on-screen audience laugh at and applaud the play-within-the movie, *Springtime for Hitler: A Gay Romp with Adolf and Eva in Berchtesgaden.* "This turned the real audience in the theater off as though a fuse had blown."

In 1998, movie mogul David Geffen called Brooks and suggested he turn *The Producers* into a Broadway musical. "David, it's a perfectly good little film," Brooks said. "Zero's good. Gene's good. Everybody's good. Let's leave it."

Geffen called the next day. "I've been thinking . . ." he said. Brooks interrupted. "David, we have lives. I have a life. You have a life. We're not living together. Unfortunately, we're not housekeeping. Don't call me on this anymore, please." Geffen called again that afternoon. And then he started calling Brooks every day, twice a day for two months. "He was driving me crazy," Brooks said. Anne Bancroft pointed out that Brooks already had written two songs for the movie—"Springtime for Hitler" and "Prisoners of Love." Just meet with him, she said.

At the meeting Geffen said, "Your songs may not be good enough for Broadway. I want you to go meet Jerry Herman." Brooks and Herman spent the afternoon at Herman's house in Bel Air singing Frank Loesser songs. Then Herman told him that Brooks's song "I'm Tired" for Madeline Kahn in *Blazing Saddles* was terrific. "Springtime for Hitler" and "Prisoners of Love" were first-rate as well, Herman said. It was unthinkable to do a musical version of *The Producers* without them. "You're another Irving Berlin," Herman said. He picked up the phone and called Geffen. "Mel should write the score," he said. "You're crazy if you don't let him do it."

Geffen agreed reluctantly.

Around this time MGM approached Brooks about turning *Spaceballs*, his *Star Wars* parody, into an animated feature. He'd written the movie with Tom Meehan, who won a Tony for his book to *Annie* in 1977. Brooks and Meehan met in 1970 when Meehan contributed a sketch to Anne Bancroft's television special *Annie, the Women in the Life of a Man*. They later cowrote Brooks's remake of *To Be or Not to Be*. They were an odd couple—Brooks, boisterous, explosive, peripatetic; Meehan, modest, quiet, steady. But they worked well together.

Brooks was not a writer in the traditional sense. He trained on Sid Caesar's *Your Show of Shows* and *Caesar's Hour*, whose writers included Larry Gelbart, Neil Simon, Woody Allen, Carl Reiner, and Michael Stewart. During those sessions, Brooks would shout out ideas for sketches, acting out all the characters, while someone else wrote everything down. As Brooks once said, "I'm not a writer, I'm a *talker.* I wish they'd change my billing on the show so that it said 'Funny Talking by Mel Brooks.' "[2] That's how Brooks and Meehan worked. Brooks would throw out lines and ideas, while Meehan scribbled everything down on his yellow legal pad, adding his own ideas and jokes. He would then sift through the notes, keeping what was funny and throwing out all that was not. "Some people have 'yes' men," Meehan said. "I always felt that in my collaboration with Mel I'm the 'no' man. 'No, no, no, no. You're Mel Brooks. Don't embarrass yourself with that line.' "

Sitting in Brooks's Culver City offices, Brooks and Meehan were stumped on how to adapt *Spaceballs* as a cartoon. Neither wanted to do it. Brooks's friend Ronny Graham, a writer and an actor, came by to help. As the fruitless meeting came to an end, Brooks asked Graham, an accomplished jazz pianist, to play a song Brooks had just written—"Where Did We Go Right?"

What do you think, Brooks asked Meehan.

"It's funny. I like it. But what is it?"[3]

"You know, I got this call from David Geffen," Brooks said. "He thinks I should do a musical of *The Producers*. That's a song I wrote. Would you want to work with me on it?"

Meehan loved the movie, but saw a flaw right away. It's set in the 1960s and features references to flower power and psychedelic drugs. Dick Shawn, as a character named LSD who's cast as Hitler, sings a song called "Love Power." Much of the movie, Meehan thought, seemed dated. He told Brooks they should cut LSD and set the show in 1959, the tail end of Broadway's golden age. Brooks loved the idea. Soon they began talking about who could direct *The Producers*. Brooks was shrewd enough to know he couldn't do it. "I didn't know the lighting, the transitions. It's very complicated. Broadway's a whole different medium from pictures."

An obvious candidate was Jerry Zaks. He liked the idea and met with Brooks and Meehan. Brooks sang "Where Did We Go

Right?" for him. Zaks told his friend Nathan Lane the song was fun and the show might be good. Lane thought, *Oh, maybe I'll wind up doing it.* But Zaks was going through a rough time in his personal life. He passed on the show. Meehan suggested Mike Ockrent, who staged *Me and My Girl* and *Crazy for You.* Ockrent came with a bonus—he had recently married Susan Stroman, fast becoming one of Broadway's most sought-after choreographers. Find them and set up a meeting, Brooks told Meehan. They agreed to meet Brooks during a break from rehearsals for another show. But the impulsive Brooks couldn't wait. The next day he appeared, uninvited, at their penthouse in the Parc Vendôme on West Fifty-Seventh Street. He threw his arms into the air and started singing "That Face, that face, that fabulous face," a song he'd written for the show. He danced and sang all the way down a long hallway and then jumped up on a couch in the living room and said, "Hello, I'm Mel Brooks!" Stroman thought to herself, *No matter what this is, it's going to be the time of our lives.*

Born and raised in Wilmington, Delaware, Stroman grew up enveloped in music. Her father, a traveling salesman, was also an accomplished pianist. He played Gershwin, Porter, Kern, and Rodgers and Hart while Stroman "danced around the living room," she said. Whenever a Fred Astaire movie was on television "everything in our house would stop and you'd sit with your TV tray and your dinner and watch it." Of all Astaire's dances, her favorite was "Sunday Jumps" from *Royal Wedding.* Astaire is waiting to rehearse with his partner (Jane Powell). When she doesn't turn up he dances with a hat rack. The use of the prop came from a dramatic situation. It wasn't extraneous. "I was able to clock that at a very young age," Stroman said.

Stroman arrived in New York in 1976, wanting to be a director and a choreographer. She made her living performing in commercials and industrial shows. She played one of the merry murderesses in the national tour of *Chicago*. In 1980, she and her friend Scott Ellis appeared on Broadway in *Musical Chairs*. Frank Rich called it the worst musical of the season. Ellis knew John Kander and Fred Ebb—he'd been in their musical *The Rink*—and asked them if he could direct a revival of their 1965 show *Flora the Red Menace*. Stroman choreographed it. The modest Off-Broadway production was a hit. That led them to stage the Kander and Ebb revue *And the World Goes 'Round*, which won raves. Based on its success, Ockrent hired Stroman to choreograph *Crazy for You*, for which she won her first Tony Award. After the show opened, Ockrent went back to England to begin a separation from his wife. A few weeks later he called Stroman and said, "I have to come back."

"You want to look at the understudies?" she asked.

"I have to come back because I've fallen in love with you," he said.

"I was shocked," Stroman recalled. "I admired him as a collaborator—I'd been through tech with this man—but I had no idea he was in love with me. When he said he was coming back I just said, 'Okay.' So we started to date and I quickly fell in love with him in more ways than just as a collaborator." They married on New Year's Day 1996.

Brooks, Meehan, Ockrent, and Stroman met on and off in London and New York throughout 1998 to work on the show. Glen Kelly, a composer and music arranger, helped Brooks with the score. Brooks doesn't write music sitting at the piano. He gets "a little melody in my head that strikes me" and then hums it or picks it out with one or two fingers on a keyboard. Kelly was instrumental in turning those "little melodies" into full-fledged songs. As for lyrics, Brooks begins with "a little poem about what the character's feeling" and then shapes the words to fit his tune.

Ockrent, skilled at structuring shows, helped Brooks and Meehan lay out the floor plan of *The Producers*. With LSD gone, the show needed someone who, to paraphrase the movie, could be its Hitler. Ockrent had an idea: Why not have Roger De Bris, the flamboyant and supremely untalented director, play Hitler? Missing from the movie—and essential to a musical—is a love story. So they beefed up the part of Ulla, the Swedish secretary, and had her fall in love with Leo. But they began to realize that the real love story is between Max and Leo. Max helps Leo, the caterpillar, become the butterfly. In so doing Max comes to care about someone other than himself. It's a nonsexual love story to be sure, but a love story nonetheless. As Stroman put it, "You not only root for them to become great producers, but you root for them to become dear friends."

In March 1999, Meehan got a message to call Ockrent at a number he didn't recognize. It was Sloan Kettering Cancer Center. Ockrent and Stroman thought a rash covering his arms and face was an allergic reaction. It was leukemia. Ockrent told Meehan he'd be fine. He did go into remission, but the cancer came back, killing him on December 2, 1999. Before he died, he told Stroman to continue working on *The Producers*. "You need to finish this off," he said. But she couldn't. "I wasn't interested in doing anything," she said. "I thought if I squeezed my skin, I could see grief coming out. It was deep."

Work on *The Producers* stopped. But then Brooks saw *Contact*, a dance musical Stroman directed and choreographed for Lincoln Center. It won the Tony for Best Musical in 2000. He called Stroman and said he wanted to see her about something. He came over to her apartment and asked her to take over *The Producers* as director and choreographer. Stroman didn't think she was up to it. "Listen to me," Brooks told her. "You'll meet us in the morning, we'll have coffee, we'll work, you'll do rehearsals and you'll go home and you'll cry your fucking eyes out. But you'll come back the next morning and you'll smile, you'll laugh, and then you'll go home and cry. But when you're with me you'll have fun. And that's how you'll get through this. Because if you just cry you'll wither away."

It was an offer she couldn't refuse.

Work resumed on *The Producers* in the winter of 2000. Three times a week Brooks, Meehan, and Kelly met in Stroman's penthouse to hash out the show. The morning always began in the kitchen with coffee and bagels, which Brooks insisted on slicing because he considered himself a "master bagel cutter." Then they'd head to the living room to work. Brooks became the characters while the others fed him a setup until he nailed a joke. Meehan scribbled everything down on his yellow legal pad. Kelly sat at the Steinway ready to turn Brooks's little melodies into songs. Stroman oversaw it all, envisioning production numbers in her head.

Meehan knew musicals needed to be front-loaded with an "I Want" song for the central characters. The song tells the audience where the characters are in their lives and where they want to be. And so Tevye sings "If I Were a Rich Man," Orphan Annie sings "Maybe" (imagining being reunited with her parents), and Eliza Doolittle sings "Wouldn't It Be Loverly." What does Max Bialystock want? To be back on top, to be "The King of Broadway." What does Leo Bloom want? "I Wanna Be a Producer."

"No 'I Want' song has ever been more on the nose than 'I Wanna Be a Producer,'" Meehan said. In the song, Leo sports a top hat and cane and drives "those chorus girls insane," as Brooks wrote. Stroman saw chorus girls stepping out of tall filing cabinets in Bloom's drab accounting office.

Not every idea made the cut. Brooks wrote a song for Liebkind called "Brownshirts on Broadway," about Hitler winning the war. It was a funny song, though probably even more tasteless than "Springtime for Hitler."

Of those working sessions in her apartment, Stroman said, "It was wonderful, it was thrilling." But when they were over and everyone had left, she did cry.

Mel Brooks and political correctness have only a passing acquaintance, and so he could write a song called "Keep It Gay," in which Roger De Bris introduces his theatrical associates, all flamboyant gay men but for the lighting designer, Shirley Markowitz, a stocky lesbian. Geffen didn't like it.

Brooks, Meehan, and Stroman wanted to show Geffen what they had, so they arranged a stage reading with some top Broadway talent, including Gary Beach as Roger De Bris, Cady Huffman as Ulla, and Evan Pappas as Leo Bloom. For Max, everybody wanted Nathan Lane. Brooks had met him in the pool of the Ritz in Paris the weekend Princess Diana was killed. "He came floating up to me like a friendly seal," Brooks said. Brooks told Lane he was working on a musical of *The Producers* and that Lane should do it with Martin Short. "That would be a great honor," Lane said. And that was the last he heard of it until Jerry Zaks mentioned it to him. He was pleased to be asked to do the reading.

A few days before the reading, Geffen called Brooks to tell him he could not produce *The Producers*. The problem wasn't "Keep It Gay." The problem was that he'd just formed DreamWorks with Jeffrey Katzenberg and Steven Spielberg, and the new company was taking up all his time. Geffen also knew Brooks would be a handful. As he told a friend, "The care and feeding that goes into Mel Brooks you can't believe." Geffen did not have the strength to run DreamWorks and manage Mel Brooks. "I'll give you money," he told Brooks, "but I can't put on your show right now." Brooks almost canceled the reading, but Stroman and Meehan knew a lot of producers. Why not invite them? Maybe one of them would pick up the show.

Rocco Landesman was not happy about having to cut short his weekend in the country on a cold Sunday afternoon in April to attend a reading of *The Producers*. But Geffen had called and asked him to take a look. Brooks's lawyer, Alan Schwartz ("May the Schwartz be with you," Brooks said), also urged him to come. Gerald Schoenfeld was there, too. So were Tom Viertel and Richard Frankel, who ran a producing and general management company. They'd done a number of shows, including the hit *Smokey Joe's Cafe*. They specialized in revues and revivals, raising money in $10,000 units from hundreds of investors. But they had never produced an original-book musical.

The reading began and Landesman started laughing. And then he started laughing so hard he was crying. At the intermission, he ran over to Brooks and offered him the St. James Theatre. "Don't you want to wait until after the second act?" Brooks asked. "The second act's going to have to be pretty bad for this not to be a big hit," Landesman said. The second act did not disappoint. Leaving the reading, Landesman asked Schoenfeld what he thought. "It's an insider show," he said. "It'll never work."

Frankel and Viertel loved the show, too, but they did not have an in with Brooks. At one point Frankel spoke to Brooks "and he was looking over my shoulder at somebody more important. I was just fucking bummed. I was so depressed. This is a fantastic show and there's no way on earth I'm going to get this." He went home and wrote Brooks a letter pointing out that his company was good in the trenches of managing shows on Broadway and on tour. "We do everything," he wrote. "We can exploit this show better than anybody else." He noted that he'd loved the movie ever since he saw it at the Cinémathèque when he was living in Paris in 1972. He knew the musical would be a big hit and, quoting Max Bialystock, added: "I WANT THAT MONEY!" The next day the phone rang. It was Brooks. He wanted a meeting.

Frankel and Viertel's offices were large and bustling. Their company employed more than sixty people. Show posters adorned the walls. *Surely, Brooks would be impressed,* Frankel thought. Brooks arrived, looked around, and said, "Where do you sit?" Frankel brought him to his modest office. Brooks closed the door, sat on the couch, and said, "Okay, now we'll talk."

As shrewdly as he assembled his creative team, Brooks put together his producing team. With Landesman he had a theater—the fabled St. James, once home to *Oklahoma!* and *Hello, Dolly!* With Frankel's company he'd have a general manager that, with *The Producers* being its first original musical comedy (and a high-profile one at that), would give the show its undivided attention. To replace Geffen's money, Brooks brought in a friend from the Hamptons, Robert Sillerman, the billionaire founder of SFX Entertainment. Harvey and Bob Weinstein joined the team, and Brooks himself invested.

Frankel drew up a budget for the show: $10.5 million. It would be the biggest and most expensive show his company had ever done. If not monitored closely, the cost of a show can balloon. Sets and costumes come at a hefty price, especially when created by designers who have a reputation for being expensive. Ockrent and Stroman wanted two of the best in the business—set designer Robin Wagner and costume designer William Ivey Long—with whom they'd done *Crazy for You.* During that show's tryout in Washington, D.C., Stroman once arrived at the theater at 8:30 a.m. to work out some choreography. The theater appeared to be empty, but then she noticed Wagner with a can of green paint on a ladder painting one of his sets. She went backstage. It was deserted but for Long, who was down on all fours painting the showgirls' shoes. "I knew then these were the two men I would always want to work with," she said. But she began to sense that some of the producers of *The Producers* were uneasy about them. "It was always me and ten men in suits around a table," she said.

"And they'd say, 'You know, William's so expensive. Maybe we should use somebody else.' And I said, 'When I'm gone from the meeting you can talk about using someone else, but if you don't use William, I'm not going to direct *The Producers.*'"

One of the "suits" suggested using someone less expensive than Wagner. Stroman replied, "I need to use Robin Wagner, so after we finish our meeting I'm going to go and you can talk about it, but I'm not going to direct *The Producers* unless I use Robin Wagner."

It was Ockrent's death, and her grief, that emboldened her. "I was in the position where doing a show didn't fucking matter," she said. "So if I was going to do it, then nobody get in my fucking way." She got Long and Wagner.

Matthew Broderick started reading in theater columns that the creators of *The Producers* wanted him to play Leo Bloom. One day he ran into Tom Meehan, who said, "You know, they're interested in you." *That's nice,* Broderick thought, *but nobody's approached me.* Then he got a call about appearing in a movie with Mel Brooks. He met Brooks and the movie people at the Regency Hotel on Park Avenue. When the meeting was over, Brooks took him aside and told him about *The Producers.* He asked Broderick to join him the next day at Glen Kelly's apartment so he could hear the score. Broderick knew what was up. "I'm going to go over there, and they're going to say, 'Why don't you sing a little bit?' And I'm really auditioning." But nobody asked him to sing. Brooks just wanted him to hear the score. He liked it. Then he was invited to take part in a reading at Stroman's apartment with Cady Huffman, cast as Ulla, and Nathan Lane, who had signed on to play Bialystock. Broderick misread his second line, "Scared. Can't talk." He said, "I can't talk." During a break Brooks rushed over to him and said, "It's 'Scared. Can't talk.' 'I can't talk' is wrong."

Aside from the minor slipup (Brooks caught even the slightest change to the rhythms of his lines), the reading went well, though Lane and Broderick thought some of the jokes and gags were from another era and might land with a thud in 1999. "Keep It Gay" was especially dicey. "Mel's gay guys are like extraterrestrials," Lane said. After the reading, he and Broderick went to lunch. "This is either going to be the biggest hit or the biggest flop ever," Lane said.

The first day of rehearsals Lane showed up, as he always does, off book. Not only did he know his lines, but he knew everyone else's as well. Broderick worked at a slower pace, developing his character and learning his lines during rehearsals. Although he won a Tony in 1994 in a revival of *How to Succeed in Business Without Really Trying*, he did not consider himself a musical comedy actor. One day he came to rehearsals and saw the assistant choreographers working on a dance break in "That Face," which he sang with Huffman. "So Cady and I will sing the song, then exit, and some dancers will come out and dance, right?" he asked. No, they told him. He and Huffman would do the dance. "When do I start doing that?" he asked. Tomorrow, they said. "Oh," he replied. "I'm glad I have some time."

Brooks was a big presence in rehearsals, shouting out new jokes and running up to the actors to tell them how to deliver a line. That's not something writers usually do in the theater, but it was Mel Brooks so nobody minded. Lane, one of the funniest men in show business, contributed his own lines to the script. A speech about being down on his luck ended with a joke that didn't quite land. "When you're down and out, and everybody thinks you're finished, that's the time to stand up on your own two feet and shout . . ." Lane ad-libbed: *"Who do you have to fuck to get a break in this town?"* There were big laughs all around. From the back of the studio Brooks yelled, "No recognition, no royalties!"

Stroman worked with the efficiency of a five-star general commanding an army. She worked out the choreography with her assistant choreographers way ahead of time and then dispatched them to teach the steps to the ensemble. She worked with the leads, teaching them the steps and adjusting the steps to suit the actors' particular physical characteristics. When the company performed a big number, Stroman appeared to be watching every single person at the same time. She didn't miss a thing—a slight misstep, a hand gesture that wasn't quite high enough. Then she'd confer with her assistants, armed with notepads to write down everything she said. At the end of the day the assistants fanned out to give the cast index cards with notes about their performances. Each card contained one note. "You always felt sorry for the girl who got the most cards," Angie Schworer, a chorus member, said.

The trickiest number to tackle was "Springtime for Hitler." It had to be tasteless, of course—the most tasteless number in the history of the musical theater. But it could not be offensive. Gary Beach, as Roger De Bris, played Hitler in the number, making his entrance saying, "Heil, myself!" Stroman hit on the idea of having him sit on the edge of the stage in a spotlight and sing to the audience. It was Hitler as Judy Garland. Everyone loved it. Still, whenever she rehearsed "Springtime for Hitler" she had the stage managers pull down the blinds in the Forty-Second Street rehearsal studios. She didn't want people in neighboring office buildings looking in "to see me lined up with everybody going, 'Sieg Heil!'"

William Ivey Long's costumes would go a long way to making "Springtime for Hitler" so over the top and hilarious it couldn't possibly be offensive. He added the hoariest of German clichés to the costumes for the Ziegfeldian chorus girls. One had a giant beer mug on her head. Another sported a huge pretzel. A third had a Valkyrie helmet, while a fourth wore a giant bratwurst headdress.

As for "Keep It Gay," Long thought, *Well, if we're going to go there we might as well go all the way.* His costumes for Roger De Bris's flamboyant production team included a BDSM leather outfit for Bryan, the set designer; a lavender suit (complete with lavender shoes and lavender-tinted sunglasses) for Kevin, the costume designer; and a tight crop top and bell-bottomed pants for Scott, the choreographer. For kicks, Long threw in the sailor and the Indian chief from the Village People. He clad Shirley Markowitz, the lesbian lighting designer, in a baggy flannel shirt and work boots. By the time *The Producers* reached Broadway, Long had designed 497 costumes.

Robin Wagner, meanwhile, was building models of the show's twelve sets in his studios at 890 Broadway. *The Producers* contained many tips of the hat to musicals of the past. So Wagner designed sets that evoked classic Broadway shows. "Little Old Lady Land" with its huge Valentine heart was "Loveland" from *Follies.* The backstage wall of an empty theater conjured up two celebrated backstage musicals—*Kiss Me, Kate* and *Gypsy.* Wagner modeled the castle on the Alpine scrim at the start of "Springtime for Hitler" on Cinderella's castle in Disneyland. And the huge mirrors that appear during "Springtime for Hitler" would remind musical theater fans of the giant mirror Hal Prince deployed in *Cabaret* and the mirrors Wagner designed for "The Music and the Mirror" in *A Chorus Line.* Brooks, Meehan, and Wagner came up with funny titles of shows Max and Leo would one day produce—*Maim, Katz, 47th Street, High Button Jews, She Shtups to Conquer.* Wagner put them on marquees that would light up at the end of the show. Brooks loved them. Except for one. "Are you crazy?" he said. "That's not how you spell *shtups*!" Wagner had it spelled *schtupps.*

During a final run-through of the show in New York, Harvey Weinstein nearly fell out of his chair laughing. "This gives bad taste a good name," he said.

In January 2001, *The Producers* headed to Chicago for its out-of-town tryout at the 2,300-seat Cadillac Palace Theatre. In the basement, Long stitched costumes, while Wagner painted his sets. Brooks and Meehan made jokes funnier. Stroman tightened dances. Index cards piled up on the actors' dressing room tables. "Oh, my God. I had thousands of them," Broderick recalled. "After a while it was like, 'Put them on my desk. I'm probably not going to look at them anyway.'"

Lane was a "hydrogen bomb," Long said, landing every joke, his energy never flagging. But Broderick seemed hesitant, sometimes vacant. And he didn't know all his lines. Frustration was building with his performance. Stroman gave him bits of business—shuffling papers, moving chairs—"because if he stands to the side he goes to sleep," she told Long.

"I tend to look very dimwitted and stupid to others watching the rehearsal process," Broderick said. "I take a while. I think about things. I catch up. That's what I do."

Brooks couldn't contain his frustration. Broderick appeared so vacant in one scene, Brooks barked at Long, "Take his suit out and drive a car over it so it has some character!"

"Mel seemed to think I'd never been in a musical," Broderick said. "And I had a Tony Award for Best Actor in a Musical."

There was some discussion of replacing Broderick, but it was quickly dropped. He was an enormous draw in Chicago, having starred in one of the city's favorite movies, *Ferris Bueller's Day Off*.

Lane was the only person who wasn't worried. As Broderick said, "Nathan seemed perfectly happy for me to frump around and take my time, because sometimes I threw him a curveball." With nothing to do in a frigid Chicago but rehearse and hang out together at their hotel, Lane and Broderick developed a strong friendship. The chemistry between them offstage was even stronger onstage, and Lane sensed it would elevate the whole show. It was there, no matter how long it took Broderick to learn his lines.*

* Broderick got a boost one day when Anne Bancroft appeared backstage, pointed at him, and said, "That's a funny man."

The day before the first public performance of *The Producers*, people who worked in the hotels where the cast and crew were staying were invited to watch a run-through. The orchestra section of the theater was full of technical people in headsets, so the hotel workers sat up in the theater's enormous balcony. The show began and gales of laugher came swooping down from the balcony. Broderick thought, *What's going on up there—did somebody slip on a banana peel?* "It's not *that* funny," Lane said under his breath to Broderick.

Brooks was on edge at the first preview the next night. He tracked down Long and asked if the swastikas worn on the cast's armbands during "Springtime for Hitler" had been sown on. No, Long told him, "they're snapped on for dry cleaning, but they'll stay on if that's what's worrying you."

"No, no, no," said Brooks. "I just want to know if it's too much, we can take them off."

"Yes, Mel, we can take them off," Long said. "But you know they're in black sequins and red jewels and diamonds, so they're musical comedy swastikas."

"Nonetheless, we can take them off, right?"

"Yes, sir," Long said.

The laughs at the first paid performance of *The Producers* started as soon as the chorus pronounced Max Bialystock's new show *Funny Boy!*, a musical version of *Hamlet*, "the worst show in town." The laughter continued through every scene, even "Der Guten Tag Hop-Clop," when Max and Leo meet Franz Liebkind, who keeps pigeons on his roof in Greenwich Village. Everybody in the show thought the number went on too long, but the audience didn't seem to mind. And they roared when Liebkind's pigeons raised their right wings to reveal swastika wing bands. The laughter and cheering that greeted "Little Old Lady Land" spilled over into intermission, as Lane told Terrence McNally. "Springtime for Hitler" in the second act left the audience delirious. No one was offended by the "musical comedy swastikas." The standing ovation at the end was "pandemonium," producer Tom Viertel recalled. The audience refused to leave the theater. Nobody involved with the show had ever experienced anything like it. "The actors were in shock that there was so much laughter," Stroman recalled. "They were covering up jokes because they didn't know whether to go forward or not. The only person who knew what to do was Nathan. He can feel the breath of the audience. He knows when to go forward. He knows when to stop. He knows if he touches his face, he'll get a bigger laugh. You just cannot teach what he has."

Brooks has only a vague memory of that first preview "because I was looking through tears. Anne and I just cried in each other's arms. It had nothing to do with business, with success, with money. It was hard work being saluted."

When the theater finally emptied, the company went to Petterino's, the Sardi's of Chicago. Brooks and Bancroft led everyone in a conga line.

After another preview in Chicago, one of the producers approached Brooks with some notes. "I'm the funny man around here," Brooks said. "I'll give the notes."* Brooks, Meehan, and Stroman knew exactly what to do. The show was running too long, so they cut out all the jokes that didn't get big laughs. The running time, though, never got much shorter. With the second-tier jokes gone the first-tier jokes got even bigger laughs. Chris Jones, the critic for *Variety*, raved about the show, but put his finger on its major

* "They all had notes," Brooks said of his producers. "So I just kept giving notes back to them. They were into the stock market and all that shit, so I'd write them phony notes about money: 'GM is moving up!' 'Sell all your Ossia stock!' 'Put your money in your mattress because we're going to have a crash!' That was the only one I was right about."

problem—the last fifteen minutes didn't live up to the rest of the show. And Lane's big 11 o'clock number, "Betrayed," suffered from "unnecessary clutter" surrounding it. Brooks and Meehan had spent a lot of time on the number. At one point they came up with a parody of "Rose's Turn" from *Gypsy*. They ran it by Arthur Laurents, who wrote the book to *Gypsy*, for approval. He sent back a terse "no." In the end they put Max in a jail cell where he recapped all he'd gone through with Leo. He feels "betrayed" because Leo ran off to Brazil with Ulla. But Leo comes back, cementing the friendship—the love story—at the heart of the musical.

By the time the Chicago run was over, *The Producers* was pretty much musical comedy perfection. It left town with a profit of $1 million. In New York, the advance was climbing past $20 million (it would eventually hit $37.8 million). The show began previews at the St. James in March. Audiences loved it. And then one night what Stroman and Brooks feared most happened. Gary Beach, as Hitler, sat down on the edge of the stage to do his Judy Garland bit in "Springtime for Hitler." An old man in the front row leapt from his seat and ran up the aisle screaming, "How dare you do this, how dare you do this!" He got to the back of the theater, spotted Brooks, ran over to him and shouted, "How dare you put Hitler onstage. I was in World War II." Brooks jumped up. Stroman held her breath. "You were in World War Two?" Brooks said. "I was in World War Two. And I didn't see you there!" They started to go at it until the company manager grabbed them both by the back of their necks and "threw these two alte kakers out in the street," Stroman said.

David Geffen caught one of the last previews. Over dinner after the show at Angus McIndoe, then a popular theater restaurant, he told Brooks, Stroman, and Meehan, "You have a big problem in the show. Matthew Broderick should be fired." Everyone was too shocked to respond. Lane and Broderick were the best double act Broadway had seen since Adele and Fred Astaire. Brooks politely changed the subject, but when Geffen left he said, "David's crazy. Matthew is wonderful."

The Producers opened to predictably spectacular reviews, undercut slightly by the news that the producers, confident in the show, raised their top ticket price to a then unheard of one hundred dollars. The press piled on, but it didn't matter. The demand for the show was huge. Scalpers were getting $500 to a $1,000 a ticket. The day the reviews came out the Shuberts sold tickets out of their box office at the Majestic Theatre to help ease the demand at the St. James across the street. Broderick rode his Vespa to the St. James that morning, hid in an alleyway, and looked at the line of ticket buyers snaking down West Forty-Fourth Street from Eighth Avenue to Broadway. "It felt like Broadway in the 1950s," he said. The box office took in $3 million that day.

The Producers received fifteen Tony Award nominations, beating the record set by Stephen Sondheim's *Company*, which received fourteen in 1971. *The Full Monty*, now an asterisk, picked up ten.

Lane and Broderick, both up for Best Actor in a Musical, hosted the telecast that year. Brooks and Meehan collected the award for their book. "I'm going to have to do the hardest thing I've ever done in my life," Brooks said. "Act humble." He was back a few minutes later to pick up Best Score. "I want to thank Stephen Sondheim for not writing a show this year. Thanks, Steve." As the orchestra played under him (the Tony's version of the hook), he quipped, "Stop with the music, will ya? Unless it's mine." Then he said, "Thank you all. It's been wonderful being here. I'll see you in a couple minutes. Good-bye!" Accepting the award for direction, Stroman, acknowledging Mike Ockrent's contribution to the show, said, "May you all be blessed with the laughter I have had over the last year."

As for Best Actor, Broderick knew Lane would win. But every now and then he allowed himself to think, *Maybe I can beat that* *guy*. Dame Edna Everage (Barry Humphries in purple wig and rhinestone-encrusted cat glasses) presented the award. She ran into Broderick backstage. "I've had a look in this envelope," she said with a trace of incredibly insincere sadness in her voice, "and I'm afraid you're going to be very disappointed." Sure enough, Lane won. But he brought Broderick onstage with him and said, "I can only accept this on behalf of the two of us. Believe me, without him I'm nothing."*

When *The Producers* won Best Musical, it set a record for the most Tony Awards ever—twelve, two more than *Hello, Dolly!* had collected in 1964.

"I want to thank Hitler for being such a funny guy on stage," Brooks said.

The summer of 2001 was a heady time for *The Producers*. The show was sold out for the duration of Lane's and Broderick's contracts. Scalpers had tickets (they always do), but the price was now $1,500 and climbing. Brooks, Meehan, and Stroman frequently stopped by the theater, sat on a flight of stairs at the back of the orchestra, and watched 1,700 people split their sides laughing. Broderick and Lane were on the covers of magazines and newspapers and in constant demand on the talk show circuit. Meehan and his wife, Carolyn, often ate at Angus McIndoe, which was next door to the theater. I joined them one night, and Meehan and I thought up taglines for all the shows dwarfed by *The Producers*. The only one I still remember was Meehan's—"*42nd Street*—where the line to buy tickets to *The Producers* begins!" Whenever Brooks came into

* At the Tony ball after the ceremony, Humphries, no longer in drag, grabbed Broderick's arm and said, "I hear my client may have said something that might have offended you." Broderick replied, "No, no. I laughed. Tell her not to feel bad at all."

Angus McIndoe, Orso, or Joe Allen, he hopped from table to table, accepting praise for his show. Bancroft, waiting patiently at their table, would let him lap it up for a bit and then yell, "Mel—eat!"

Though *The Producers* was the undisputed king of Times Square that summer, it helped all the other shows by putting Broadway squarely in the mainstream of American popular culture. The total box office gross for the 2000–01 theater season hit an all-time high of $665 million, a 10.3 percent jump from the previous season. Paid attendance soared five hundred thousand to set another record—11.9 million. It was the tenth year in a row that Broadway had smashed its own records.[4]

Attendance dipped slightly during the summer as the economy began to sag. Jed Bernstein, the head of the League of American Theatres and Producers, said, "We are far from a panic situation, but it certainly bears watching. It means keeping the marketing pressure on."[5] Nobody was too concerned, especially since another blockbuster was around the corner—*Mamma Mia!*, the ABBA musical from London, set to open October 18, 2001, at the Winter Garden. It already had an advance of $20 million.

On Sunday, September 9, Broadway kicked off the fall theater season with "Broadway on Broadway," an annual free concert in Times Square featuring performances from all the shows. "You know what the number one attraction in the city of New York is?" Mayor Rudolph Giuliani asked the crowd. "Broadway!" Bernstein thought the mayor looked tired. He was coming to the end of his term—and his marriage to Donna Hanover. The tabloids had relished the news of his affair with Judith Nathan. He'd battled cancer and ended a lackluster bid for the United States Senate. "It was obvious he wasn't having any fun," Bernstein said. Everybody else was, however. Joe Bologna, starring on Broadway with his wife, Renée Taylor, in *If you ever leave me . . . I'm going with you!*, summed up the afternoon: "On this beautiful, perfect New York September day to be on Broadway . . . there is nothing more exciting."

On Tuesday—another "beautiful, perfect New York September day"—Bernstein was having breakfast with Paige Price, the star of the musical version of *Saturday Night Fever*, at the Polish Tea Room. Price was thinking of becoming a producer, and Bernstein was giving her advice. Harry Edelstein, the owner of Cafe Edison, came over to their table and said, "A plane just hit one of the World Trade Center towers." Bernstein thought, as so many people did, it must be a small plane. He remembered that in 1945 a plane crashed into the Empire State Building. He finished breakfast and went to his office at the League. Everybody was in the conference room watching television. The south tower had just collapsed. Bernstein sent all but a few people home and then arranged a conference call with the Shuberts, the Nederlanders, and Jujamcyn Theaters to consider the threat to Times Square. Some planes were still unaccounted for. They also had to decide if the shows would go on that night, and what they should tell the press. As events unfolded, it became clear Broadway would have to shut down. The city was cordoned off, all bridges and tunnels closed, the Manhattan sky ringed by fighter jets.

I spoke to Gerald Schoenfeld that morning. "Broadway is world famous and as much a target as any other landmark," he said, adding that he and the other theater owners would talk to city officials before deciding when—or if—to reopen.

All through that day, Rudy Giuliani kept thinking, *Where can I go for guidance on this?* Two places came to mind: Israel and London during the Battle of Britain. After the Jaffa Road bus bombings in 1996, Giuliani went to Israel to ride the bus with Jerusalem mayor Ehud Olmert. "They got that bus running as quickly as possible to show the terrorists you can't deter the Israelis," Giuliani said. When the attack on New York occurred, Giuliani was reading Roy Jenkins's new biography of Winston Churchill. He tried to get an hour or so of sleep in the early morning of September 12, but couldn't. He picked up the Churchill biography and read that, during the Battle of Britain, Churchill insisted the theater, the opera, the ballet, the orchestra go on as usual "to show the Germans that you can't defeat our spirit," Giuliani said.

The next morning Bernstein got a call from Cristyne Nicholas, the head of NYC & Company, the city's tourism office. She summoned him to a meeting with the mayor at the Police Academy on East Twentieth Street. Richard Grasso, the head of the New York Stock Exchange was there, along with officials from the Metropolitan Museum and the hotel industry. A grim Giuliani said, "We have to put our emotions aside for a moment and figure out how we are going to save New York." He turned to Grasso. "When can you get the stock market reopened?"

"If you can give us power, we can reopen," Grasso said. (The stock market opened one week later.)

Giuliani turned to Bernstein and Nicholas. "When can Broadway reopen?" Bernstein and Nicholas hesitated and then outlined the problem. Many people who work on Broadway live in the suburbs. With the bridges and tunnels closed they would not be able to get to work. "If you can get our employees over the bridges, we can reopen," Bernstein said.

"Thursday," Giuliani said.

"This isn't going to be as easy as Rudy thinks," Bernstein told Nicholas as they were leaving the meeting. "I don't know if we can just flip the switch, turn on the lights, and have a Broadway show."

Bernstein convened a meeting of producers, union heads, and press agents—more than a hundred people stuffed into the League's conference room. He told them the mayor wanted Broadway open on Thursday. There were questions about safety, logistics, economics, whether there would even be an audience. But in the end, everyone agreed to light the lights of Broadway Thursday night. Someone mentioned that on Tuesday night all the members of Congress had gathered on the steps of the Capitol and sang Irving Berlin's "God Bless America." Why not have the casts of every show sing the song during the curtain call, the person suggested.

Nicholas met with more than two hundred actors, musicians, stagehands, stage mangers, and press agents that afternoon in a Broadway theater to tell them the mayor wanted them at work Thursday night. There was resistance—concerns, again, about safety and getting into the city. An actor stood up and said, "You're not the one who has to get up there and perform. You have no idea how hard it is. We're human beings. We're hurting, we're suffering." Nicholas understood, but said, "Please do your best, for the city."

She relayed concerns about safety and being able to get into the city to Giuliani. He had already stepped up the police presence in Times Square as it was on his list of the city's top ten potential targets. As for getting into the city, he said, "Tell them to show their union card at the bridges and tunnels and I guarantee they will get in," he said. "I want Broadway open on Thursday."

"The focus was on New Jersey," Giuliani recalled years later, "because that's where the terrorists came from that did the first bombing of the World Trade Center in 1993. But I thought if people say they're working on Broadway and we examine them a little bit, we could let them in without too much of a risk."

Giuliani called the big three theater owners—Gerald Schoenfeld, James L. Nederlander Jr., and Rocco Landesman—to enlist their help in getting Broadway up and running on Thursday night. He told Landesman, "Get *The Producers* back up because then everybody will follow suit." Landesman said he would.

It was clear by the end of the day on Wednesday that Broadway could reopen. But would there be an audience? As he was dealing with the untold horrors of the attack, Giuliani, surrounded by media wherever he went, said several times, "If you want to help the city—if you want to show the terrorists that we can handle this—come to the city. Come to a play. Go to a movie. Go to a restaurant. Spend some money here. We need the money."

* * *

Matthew Broderick made his way to the St. James from his SoHo apartment Thursday afternoon. There were checkpoints everywhere, but he showed his ID and got through. *Is it okay to be in Times Square?*, he thought as he headed to the theater. *Is this still going on?* And yet "we had something to do," he said. "The world was going to go forward in some way, maybe."

The cast gathered backstage to prepare for the show. The stage manager told them the sound effects of the bombs falling during "Springtime for Hitler" would be cut. The cast rehearsed "God Bless America." Broderick didn't know all the lyrics, but he was determined to learn them.

Giuliani went to *The Lion King* for the start of the show that night. Nicholas attended *The Full Monty*. The majority of the press covering the reopening of Broadway attended the hottest show in town, *The Producers*. Reporters stood at the back of the theater with Brooks, Bancroft, Meehan, and most of the show's producers. The house, to everyone's surprise, was about two-thirds full. But it was quiet. The buzz of excitement at a hit musical before the curtain goes up was missing. Rocco Landesman walked out onstage and told the audience, "You have permission to laugh tonight. That's the best approach. We've come together and we will laugh together."

Lane got muted laughs during "The King of Broadway." "The big laughs weren't there," Jeffry Denman recalled. "We had to gradually pull people in. It was, 'We can do this, we can do this together.'" And then when Roger De Bris said to Leo, "God, if I could bottle you, I'd shove you under my armpits," and Leo hugs Max for safety, there was a big laugh. "Keep It Gay" was off and running, and the laughs came. They came for "Little Old Lady Land." And they came for "Springtime for Hitler." At the curtain call Lane and Broderick joined hands with the cast and led fifteen hundred people in tears through "God Bless America."

EPILOGUE

AND THE SHOW GOES ON

The weeks after the attack on the World Trade Center were harrowing for the Broadway community, as they were for every New Yorker, every American. Engine 54/Ladder 4/ Battalion 9 on Eighth Avenue and West Forty-Eighth Street—long known as Broadway's firehouse—lost fifteen firefighters. They were among the first to arrive at the Trade Center.

Many on Broadway lost friends and loved ones. A phone call from a family member jolted LaChanze, the Tony Award–winning star of *Once on This Island* and *The Color Purple*, out of sleep on the morning of September 11. The family member told her a plane had hit the north tower of the World Trade Center. She turned on the television and counted down the windows to floors 105 through 101 where her husband, Calvin Gooding, worked as a trader for Cantor Fitzgerald. His office was directly above the impact zone of American Airlines Flight 11. Gooding and LaChanze had a one-and-a-half-year-old daughter, and she was seven months pregnant with a second.

Financially, Broadway was in its most precarious position since the Great Depression. Times Square was a ghost town. Most shows played to houses that were only a quarter full. Broadway lost nearly $5 million the week following the attack. "We are in complete crisis," Jeffrey Seller, a producer of *Rent*, told the *New York Times*. "This is disaster mode."[1] A number of shows that were in trouble before the attacks closed quickly, throwing a hundred actors and dozens of crew members out of work. Long-running shows such as *The Phantom of the Opera* and *Les Misérables* were dangerously close to collapse.

The League of American Theatres and Producers convened meetings with union officials to negotiate reduced running costs. Philip J. Smith, the president of the Shubert Organization, called his friend Thomas Short, the powerful head of the International Alliance of Theatrical Stage Employees. "We're in trouble and we need some relief," he told Short. He asked for a 35 percent cut in wages for the shows in jeopardy, to be paid back when, and if, business recovered. "You can either be a hero or a spoiler," Smith said. Short counteroffered with a 25 percent cut in wages for four weeks. The other unions agreed to the same deal.

There was some grumbling about "millionaire producers" getting concessions from Broadway's rank and file. *New York Post* columnist Liz Smith accused Cameron Mackintosh of using the crisis to "crunch costs" on *Phantom* and *Les Misérables*. A furious Mackintosh called Smith's column "erroneous" and "highly damaging." He wrangled a correction from her.[2]

The League also put together an aggressive marketing campaign to encourage people to support New York by coming to see a show. Jed Bernstein and Barry Weissler thought the industry needed another television commercial such as the "I Love New York" campaign that helped revive Broadway in the 1970s. They proposed bringing every actor on Broadway to Times Square to film them singing a song that would tell the world Broadway was open for business. Weissler thought all of the actors should be in the costumes they wore in their shows. They told Nancy Coyne about the idea. "I'm going to call Nathan Lane," Coyne said. "If he'll do it, everybody else will, too." Lane was in. Weissler thought the song should be "New York, New York." John Kander and Fred Ebb waived their royalties.

On September 27, 2001, the actors, dressed in their costumes, met at the Booth Theatre to learn some steps devised by Jerry Mitchell, the choreographer of *The Full Monty*, and brush up on "New York, New York." Several Broadway stars not in a show joined them—Bernadette Peters, Bebe Neuwirth, Joel Grey, Tommy Tune, Alan Alda, Glenn Close, Betty Buckley, Harvey Fierstein. Every union waived its fees. The media, which was covering the filming of the commercial (thus giving the event millions of dollars' worth of free publicity), stood atop double-decker Gray Line buses parked on either side of Duffy Square (the small square in the middle of Times Square).

The Rockettes joined the actors. Lane and Broderick, dressed as Bialystock and Bloom, were front and center, flanked by Cady Huffman, in her slinky white Ulla dress, and Roger Bart, in his campy Carmen Ghia costume. Minutes before the cameras rolled, Elaine Stritch, in a white blazer and white porkpie hat, appeared. She marched to the front of the line and stood next to Lane. But she didn't know the steps. Lane tried to teach them to her, but it was hopeless. At one point her hand went up at the wrong time and hit him in the face. The producers shot a few takes, but there was Stritch, front and center, several beats behind everyone else. "We gotta move her," one of the producers told Jed Bernstein, who was in the broadcast booth. They devised a plan. They would tell Stritch that since both she and Huffman were in white, the cameras were picking up a strobe-lighting effect. Would she mind if they moved her a few paces to the right? "We thought this was very clever," Bernstein said. "But being the Broadway heavyweights that we were, we sent a production assistant to tell her." They moved Stritch, but when Jerry Mitchell yelled, "Action," she ran right back to Lane's side.

The network news outlets ran the sixty-second "New York, New York" video in its entirety. Local and international outlets picked it up and also ran it in its entirety. "We stopped counting around forty million dollars of free media that we knew about," Bernstein said. The League and NYC & Company devised another campaign: "Spend Your Regards to Broadway." The city, though strapped for cash, bought $2.5 million worth of theater tickets at $50 apiece. NYC & Company put out the word that if you spent $500 in New York City, you could take the receipts to the Visitor Center in Times Square and get two tickets to a Broadway show. "Nobody values a free ticket," said Cristyne Nicholas. "So we made them work for the ticket."

The "I Love New York Theater" and "Spend Your Regards to Broadway" campaigns—as well as $1 million worth of ads for the theater paid for by New York State—worked so well that by May 2002 Broadway was setting box office records once again. Most of the shows recovered quickly enough that the League wound up returning $1 million of the $2.5 million it had received in ticket subsidies. Off-Broadway and nonprofit theaters felt left out, but the world identified Broadway with New York. If Broadway was up and running, so was the city.

Mamma Mia! was in rehearsals on September 11. It was scheduled to open in October, but producer Judy Craymer thought she should postpone. Giuliani called, requesting she open as planned. "It was traumatic, and we felt inadequate because all we were doing was *Mamma Mia!*, but we just got on with it," Craymer said.[3] A jukebox musical that squeezed ABBA's songs into a charming if slight plot, it was the kind of show that in normal times might make a *New York Times* critic cringe. But these were not normal times, and so Ben Branltey wrote, "Those in need of such solace—and who doesn't that include in New York these days—will be glad to learn that a giant singing Hostess cupcake opened at the Winter Garden Theatre last night. It's called 'Mamma Mia!,' and it may be the unlikeliest hit ever to win over cynical, sentiment shy New Yorkers."[4]

The one show whose box office barely dipped during the crisis was *The Producers.* Less than two months after September 11, Rocco Landesman announced that *The Producers* would charge the unheard of price of $480 a ticket for fifty of the best seats in the house at every performance. Broadway was aghast. Gerald Schoenfeld told him, "You can't do this. There will be the perception that Broadway tickets are five hundred dollars now. It will ruin this business." But Landesman knew that ticket brokers were getting nearly $2,000 a ticket, and none of that money was going to the show's investors or creators.

Landesman had a point. Brokers—or scalpers, to be less polite about it—had been a part of the Broadway food chain since Oscar Hammerstein I opened the Olympia, the first theater in Times Square, in 1895. Brokers snapped up as many tickets as they could at face value and then, if the show was a hit, sold them to the public at substantial markups. Brokers got many tickets from box office workers, producers, and theater owners, paying them kickbacks. Hotel concierges funneled many a rich out-of-towner to the brokers. The concierges got their kickbacks, too. It was an all-cash transaction, so the kickbacks disappeared like ice, which gave the whole murky business its name. Over the years there were several investigations into "ice," including one in 1963 that nearly brought down the Shubert Organization. Attempts were made to clean it up, but most were halfhearted. There was simply too much ice to go around. By the 1980s, brokers (and others with access to tickets) were making startling amounts of money. One broker even left a lucrative career on Wall Street because "there was more reliability with tickets than with the stock market," he said. That was largely due to one show—*The Phantom of the Opera.*

The top ticket was $50. Brokers were selling them for $600. Even seats in the rear mezzanine were going for $300. The show was such a hit that those inflated prices held for years. One person close to the show with regular access to orchestra seats "must have had the biggest safety deposit box God ever created with a lot of cash in there," said a broker who did business with this person.

The bigger the hit, the more ice. At its height in 1994, with Glenn Close in the lead, orchestra seats to *Sunset Boulevard* fetched $1,000 on a Saturday night. *Rent* was another boon to brokers. They even figured out ways to get their hands on the twenty-dollar tickets set aside for the kids willing to camp out all night in front of the theater. A lot of those "kids" were in fact working for brokers. In the business, they're called *diggers* (they "dig" out tickets). When the producers of *Rent*, concerned about safety and the unsightliness of people sleeping outside their theater, instituted the lottery system, the brokers got their hooks into that as well. Hopeful *Rent*-heads showed up early in the morning to fill out slips of paper with numbers on them. They'd come back late in the afternoon and someone from the show would pick the numbers out of a hat. Holders of the lucky numbers got two tickets. The brokers would send word to their crony at the show that their diggers were, say, two, five, seven, and nine. The crony would then put those slips of paper into a freezer. When the crony reached into the hat he felt for the cold slips. About half the tickets in the lottery went to brokers, the rest to real *Rent*-heads. "It had to look legitimate. So you couldn't get too greedy," a person familiar with the practice said.

Landesman knew about some of these tricks. The $480 premium-priced seat to *The Producers*, he said, would "strike a blow at the heart of the scalping operation."[5] Though Schoenfeld and the press balked at the price, the public snapped up the tickets (the brokers got some, too, and sold them at higher prices, though Landesman did cut into their margins).

As long as Lane and Broderick were above the title, *The Producers* sold out every night. But would it do so after they departed? Nancy Coyne feared that if both left at the same time, it could damage the show. But Lane and Broderick were exhausted. And Lane developed a polyp on his left vocal chord and had to scale back his schedule to six performances a week. "That show almost killed me," he said. "I had no voice. My back, my everything had gone." They gave their final performance (or so they thought) on March 17, 2002. Steven Weber, a television actor, replaced Broderick. Henry Goodman, a celebrated British actor, stepped in for Lane. Weber, in rehearsals, was competent and charming. Goodman, a Shakespearean actor, was in trouble. He did not inhabit the world of Mel Brooks. His lines fell flat. He couldn't even get a laugh on "When I was young and gay—but straight!" Goodman was frustrated that the assistant directors told him to do everything the way Lane had done it. He wanted to create his own Max Bialystock. Stroman and Brooks worked with him and, he would later say, seemed encouraging. But there was growing unease. At an early preview when Goodman failed to get a laugh, Brooks whispered to Landesman, "Don't panic." He paused then added, "Panic."

In early April 2002, I got word that Goodman was in trouble. He'd been performing the show for two weeks. Audience response was lackluster. I bought a ticket to a Wednesday matinee, taking my seat in the rear of the orchestra. The critics would soon be re-reviewing the show. Early on it was clear that what had once been the funniest show on Broadway was no longer. Goodman was lost. He tried for a joke, but missed. I heard a bang behind me. It was Brooks, pounding the wall. I called John Barlow, the shows' press agent, and said I'd be writing a column that Friday about the concerns surrounding Goodman's performance—and how a round of bad reviews would irreparably damage the show. Barlow called back a few minutes later. "Henry Goodman is going to be fired after the matinee on Sunday," he said. "We're asking you not to write about him on Friday, and we will give you the exclusive story on Sunday." Deal, I said. Barlow called after the matinee. "Goodman's been fired. Go with the story."

Nobody had the guts to fire Goodman to his face. He heard the news from his agent in London, who called him backstage after the performance.

BRIT STAR FIRED FOR FAILING TO "PRODUCE," the *Post* blared the next day. "Max has gotten the ax." Brad Oscar, who played Franz Liebkind and understudied Bialystock, took over the role. He got fine reviews, but the damage was done. Goodman's firing created the perception that without Lane and Broderick *The Producers* was no longer a hot ticket. And Goodman's firing was costly. The show had to pay out his eight-month contract, which guaranteed him $15,000 a week.

The Producers' box office began to sag in 2003. It had recouped its $10.5 million in record time and was still profitable. But a show that once looked as if it would run as long as an Andrew Lloyd Webber smash was beginning to wind down. There was one way to save it: bring back Lane and Broderick. Lane was reluctant, but he knew the show needed help. There was something else as well. "I believe it was the money," Lane said years later. "I believe they offered us a great deal of money. And then there was the money." They made a deal to rejoin the show for three months starting in January 2004. They would each make more than $100,000 a week during their return engagement. When the *New York Post* broke the news they were coming back, there were lines around the block to buy tickets.

Asked to open the show in London in November 2004, Lane said no. *The Producers* changed his life, but it was time to move on. Richard Dreyfuss got the part of Bialystock. Lane ran into him at a benefit in New York shortly after he'd been cast.

"I'm going to be playing your part in London," he told Lane.

"Great," Lane said. "Have you ever done a musical before?"

"No, but it just looks like it'll be a lot fun."

"Fun is a part of the quotient," Lane replied. "But you should really start preparing now. Get a trainer, get lots of rest, drink lots of fluids, and learn your lines."

Several weeks later, having finished up a run in Stephen Sondheim's *The Frogs*, an exhausted Lane arrived at his house in East Hampton for a much-needed vacation. The phone rang. It was Stroman. "I need to talk to you about something," she said. Dreyfuss wasn't working out. Would Lane be willing to replace him? Lane discussed it with his partner and decided to say no. He was going to shoot the film version of *The Producers* in a few months and wanted time to prepare. He called Stroman the next day to tell her. She burst into tears. "It's a disaster," she said. "I don't know what's going to happen."

Dreyfuss was, in fact, far worse than Goodman. A week before previews at the Drury Lane, he didn't know his lines or his blocking, and often seemed to be in a fog.

"Okay," Lane told the sobbing Stroman, "I'll be there Monday."

"Of course, Mel always says, 'I told her to cry,'" Lane recalled with a laugh years later. He rehearsed just three days before the first preview at the Theatre Royal, Drury Lane. Brooks and Bancroft arrived to support him and Stroman. "We were all together again. It was a wonderful time," Lane said. He received raves, and although he was only in the show a few months, he launched what turned out to be a successful run.

Back in New York, however, *The Producers* was in trouble. Lane and Broderick's return gave the show a huge lift, but at the same time doomed it. The perception that if you missed them in the show why bother now, really took hold. *The Producers* closed on April 22, 2007, after a run of just six years. Its producers acknowledged mistakes along the way, but maybe, as Jerry Schoenfeld said after that first reading, the show was "too insider." *The Producers* was a New York musical about showbiz. Leo delivers one of its best lines after he decides to quit his accounting firm. His boss says, "Bloom, where do you think you're going? You've already had your toilet break!"

"I'm not going into the toilet!" Leo replies. "I'm going into show business!" The line drew huge laughs in New York that first year. But producer Tom Viertel noticed something: "The further away from opening night, the less of a laugh that line got. And then when we opened the tour in Pittsburgh there was no laugh whatsoever."

The Producers did establish that musical comedy was back in style. In 1998, Margo Lion, a producer of *Angels in America* who sometimes used her West End apartment as collateral to back shows, came down with a bad cold. To pass the time in bed, she popped a video of John Waters's movie *Hairspray* into the VCR. She'd seen it when it came out in 1988, but wasn't impressed. Watching it a second time, she thought, *This is a musical comedy.* She recruited Marc Shaiman, who wrote the music for *South Park*, and his then partner and collaborator, lyricist Scott Wittman, to write four songs on spec, including one called "Good Morning Baltimore." Tom Meehan and Mark O'Donnell, a writer from *Saturday Night Live*, wrote the script. Harvey Fierstein signed up to play, in drag, Edna Turnblad. *Hairspray* opened on Broadway in 2002, won eight Tony Awards, and ran seven years.

At a Hanukkah party in 2002, a young man came up to me and said he was a fan of my *New York Post* theater column. His name was Robert Lopez. He said he was at work on a new musical with his collaborator Jeff Marx. "It's a small show," he said, "with puppets. Sort of an X-rated *Sesame Street*. I hope you'll come see it." *Avenue Q* opened in 2003 at the Vineyard Theatre. The reviews were glowing. Jeffrey Seller and Kevin McCollum moved it to Broadway a few months later. In *ShowBusiness: The Road to Broadway*, a documentary about the 2003–04 theater season, I called *Avenue Q* a puppet show that could not possibly last more than a few months on Broadway. It won three Tonys, including Best Musical, and ran for six years.

In 2002, Eric Idle finally got around to an idea he'd had for years: Turning *Monty Python and the Holy Grail* into a musical. He wanted Mike Nichols to direct. "Forget it," said Bill Haber, the show's producer, "he doesn't want to work this hard."[6] As soon as Nichols read the script and heard the score, he said, "I'm screwed. I have to do this."[7] *Spamalot* played its out-of-town tryout in Chicago. "I have seen the next *Producers*, and its name is *Spamalot*," the critic for the *Chicago Sun-Times* wrote. The musical opened on Broadway in 2005 with an $18 million advance, ran 1,575 performances, and grossed nearly $200 million.

In February 2011, the producer Scott Rudin invited me to a rehearsal of his new musical, *The Book of Mormon*, written by *South Park* creators Matt Stone and Trey Parker, and Robert Lopez. I watched as two actors playing Mormon missionaries arrived in Uganda to spread the word of God. Some thugs stole their luggage, but as the poor but happy villagers tell them, when things go wrong in Uganda, you just throw up your hands and sing "Hasa Diga Eebowai." Everybody sang and danced to this peppy tune, a send-up of "Hakuna Matata" from *The Lion King*. And then a cheery black man introduced the missionaries to the people in the village: "Here's the butcher. He has AIDS. Here's the doctor. He has AIDS. Here's my daughter. She has . . . a lovely personality. But if you touch her, I'll give you my AIDS." When one of the missionaries asked the happy villager what "Hasa Diga Eebowai" means in English, he replied, "Fuck you, God!"

Oh, my God, I thought. The Book of Mormon *may be the most subversive musical ever to hit Broadway, and yet it's as peppy as* Bye Bye Birdie.

Later that day I got a call from a ticket broker friend. I told him I'd just seen a rehearsal of *The Book of Mormon.* "I have no idea how Broadway audiences are going to react, but if I were you I'd buy every ticket in sight," I said. The show is now in its tenth year on Broadway. It has grossed more than $500 million in New York alone. My ticket broker friend has a red Ferrari with the license plate "BOM," for *Book of Mormon.*

Garth Drabinsky, the first producer to sell VIP tickets (for a mere $125), spent the 2000s in Toronto courtrooms battling charges of fraud and forgery. He was also under indictment in the United States and could not cross the border without being arrested. During his trial, it emerged that when he was tossed out of Livent's offices he left behind a briefcase containing ledgers with notes in his handwriting directing accounting changes.[8] In 2009, he and Myron Gottlieb were found guilty and sentenced to seven years in jail. Drabinsky appealed and lost. In 2011, he entered the Millhaven Institution, a maximum-security prison in Ontario. While there some inmates reportedly beat him up, though Drabinsky said that was not true. He was treated "as well as you can expect to be treated in that circumstance," he said. He served out most of his sentence, which was reduced, at Beaver Creek, a minimum-security prison. Released on parole in 2013, he returned to producing. A musical version of his movie *Madame Sousatzka* flopped in Toronto in 2017. Several people who worked on the show said that when it closed Drabinsky owed them money.

In a 2020 interview for this book, Drabinsky conceded he'd made some mistakes at Livent, namely that his tours of *Show Boat* and *Ragtime* were too expensive. "The touring division was a disaster," he said. "I know that. I had never taken the time to scale shows down." He had successfully toured a full-scale *Phantom* that didn't compromise the show so his "instinct," he said, was to do the same with *Show Boat* and *Ragtime.* He projected more profitable weeks in each city than there were and eventually "you get hurt." He refused to discuss his legal problems, but pointedly noted that the U.S. Attorney for the Southern District of New York dismissed all charges against him in 2018. The case was on hold while Drabinsky was prosecuted and convicted for his crimes in Canada.

"Because Drabinsky has already served a term of imprisonment for crimes arising from the same underlying cause of indictment, and because the interests of justice would not be served by further prosecution of this matter, the government has determined that dismissal of the indictment is warranted," assistant U.S. attorney Sarah Eddy said.

One of the shows SFX Entertainment acquired when it bought what was left of Livent was *Seussical* by Lynn Ahrens and Stephen Flaherty, fashioned from the Dr. Seuss books. A workshop in Toronto drew raves from Broadway insiders. Jerry Schoenfeld told me it had the potential to be the next *Cats.* SFX teamed up with Fran and Barry Weissler to produce the $10 million show on Broadway. *Seussical* tried out in Boston, and what looked adorable in the workshop was muddled and charmless in the Colonial Theatre. The Weisslers fired much of the creative team ("Heads Are Rolling in Whoville," I gleefully noted in the *New York Post*), including director Frank Galati. Rob Marshall, who would go on to direct the Oscar-winning movie of *Chicago*, replaced him. But even he couldn't save *Seussical.* Before the curtain went up on opening night in New York, Barry Weissler pulled me aside and said, "We're going to get killed, right?" I'd spoken to several critics that day so I knew what the verdict would be. "Yes," I said. Horton heard a *boo* when the reviews came out.

Seussical only ran 198 performances, but it has a place in theater history: it was the first show to be done in not only by the critics but also by the Internet.

On January 28, 1997, V. J. John Gillespie, a former decorator who outfitted dressing rooms for Broadway stars, launched a website called Talkin' Broadway where he and other theater fans could tell stories about shows they loved and theater people they knew. At the last minute, Gillespie's web designer added a message board called All That Chat. Nobody paid much attention to it at first. It was a place where devoted theater fans could discuss what songs had been cut from Sondheim shows during out-of-town tryouts. But some posters began reviewing Broadway-bound shows out of town. They savaged *Seussical* in Boston.

"I felt bad about it because I wish every Broadway show the greatest success, but that just doesn't happen," Gillespie said. The "dear shits," as Alan Jay Lerner once dubbed theater fans who rush to see a disaster in the making, had found their outlet on All That Chat. Producers and press agents were appalled. The old rule of letting a show work out its problems during a tryout with little or no notice from the New York press was smashed to smithereens. As Jeremy Gerard wrote in *New York*, "the Web is the Fisher-Price baby monitor of Broadway, broadcasting each night's mewling to an audience of voyeurs before the cherished child is ready to seek its fortune in the world."[9]

Newspaper critics dismissed All That Chat as nothing but a forum for bitter show queens who probably dreamed of a career in the theater but never had one. Critics, on the other hand, were professional writers with experience, knowledge, and judgment. But even they could not withstand the onslaught of All That Chat. By the time their reviews came out, anybody who cared to know what was going on in the theater knew from the message board if a show was good or bad. The critics were now late to the game. The Internet decimated newspapers in the 2000s, and when the recession hit in 2008, many critics whose quotations and names once emblazoned the sides of buses found themselves on the unemployment line. "Old newspaper critics used to get a certain amount of respect," said Gannett Newspaper's Jacques le Sourd after he'd been let go after thirty-five years. "Now we're tossed onto the slag heap in the alley like old computer monitors. We're obsolete equipment."[10]

In a last-ditch effort to save *Seussical*, Fran and Barry Weissler put Broadway's number one fan—Rosie O'Donnell—in the role of the Cat in the Hat. O'Donnell was winding up her TV show, and wanted to work in the theater. In 2003, she produced *Taboo*, a musical about the fashion designer and performance artist Leigh Bowery, who died of AIDS in 1995. Boy George wrote the score and played Bowery. Plagued by backstage battles and a volatile O'Donnell, who frequently dressed down her creative team, the show was a disaster. O'Donnell put up most of the $10 million investment, and lost it all.

But her favorite musical, *The Lion King*, is still on Broadway after twenty-two years. It's been produced in nearly thirty countries, and with a worldwide gross of $8.2 billion is thought to be the most lucrative entertainment property ever. Disney's next show, *Aida*, received mixed reviews but, with a score by Elton John and Tim Rice, ran a profitable four years. Disney stumbled with *The Little Mermaid*, *Tarzan*, and *Mary Poppins*, but recovered with the charming *Newsies* and the lucrative *Aladdin*. Peter Schneider became the chairman of Walt Disney Studios in 1999. It was a job he did not want. He lasted eighteen months before resigning to produce and direct in the theater. Thomas Schumacher runs Disney's vast theatrical empire from his all-glass office atop the New Amsterdam Theatre. Julie Taymor has directed operas and plays all over the world, but her monumental Broadway flop, *Spider-Man: Turn Off the Dark*, eclipsed them all. She wrote the musical with Bono and The Edge. When it was in dire straits in previews, Bono and The Edge were collecting millions touring

New Zealand. Taymor tried to save the show amid multiple cast injuries, technical mishaps, opening-night postponements, mounting financial losses, and brutal press coverage. She shouldered much of the blame (somewhat unfairly) and suffered the humiliation of being bounced from the show in 2011. *Spider-Man* stumbled along for a few years before closing at a loss of nearly $100 million.

Mel Brooks, Tom Meehan, and Susan Stroman teamed up again on a $16 million stage production of *Young Frankenstein* in 2007. Meehan had misgivings while he and Brooks were writing the show. Anne Bancroft had died unexpectedly of cancer in 2005 and Brooks "was angry at the world," said Meehan. "He was just not in the right frame of mind to write a musical comedy." Nonetheless, the producers of *Young Frankenstein: The New Mel Brooks Musical* were so confident it would be a hit they priced orchestra seats at $450. The show opened to lackluster reviews and eked out a run of just over a year. A revised version opened to strong reviews in Newcastle, England, in 2017. Brooks appeared at the curtain call and told cheering fans, "It's working. We can take it right to the Garrick Theatre. But the problem is: How are we going to get you all on the bus?"[11] The show received another round of glowing reviews at the Garrick in London a month later. But Tom Meehan was not there to celebrate. He died August 21, 2017. He was eighty-eight.

Neil Simon wrote no more hits after *Lost in Yonkers*, though a revival of *The Odd Couple* in 2005 starring Broderick and Lane opened with a $20 million advance. In 2009, Emanuel Azenberg set out to produce in repertory *Brighton Beach Memoirs* and *Broadway Bound*. Only *Brighton Beach*, starring Laurie Metcalf, made it to the stage, and only for one week. The reviews were good, but ticket sales were terrible. The audience for a Neil Simon play was either in Florida or dead. And tastes in comedy had changed.

David Letterman, Larry David, Howard Stern, Lewis Black, the plays of Martin McDonagh, and television shows such as *The Office* offered a more biting, darker, and satirical brand of humor than *Barefoot in the Park* or *The Sunshine Boys*.

Many theater people, including producer Scott Rudin, Frank Rich, Alex Witchel, and I—people who remembered when Simon was on top—attended the final performance of *Brighton Beach Memoirs*. Azenberg was crying as he greeted us. Simon, sitting by himself in the last row of the orchestra off to the right, watched as his era came to an end. He died August 26, 2018.

Tony Kushner has written several political plays—*Slavs!*, *Homebody/Kabul*—but none has approached the success and impact of *Angels in America*. His musical *Caroline, or Change* flopped on Broadway. His ambitious (and long-winded) *The Intelligent Homosexual's Guide to Capitalism and Socialism with a Key to the Scriptures* had a brief run at the Public Theater in 2011. *Angels in America* is still performed all over the world. It was revived on Broadway in 2018 with Nathan Lane receiving a Tony nomination as Roy Cohn.

Edward Albee followed up *The Goat, or Who Is Sylvia?* with several experimental plays and enjoyed two critically acclaimed Broadway revivals of *Who's Afraid of Virginia Woolf?* in 2005 (starring Kathleen Turner as Martha) and in 2011 (starring Tracy Letts as George). Albee's health began to fail in 2014, and he withdrew from public appearances. On March 13, 2016, one day after Albee turned eighty-eight, Sardi's corrected a long-standing oversight and unveiled his caricature. He was too ill to attend the ceremony, but a select group of friends—among them Terrence McNally, Angela Lansbury, Mercedes Ruehl, critic Linda Winer, Elizabeth I. McCann, and press agent Sam Rudy—gathered to share stories of the playwright. McNally recalled the night he met Albee at a party in 1959. Albee offered to give him a ride home and then invited him up to his apartment for a drink. *It's so late—won't his wife mind?* McNally thought. "Shows you how good my gaydar was back then," he said.

Albee died September 16, 2016, at his house in Montauk, attended by a health aid from Guyana. She didn't understand why his friends laughed after learning that her name was Martha.

As good as *Titanic* was, it only lasted two years on Broadway and failed to recoup its $10 million investment. After that, Michael David and the Dodgers had a run of critically maligned and money-losing shows—*Footloose*; *High Society*; *Dracula, the Musical*; *Good Vibrations*. The Dodgers' biggest backer, Joop van den Ende, severed ties with the company in 2005. The Dodgers dismissed three-quarters of its staff and moved from swanky offices above Times Square to an old rehearsal studio in a drab building on a side street of the theater district. The *New York Times* chronicled the company's fall in a front-page story titled STARVED FOR HITS, PRODUCER FINDS HARD TIMES ON STREET OF DREAMS. The article mentioned in passing the Dodgers' next show—*Jersey Boys*, a bio musical about the Four Seasons. I attended an early preview in New York. At intermission a man in front of me turned around and said, "I've invested in a lot of shows with the Dodgers. Do you think we finally have a hit here?"

"I think you're going to be okay with this one," I said.

Jersey Boys ran twelve years on Broadway and spawned productions all over the world that to date have grossed more than $2 billion. It also created an industry of bio musicals that have invaded Broadway—*Beautiful: The Carol King Musical*; *On Your Feet!*, the Gloria Estefan musical; *Summer: The Donna Summer Musical*; *The Cher Show*; *Tina: The Tina Turner Musical*; *Ain't Too Proud: The Life and Times of the Temptations;* and *MJ The Musical*, the Michael Jackson musical, which, with any luck, will bring an end to it all.

When James H. Binger, the chairman of Jujamcyn Theaters, died in 2004, Rocco Landesman exercised his right to buy the chain for what many considered the undervalued price of $30 million. In 2009, Landesman sold a 50 percent stake in the company to Jordan Roth, the son of billionaire real estate developer Steve Roth and Broadway producer Daryl Roth. (Jordan Roth would eventually acquire 100 percent of the company.) That same year President Barak Obama appointed Landesman chairman of the National Endowment for the Arts. Landesman put a memento from *The Producers* on his desk—a puppet pigeon with a swastika on its wing. It was the first thing his staff "cleared off my desk and put in storage," he said. "You can't do that, they told me. Not here in D.C."

In the 1980s, Andrew Lloyd Webber and producer Cameron Mackintosh nudged Broadway from the backwaters of the entertainment business to more mainstream popularity with shows such as *Cats, Les Misérables,* and *The Phantom of the Opera.* The 1990s put Broadway at the center of American popular culture in a way it had not been since the 1950s. *Rent, Angels in America, Chicago, The Lion King,* and Matthew Broderick and Nathan Lane in *The Producers* were as famous and popular as *Friends* and *Frasier, Pulp Fiction* and *Forrest Gump.* That popularity continues with the rise of shows such as *Wicked, Avenue Q, Jersey Boys, The Book of Mormon, Dear Evan Hansen,* and that cultural phenomenon that has rivaled any TV show or movie, *Hamilton.*

Broadway is in the midst of its new Golden Age.

ACKNOWLEDGMENTS

I did not intend to write this book. After *Razzle Dazzle: The Battle for Broadway* came out in 2015, I thought I'd take a break from writing about the theater and tackle another subject. I had a few ideas, but when I ran them by my editor and friend, Ben Loehnen, his response was a polite "That's interesting." To be honest, none of my ideas excited me that much, either. Then one afternoon over drinks (always the best way to do some thinking), Ben said, "You know what I would like? A sequel." In an instant, all the shows and colorful theater people I'd covered in my career flashed through my mind. The material was there, and Ben knew it. So if you like *Singular Sensation: The Triumph of Broadway*, thank Ben. If you don't, blame him.

Ben was enthusiastic about the book from the first chapters. But when it came time to edit, he pulled out his red pen and slashed away all the fat. Once again, he made me a better writer than I ever thought I could be. I can't imagine working with anyone else.

I want to thank Jonathan Karp, who loves the theater as much as I do. He signed up and championed *Razzle Dazzle*, and then, based on a brief outline I dashed off on a plane, signed up *Singular*

Sensation. He signed up a third book, too. It doesn't exist yet, but I appreciate his faith in me. I also want to thank Jonathan Evans and Tony Newfield, excellent copyeditors and fact-checkers who know more about the theater than I do.

Back in 2011, David Kuhn, my agent, convinced this old newspaperman he had a book in him. Who knew I had two? He gave me a new career, and I am deeply grateful. My thanks to his colleagues at Aevitas Creative Management, who kept on top of things that had slipped my mind.

Singular Sensation would not exist without the memories, stories, and insights from its cast of characters. Andrew Lloyd Webber gave me a thoughtful and candid interview about the saga of *Sunset Boulevard*. Patti LuPone was equally candid (and uproarious) when she told me her side of the story as she sat in front of a mirror doing her makeup before a performance of *War Paint*. I spent a delightful afternoon with Jonathan Larson's sister, Julie, and his father, Al, at Julie's house in Cheviot Hills, Los Angeles. They brought Jonathan to vivid life, and I hope I have captured something of his indomitable spirit in the chapters on *Rent*. I also want to thank my friend Don Summa for a long and thoughtful interview about Jonathan and the show, and for putting me in touch with several other sources. Rocco Landesman was never a big fan of mine when I was writing a theater column for the *New York Post*, but he liked *Razzle Dazzle* and gave me a fun and colorful interview for this book. I hope he'll let me take him out for drinks one day. Jack Viertel is not only a terrific source but a terrific writer as well. His *The Secret Life of the American Musical: How Broadway Shows Are Built* is right up there with, well, *Razzle Dazzle: The Battle for Broadway*. Michael David regaled me with stories of *Guys and Dolls*, and rifled through his files to find notes he gave Jerry Zaks during previews. He also had great stories about raising the *Titanic*, as did one of my favorite Broadway composers, Maury Yeston. Fran and Barry Weissler are two of the funniest and shrewdest people I've ever met. The stories of how they made their way to the top of Broadway, and of how they managed to produce *Chicago* when no one thought it could survive beyond a few performances, greatly enlivened *Singular Sensation*. Interviews with William Ivey Long are painful because he makes you laugh so hard. He remembers everything in side-splitting detail. Tom Schumacher remembers everything as well, and tells it with flair. I'm grateful to him for easing the way to Julie Taymor, who was wary of me after some tough columns I wrote about her show *Spider-Man: Turn Off the Dark*. She is a towering talent. The first time I saw the opening of *The Lion King* remains the single most thrilling moment in all the years I've spent in the theater. I also want to thank the man who gave Tom Schumacher his job at Disney, my good friend Peter Schneider. Jon Wilner lost his business when Livent went bankrupt. He remembers every detail of that wild ride. It was painful for him to recount, but he did it with honesty and humor. I always enjoyed sparring with Garth Drabinsky when he ran Livent, and I'm grateful he gave me an interview for this book. It was good to see him after all these years, and though the interview got a little contentious in the end, I still admire his intelligence, ambition, and taste. Jed Bernstein gave me a sweeping assessment of the changes Broadway underwent in the 1990s. He also, along with Cristyne Nicholas and Rudy Giuliani, delivered a riveting, blow-by-blow account of September 11th and how Broadway staged its recovery.

I would also like to thank the following people for their time and their memories: Lynn Ahrens, Barry Avrich, Emanuel Azenberg, Jordan Baker, John Barlow, Marty Bell, Jeff Berger, Andre Bishop, Don Black, Walter Bobbie, Chris Boneau, Dan Brambilla, John Breglio, Matthew Broderick, Mel Brooks, Peter Brown, Adrian Bryan-Brown, David Caddick, Kevin Cahoon, Glenn Close, Michael Cohl, Nancy Coyne, Jeffry Denman, Edgar

Dobie, Robert Duva, Michael Eisner, Rick Elice, Jordan Fiksenbaum, David Fingold, Robert Fox, Richard Frankel, Alex Fraser, Jeremy Gerard, Ron Gibbs, Len Gill, V. J. John Gillespie, Eleanor Goldhar, Robyn Goodman, Michael Greif, Joel Grey, Christopher Hampton, David Hare, John Hart, Drew Hodges, Geoff Hoyle, Hugh Jackman, Chris Jones, John Kander, Richard Kornberg, Judy Kuhn, Nathan Lane, Chris Loudon, Hailey Lustig, Cameron Mackintosh, Richard Maltby Jr., Elizabeth I. McCann, Kevin McCollum, Anne Miner, Rick Miramontez, James Nadeaux, James C. Nicola, Richard Ouzounian, Amy Powers, Janice Price, Ann Reinking, Daphne Rubin-Vega, Sam Rudy, Pete Sanders, Eric Schnall, Jeffrey Seller, Stephen Sondheim, Susan Stroman, Bill Taylor, Robert Topol, John Vickery, Tom Viertel, George Wachtel, Robin Wagner, Tim Weil, Angela Wendt, Miles Wilkin, Norman Zaiger, Jerry Zaks, and Scott Zeiger.

Three sources died before this book came out: Thomas Meehan, a gentle man with the slyest of wits; Terrence McNally, who knew Edward Albee better than anyone else; and Roger Horchow, whose Texas drawl I hear every time I recall that story he told me about listening to George Gershwin play the piano in his living room when he was six years old. It was a pleasure to spend time with them before they left.

Several friends supported me throughout the four years it took to report and write *Singular Sensation*. David Stone read every chapter as I finished it. We grew up together in this business in the 1990s, so he knew what I was aiming at. I am indebted to him for his encouragement, his jokes (usually at my expense), his criticisms, and his corrections. Every writer should have a friend as wise and generous as Scott Rudin. He instantly grasps where you're headed, and when you veer off, puts you back on track. As I was writing this book, I had many dinners at Sette Mezzo with Scott and Phil Smith. Every time I told them a story I thought I had unearthed for the first time in years, Phil knew all about it, and added a little bit more color and detail. Nobody alive today knows as much about Broadway as Phil Smith does. George Lane dealt with nearly everyone in this book. If he laughed when I read him scenes, I knew they were true. And Imogen Lloyd Webber was always available for a drink and a few laughs when I needed to hash something out. She's a fine writer and broadcaster herself, and a true friend.

I must thank my cohost Len Berman for not paying the slightest bit of attention to me as I yammered on about this book every weekday morning between commercial breaks. I also inflicted that particular torture on my colleagues Joe Bartlett, Natalie Vacca, Lou Rufino, Alice Stockton Rossini, Anthony Fillippleo, and Terry Trahim. They got through it, I believe, by plugging their ears. Thanks also to Tom Cuddy and Scott Lakefield, my bosses and friends at WOR.

I am grateful to the following friends, who have always supported so much of what I've tried to do: William Bratton, Tita Cahn, Margi Conklin, Clive Davis, Clive Hirschhorn, Katie and Peter Hermant, Barbara Hoffman, Charles Isherwood, Wendy Kidd, Rikki Klieman, Steve and Michelle Lichtman, Jimmy and Margo Nederlander, Patrick Pacheco, Albert Poland, Nick Scandalious, Greg Schriefer, Mark Simone, and Robert Wankel.

Christina Amoroso came into my life when I started *Razzle Dazzle* and stuck around for *Singular Sensation*. At times I got so busy with this book that it distracted me from my daily calls to her, while she was at work, to ask, "Anything to report?" For some reason, that didn't seem to bother her. Well, I have news, CA: I'm back, and I have a feeling I'll be asking "Anything to report?" for a long time to come.

My sister, Leslie Riedel, and her husband, Scott Friend, saw me through *Razzle Dazzle* when I had doubts about my ability to write it. I had no doubts this time around, but that's because I knew they'd be there if I did.

Most of all, I thank my parents, for everything. I wrote the first and last chapters of this book on their lanai in Sarasota. It was my own little Yaddo colony. There is no better place to write, and no better parents to have around when you're writing.

NOTES

FOREWORD

1 Michael Riedel, "'Company' Producer Strives to Keep It Together," *New York Post*, April 2, 2020.
2 Michael Riedel, "Darkness Falls," *Air Mail*, May 9, 2020.

CHAPTER ONE: **I'M READY FOR MY CLOSE-UP, MR. LLOYD WEBBER**

1 Patti LuPone, interview with author.
2 Michael Riedel, "Backstage at 'Boulevard,'" *New York Daily News*, November 6, 1994.

CHAPTER TWO: **BOULEVARD OF BROKEN DREAMS**

1 Mervyn Rothstein, "Producer Cancels 'Miss Saigon'; 140 Members Challenge Equity," *New York Times*, August 9, 1990.
2 Frank Rich, "'Miss Saigon' Arrives, From the Old School," *New York Times*, April 12, 1991.
3 LuPone, *Patti LuPone: A Memoir* (New York: Crown Archetype, 2010), 214.
4 Ibid., 218.
5 Michael Riedel, "Backstage at 'Boulevard,'" *New York Daily News*, November 6, 1994.
6 Bruce Weber, "Close Is Given LuPone's Place in 'Sunset' Cast for Broadway," *New York Times*, February 18, 1994.

7 Peter Brown, interview with author.
8 Andrew Lloyd Webber, interview with author.
9 Michael Riedel, "Who'll Be a Close Second?" *New York Daily News*, October 2, 1994.
10 Bernard Weinraub, "When Egos Collide: Twilight at 'Sunset,'" *New York Times*, July 5, 1994.
11 Edgar Dobie, interview with author.
12 Michael Riedel, "Walters Entangled in a Web of Conflict," *New York Daily News*, February 19, 1997.
13 Frank Rich, *Hot Seat: Theater Criticism for* The New York Times, *1980–1993* (New York: Random House, 1998), 936.

CHAPTER THREE: **508 GREENWICH, #4**

1 Julie Larson, interview with author.
2 Jonathan Larson, *Rent:* Interviews and text by Evelyn McDonnell with Katherine Silberger (New York: Rob Weisbach Books, 1997), 14.
3 Tom Rowan, *Rent FAQ: All That's Left to Know About Broadway's Blaze of Glory* (Montclair, NJ: Applause Theatre & Cinema Books, 2017), 10.
4 Daphne Rubin-Vega, interview with author.
5 Rowan, *Rent FAQ*, 44.
6 Ibid., 21
7 Ibid., 23.
8 Michael Greif, interview with author.
9 Jim Nicola, interview with author.
10 Jeffrey Seller, interview with author.
11 Larson, *Rent*, 29.
12 Ibid., 35
13 Anthony Tommasini, "A Composer's Death Echoes in His Musical," *New York Times*, February 11, 1996.
14 Larson, *Rent*, 50.
15 Daphne Rubin-Vega, interview with author.
16 Lawrence Van Gelder, "On the Eve of a New Life, an Untimely Death," *New York Times*, December 13, 1996.

CHAPTER FOUR: **LA VIE BROADWAY**

1 Jonathan Larson, *Rent:* Interviews and text by Evelyn McDonnell with Katherine Silberger (New York: Rob Weisbach Books, 1997), 52.

2 Anthony Tommasini, "A Composer's Death Echoes in His Musical," *New York Times*, February 11, 1996.
3 Ben Brantley, "A Rock Opera a la 'Boheme' and 'Hair,'" *New York Times*, February 14, 1996.
4 Larson, *Rent*, 58.
5 Kevin McCollum, interview with author.
6 Michael Riedel, "Room for *Rent*? Theater Folk Wonder If B'way Can Accommodate the Rock Musical," *New York Daily News*, February 22, 1996.
7 Tom Rowan, *Rent FAQ: All That's Left to Know About Broadway's Blaze of Glory* (Montclair, NJ: Applause Theatre & Cinema Books, 2017), 9.
8 Drew Hodges, interview with author.
9 Drew Hodges, *On Broadway: From* Rent *to Revolution* (New York: Rizzoli, 2016), 14.
10 Hodges, interview with author.
11 Peter Marks, "A Box Office Prize," *New York Times*, April 12, 1996.
12 Ben Brantley, "Enter Singing: Young, Hopeful and Taking on the Big Time," *New York Times*, April 30, 1996.
13 Michael Riedel, "Every Day a *Rent* Party: Hardcore Fans of the Hit Musical Form a Squatters Camp at the Box Office," *New York Daily News*, March 3, 1997.
14 Jeffrey A. Trachtenberg, "The Producers: How to Turn $4,000 into Many Millions," *The Wall Street Journal*, May 23, 1996.
15 Jeffrey Seller, interview with author.

CHAPTER FIVE: **THE GAMBLER**

1 Harold C. Schonberg, "The Schuberts and the Nederlanders Have a Rival," *New York Times*, March 14, 1982.
2 Frank Rich, "'Moose Murders,' A Brand of Whodunit," *New York Times*, February 23, 1983.
3 Ibid.
4 William Goldman, *The Season: A Candid Look at Broadway* (New York: Limelight Editions, 2004), 24.
5 Frank Rich, "With Huck Finn on the 'Big River,'" *New York Times*, April 26, 1985.
6 John Simon, "Splash," *New York*, May 6, 1985.
7 Walter Kerr, "Farewell to a Jaunty Gentleman of the Stage," *New York Times*, June 2, 1985.

8 Jeremy Gerard, "Rocco Landesman Named Jujamcyn Theaters Head," *New York Times*, June 10, 1987.
9 William A. Henry III, "The Biggest All-Time Flop Ever," *Time*, May 30, 1988.
10 David Owen, "Betting on Broadway," *New Yorker*, June 13, 1994.
11 Rocco Landesman, "What Price Success at Lincoln Center?" *New York Times*, December 11, 1988.

CHAPTER SIX: **I GOT THE HORSE RIGHT HERE**

1 Frank Rich, "On Broadway, the Lights Get Brighter," *New York Times*, May 31, 1992.
2 Frank Rich, "'Crazy For You,' a Musical with the Gershwin Touch," *New York Times*, February 20, 1992.
3 Ross Wetzsteon, "The Great New York Show: 'Guys and Dolls' Lights Up Broadway All Over Again," *New York*, May 4, 1992.
4 Ibid.
5 Ibid.
6 Ibid.

CHAPTER SEVEN: **WINGING IT**

1 Brooks Atkinson, *Broadway* (New York: Limelight Editions, 1985), 68.
2 Ibid., 404.
3 Ibid., 415.
4 Frank Rich, "The Great Dark Way: Slowly, the Lights Are Dimming on Broadway," *New York Times*, June 2, 1991.
5 Ibid.
6 Ibid.
7 Isaac Butler and Dan Kois, *The World Only Spins Forward: The Ascent of* Angels in America (New York: Bloomsbury, 2018), 65.
8 Ibid., 34.
9 Bruce Weber, "Angels' Angels," *New York Times*, April 25, 1993.
10 Ibid.
11 Butler and Kois, *World Only Spins Forward*, 101.
12 Frank Rich, "Marching Out of the Closet, into History," *New York Times*, November 10, 1992.
13 Butler and Kois, *World Only Spins Forward*, 139.
14 Ibid., 164.

15 Frank Rich, "Embracing All Possibilities in Life and Art," *New York Times*, May 5, 1993.
16 John Simon, "Of Wings and Webs," *New York*, May 17, 1993.
17 John Simon, "Angelic Geometry," *New York*, December 6, 1993.

CHAPTER EIGHT: **WHO'S AFRAID OF EDWARD ALBEE?**

1 John Lahr, interviewed on *Theater Talk*, December 29, 2014.
2 Edward Albee, conversation with author, March 2008.
3 Michael Riedel, "Who's Afraid of Albee?" *New York Daily News*, November 7, 1993.
4 Lyn Gardner, "Edward Albee Obituary," *The Guardian*, September 18, 2016.
5 Terrence McNally, interview with author.
6 Mel Gussow, *Edward Albee: A Singular Journey* (New York: Simon & Schuster, 1999), 341.
7 Edward Albee, interviewed on *Theater Talk*, November 3, 2007.
8 McNally, interview with author.
9 David Richards, "Critical Winds Shift for Albee, a Master of the Steady Course," *New York Times*, April 13, 1994.
10 Michael Riedel, "Oh, You Kid! Horns Lock Over Albee's Man-Goat Love Story," *New York Post*, February 22, 2002.
11 Michael Riedel, "Giving It His Albee," *New York Post*, March 12, 2008.

CHAPTER NINE: **RAZZLE DAZZLE**

1 Martin Gottfried, *All His Jazz: The Life and Death of Bob Fosse* (New York: Da Capo Press, 1990), 340.
2 John Kander, Fred Ebb, and Greg Lawrence, *Colored Lights: Forty Years of Words and Music, Show Biz, Collaboration, and All that Jazz* (New York: Faber & Faber, 2003), 126.

CHAPTER ELEVEN: **EVERYTHING'S COMING UP ROSIE**

1 Peter Marks, "Ad Official to Head the Theater League," *New York Times*, August 2, 1995.
2 Janny Scott, "Rosie Speaks, and Broadway Ticketsellers Cheer," *New York Times*, May 3, 1998.
3 Michael Riedel, "That Sinking Feeling," *New York Daily News*, October 20, 1996.

4 Michael Riedel, "Raising the 'Titanic,'" *New York Daily News*, July 22, 1997.
5 Ben Brantley, "'Titanic,' the Musical, Is Finally Launched," *New York Times*, April 24, 1997.
6 Riedel, "Raising the 'Titanic.'"
7 Ibid.
8 Scott, "Rosie Speaks."
9 Michael Riedel, "A Win-Lose Situation for Kander and Ebb," *New York Daily News*, June 4, 1997.
10 Michael Riedel, "Rosie & Tony," *New York Daily News*, June 7, 1998.

CHAPTER TWELVE: **THE MAKING OF A MOGUL**

1 Leonard Zehr, "Screen Giant," *The Wall Street Journal*, March 16, 1987.
2 *Show Stopper: The Theatrical Life of Garth Drabinsky*. A film by Barry Avrich, 2012.

CHAPTER THIRTEEN: **BE AT THE FUCKING MATINEE**

1 Dan Brambilla, interview with author.
2 Barry Avrich, *Moguls, Monsters and Madmen: An Uncensored Life in Show Business* (Toronto: ECW Press, 2016), 52.
3 Jeff Berger, interview with author.
4 Peter Marks, "Turning Two Historic Theaters into One Big One," *New York Times*, January 17, 1996.

CHAPTER FOURTEEN: **THE LION QUEEN**

1 James B. Stewart, *DisneyWar* (New York: Simon & Schuster, 2005), 108.
2 Barry Singer, "Just Two Animated Characters, Indeed," *New York Times*, October 4, 1998.
3 Tyler Spicer, "Curtain Speech: Julie Taymor," *New Musical Theatre*, October 6, 2014.
4 Samuel R. Delany, *Times Square Red, Times Square Blue* (New York: New York University Press, 1999), 10.
5 *New York Post*, November 14, 1997.

CHAPTER FIFTEEN: **THE UNMAKING OF A MOGUL**

1 Ward Morehouse III and Paul Tharp, "His Shows Must Go On," *New York Post*, January 18, 1998.
2 Ben Brantley, "'Ragtime': A Diorama with Nostalgia Rampant," *New York Times*, January 19, 1998.
3 Michael Riedel, "The World According to Garth," *New York Daily News*, February 5, 1998.
4 Chris Boneau, interview with author.
5 Christopher Byron, "A Broadway Angel?" *New York Observer*, February 10, 1997.
6 Michael Riedel, "Dealing for Dollars," *New York Daily News*, April 14, 1998.

CHAPTER SIXTEEN: **THE PLAYMAKERS**

1 Ralph Blumenthal, "Despite the Broadway Boom, Serious Plays Face Serious Peril," *New York Times*, January 9, 1997.
2 Ibid.
3 Ralph Blumenthal, "Dramas Show a Surprising Strength in Tony Nominations," *New York Times*, May 5, 1998.

CHAPTER SEVENTEEN: **IT'S GOOD TO BE THE KING**

1 Jeffry Denman, *A Year with* The Producers: One Actor's Exhausting (but Worth It) Journey from *Cats* to Mel Brooks' Mega-Hit (New York: Routledge, 2002), 25.
2 Kenneth Tynan, *Show People: Profiles in Entertainment* (New York: Simon and Schuster, 1979), 242.
3 Mel Brooks and Tom Meehan, *The Producers: How We Did It* (New York: Talk Miramax Books, 2001), 21.
4 "Broadway Record," *Crain's New York Business*, June 4, 2001.
5 Michael Kuchwara, "Broadway Attendance Dips Slightly," Associated Press, August 8, 2001.

EPILOGUE: **AND THE SHOW GOES ON**

1 Jesse McKinley, "Broadway Is in the War All the Way," *New York Times*, September 21, 2001.

2 Ibid.

3 Michael Riedel, "After 14 Years on Broadway, 'Mamma Mia!' to Close," *New York Post*, April 9, 2015.

4 Ben Brantley, "Mom Had a Trio (and a Band, Too)," *New York Times*, October 19, 2001.

5 Jesse McKinley, "For the Asking, a $480 Seat," *New York Times*, October 26, 2001.

6 Bill Zehme, "King Mike and the Quest for the Broadway Grail," *New York*, March 4, 2005.

7 Ibid.

8 *Show Stopper: The Theatrical Life of Garth Drabinsky*. A film by Barry Avrich, 2012.

9 Jeremy Gerard, "Candor and the Web," *New York*, October 16, 2000.

10 Michael Riedel, "Schwartz Again 'Pippin' Hot,'" *New York Post*, November 19, 2010.

11 Michael Riedel, "New 'Young Frankenstein' Electrifies in UK Run," *New York Post*, August 29, 2017.

BIBLIOGRAPHY

Albee, Edward. *Three Tall Women*. New York: Dutton, 1995.

———. *Selected Plays of Edward Albee*. New York: Nelson Doubleday, 1987.

Atkinson, Brooks. *Broadway*. New York: Limelight Editions, 1985.

Avrich, Barry. *Moguls, Monsters and Madmen: An Uncensored Life in Show Business*. Toronto: ECW Press, 2016.

Bentley, Eric. *Bernard Shaw*. New York: Limelight Editions, 1947.

Breglio, John. *I Wanna Be a Producer: How to Make a Killing on Broadway . . . or Get Killed*. Milwaukee: Applause Theatre and Cinema Books, 2016.

Brooks, Mel, and Tom Meehan. *The Producers: How We Did It*. New York: Talk Miramax Books, 2001.

Butler, Isaac, and Dan Kois. *The World Only Spins Forward: The Ascent of* Angels in America. New York: Bloomsbury, 2018.

Delany, Samuel R. *Times Square Red, Times Square Blue*. New York: New York University Press, 1999.

Denman, Jeffry. *A Year with* The Producers: *One Actor's Exhausting (But Worth It) Journey from* Cats *to Mel Brooks' Mega-Hit*. New York: Routledge, 2002.

Drabinsky, Garth. *Closer to the Sun: An Autobiography*. Toronto: McClelland and Stewart, 1995.

Ganzl, Kurt. *The Complete* Aspects of Love: *The New Andrew Lloyd Webber Musical*. London: Viking Studio Books, 1990.

Goldman, William. *The Season: A Candid Look at Broadway*. New York: Limelight Editions, 1969.

Gottfried, Martin. *All His Jazz: The Life and Death of Bob Fosse.* New York: Bantam Books, 1990.

Green, Stanley. *The World of Musical Comedy.* New York: Da Capo Press, 1985.

Gussow, Mel. *Edward Albee: Singular Journey.* New York: Simon & Schuster, 1999.

Hodges, Drew. *On Broadway: From* Rent *to Revolution.* New York: Rizzoli, 2016.

Isenberg, Barbara. *Making It* Big: *The Diary of a Broadway Musical.* New York: Limelight Editions, 1996.

Jackson, Kenneth T. *The Encyclopedia of New York City.* New Haven: Yale University Press, 1995.

Kander, John, and Fred Ebb (as told to Greg Lawrence). *Colored Lights: Forty Years of Words and Music, Show Biz, Collaboration, and All That Jazz.* New York: Faber & Faber, 2003.

Lahr, John. *Honky Tonk Parade:* New Yorker *Profiles of Show People.* London: Overlook Duckworth, 2005.

———. *Light Fantastic: Adventures in Theatre.* New York: Delta, 1996.

Larson, Jonathan. *Rent.* New York: Rob Weisbach Books, 1997.

Lassell, Michael. *The Lion King: Twenty Years on Broadway and Around the World.* New York: Disney Editions, 2017.

Lerner, Alan Jay. *The Street Where I Live.* New York: W. W. Norton, 1978.

LuPone, Patti (with Digby Diehl). *Patti LuPone: A Memoir.* New York: Three Rivers Press, 2010.

Mandelbaum, Ken. *Not Since Carrie: Forty Years of Broadway Musical Flops.* New York: St. Martin's Press, 1991.

Pacheco, Patrick. *American Theatre Wing: An Oral History.* Berkeley: Graphic Arts Books, 2018.

Riedel, Michael. *Razzle Dazzle: The Battle for Broadway.* New York: Simon & Schuster, 2015.

Rigg, Diana. *No Turn Unstoned: The Worst Ever Theatrical Reviews.* Los Angeles: Silman-James Press, 1982.

Rowan, Tom. *Rent FAQ: All That's Left to Know About Broadway's Blaze of Glory.* Montclair, NJ: Applause Theatre and Cinema Books, 2017.

Runyon, Damon. *Guys and Dolls and Other Writings.* New York: Penguin Books, 2008.

Siegel, Fred. *The Prince of the City: Giuliani, New York and the Genius of American Life.* New York: Encounter Books, 2005.

Stewart, James B. *DisneyWar.* New York: Simon & Schuster, 2005.

Taymor, Julie. *The Lion King: Pride Rock on Broadway.* New York: Hyperion, 1997.

Teichman, Howard. *George S. Kaufman: An Intimate Portrait.* New York: Dell Publishing, 1972.

Tepper, Jennifer Ashley. *The Untold Stories of Broadway: Volume 3.* New York: Dress Circle Publishing, 2016.

Tynan, Kenneth. *Show People: Profiles in Entertainment.* New York: Simon and Schuster, 1980.

Van Hoogstraten, Nicholas. *Lost Broadway Theatres.* New York: Princeton Architectural Press, 1991.

Wasson, Sam. *Fosse.* New York: Houghton Mifflin Harcourt, 2013.

White, Norval, and Elliot Willensky with Fran Leadon. *AIA Guide to New York City.* New York: Oxford University Press, 2010.

Zagat, Tim. *9/11: Stories of Courage, Heroism and Generosity.* New York: Zagat, 2011.

INDEX

ABOUT THE AUTHOR

MICHAEL RIEDEL is the cohost of "Len Berman and Michael Riedel in the Morning" on 710 WOR. He has been the theater columnist for the *New York Post* since 1998. *New York* magazine has called his column a "must-read" for the theater world. Michael's book *Razzle Dazzle: The Battle for Broadway* won the Marfield Prize for arts writing in 2015. A graduate of Columbia University, Michael lives in Manhattan's West Village.